MANIC STREET PREACHERS

SWEET VENOM

Revised and Updated

MARTIN CLARKE

PLEXUS, LONDON

First published in 2009
by Plexus Publishing Limited
This edition copyright © 2009
by Plexus Publishing Limited
All rights reserved including the right of
reproduction in whole or in part in any form
Martin Clarke is the author of chapters 1–12
Text copyright © 1997 by Martin Clarke
Additional material supplied by
Tom Branton for Chapters 13–18
Text copyright © 2009 by
Plexus Publishing Limited
25 Mallinson Road
London SW11 1BW
www.plexusbooks.com
First printing 2009

British Library Cataloguing in Publication Data

Clarke, Martin.
  Manic Street Preachers : sweet venom. – 2nd ed.
  1. Manic Street Preachers (Musical group) 2.
  Rock musicians – Great Britain – Biography.
  I. Title
  782.4'2166'0922-dc22

  ISBN-10: 0-89565-428-1
  ISBN-13: 978-085965-428-9

Cover photograph by Paul Slattery/Retna
Cover designed by Coco Wake-Porter
Book designed by Phil Gambrill
Printed in Great Britain by Cromwell Press Group

ACKNOWLEDGEMENTS

This book is dedicated to Alan Parker, for his
invaluable help, research and knowledge.

The following publications were extremely helpful
in the writing of this book: *NME, Melody Maker,
Sounds, Q, Vox, Select, Spiral Scratch, Kerrang!,
Smash Hits, EP magazine*

We would like to thank the following
photographers, photo agencies and publications:
Martyn Goodacre/ SIN; Hayley Madden/SIN; Joe
Dilworth/SIN; Kim Tonelli/SIN; Steve Double/
SIN; Ian Tilton/SIN; Karena Bernard/SIN; Tim
Paton/SIN; Paul Stanley/ SIN; Piers Allardyce/
SIN; Bruce Fredericks/Retna; Tony Mottram/
Retna; Matt Anker/Retna; RIP/Retna; Bernaded
Dexters/Retna; David Tonge/Retna; Martyn
Goodacre/Retna; Chris Floyd/Retna; Franck
Camhi/Vision/Retna; Steve Double/Retna; Ed
Sirrs/ Retna; Adrian Green/Retna; Paul Slattery/
Retna; Ian Tilton/Retna; Colin Bell/Retna; Nick
Tansley/All Action; Justin Thomas/All Action;
Tony Kyriacou/ Rex Features; Pascal Leopold/Rex
Features; Mick Hutson/Getty; Geoffrey Swaine/
Rex Features; Huw John/Rex Features; Dave M.
Benett/Getty; Action Press/Rex Features; Mick
Hutson/ Getty; *New Musical Express*; *The Times
Magazine*; *Melody Maker*.

CONTENTS

CHAPTER 1

*'If you built a museum to represent Blackwood all you
could put in it would be shit, rubble and shit.'*
Nicky Wire

The Miners' Strike of 1984–5 ripped the very heart out of many small British
pit communities. The union's defeat at the hands of the Iron Lady, Margaret
Thatcher, and the subsequent pit closures left dozens of traditionally
prosperous and busy mining towns shells of their former selves. Blackwood,
Gwent, was one such town. Standing on the perimeter of the Sirhowy Valley
in between the larger populaces of Newbridge and Ystrad Mynach,
Blackwood enjoyed crisp, clean air and a strong community spirit. But the
year-long miners' dispute changed everything. Men who had worked down
the pits for generations now found themselves out of work in a town that had
known no other way. Their options were grim – the dole, a token retraining
programme or menial work on production lines at the newly erected,
gleaming capitalist temples of Sony, Toshiba or, worse still, the Pot Noodle
factory. Here shrewd overseas conglomerates signed the newly
disenfranchised hordes on consecutive three-month temporary contracts,
knowing their new charges were in no position to argue, and thus avoiding
any redundancy commitments. With a population of just over 20,000, the
social impact of the union's defeat was immediate and direct. The lowering
of average incomes had a knock-on effect on the town's retail trade as the void
left by the pit closure gradually sucked the life out of the quiet backwater.
When the last gasp of trade unionism died out in the town, a thick fog of
despondency descended on Blackwood.

The same atmosphere soon pervaded Blackwood's youth culture.
There were several pubs and take-aways, a cinema and a snooker hall, but no
music venue. After a mind-numbing day's work on the production lines, there
was little to do in the evenings except drink in the pubs. Consequently, alcohol
consumption rose alarmingly high, as elsewhere in Gwent, which became the
county with the second highest level of alcohol poisoning in the UK.

With an almost ritualistic predictability, Saturday nights would see scores of people sinking pint after pint then sprawling and brawling out onto the streets in violent scuffles. There were stories of youths in one nearby area stealing syringes off the NHS and injecting cider into their arms for kicks. Other kids would hide in manholes in train tunnels, knowing that when the carriages rushed past at high speed, all the oxygen would be sucked out of their lungs by the subsequent vacuum. The general air of gloom extinguished any ambition or vitality the kids had, meaning they could be one of two things – a wage slave or a dole slave.

All this was some way off when the future members of the Manic Street Preachers were born at the end of the sixties. It was still half a decade before Mrs Thatcher was to first make her mark as the infamous 'Milk Snatcher' who stopped the free milk in schools, and back then Blackwood was still a strong mining community where a disciplined work ethic, money and optimism were all in abundance. Youngsters could happily play outside until dark without fear, usually on the imposing slag-heaps that were spattered around town. It was on these slag-heaps that James Dean Bradfield and his cousin Sean Moore spent much of their formative years. Most local events took place there, such as Halloween and Bonfire Night, even the local school fights between the two school districts of Pontllanfraith and Springfield. Later on, many kids lost their virginity there too. But by the time Bradfield and Moore had reached their mid-teens, the Miners' Strike had been lost and the mounds levelled. On the site of the main slag-heap the council built a lake called Pen-Y-Fan, which they filled with 2000 fish. All of them died after the water went stagnant. As if under a curse, the lake also claimed the lives of two people a year on average, sucking them under with its dangerous whirlpools and undercurrents.

Although Sean was in the year above James at Pontypridd Junior School, their family ties and close neighbourhood proximity made them the best of friends. This was just as well for Sean – when he was ten his parents split up and he was forced to go and live with James's family, sharing a pair of bunk beds with his cousin for the next twelve years. James himself was named after the rebel without a cause, who had narrowly beaten Clint Eastwood as his father's preferred choice. His unusual name only added to his problems at school, for James had been born with a slow eye which made him look cross-eyed, making him a perfect target for his jeering primary school peers.

They berated him daily with any one of dozens of nicknames, the most popular being 'Crossfire'. To add to his troubles, he also sang in the school choir and showed a notable musical bent from an early age – never a talent likely to win over many schoolyard bullies. As if that wasn't enough, he lived in the same street as future Labour leader, Neil Kinnock.

'You go out and get pissed and have fights, or you stay in and get on with your boredom. We were happier to go along with the boredom.' Richey

Sean was troubled by the break-up of his parents' marriage and was a much quieter child than James. Although he was bright, he clammed up in classes and often refused to answer the teachers' questions; as a result, he found himself moving up to the secondary school earmarked for the CSE rather than the GCE stream. After the marriage split, he barely saw his father – it was not until over a decade later when the Manics were on *Top Of The Pops* that Sean received a letter from his father asking for them to be friends again. Even so many years on, this upset Sean sufficiently for him to drunkenly smash up his dressing room with a pool cue.

One of James's friends in his school year was Nicky Jones, nicknamed Wire because of his gangly appearance. According to Nicky, the Manics first came together on the local football field, which was owned by the neighbouring Gossard corset factory. Wire lived on the Woodfield side of town, whereas Sean and James lived on the Pont side. Informal soccer teams were selected according to these minuscule geographical differences, with the victor carrying off a battered crown green bowls trophy which Nicky's dad had found on a rubbish tip. One week, Nicky brought along a boy who lived in his street. Like Sean, this new friend was in the year above Nicky and James at Pontypridd Junior School, having been born in December 1967. That friend was Richard James Edwards.

> *'Most people look back on their childhoods with more fondness than their early twenties or their teenage years which are pretty horrendous. As a child, you put your head on the pillow and fall asleep with no worries. From being a teenager onwards it's pretty rare that you don't end up staying awake half the night thinking about bullshit.'*
>
> *Richey Edwards*

Richard, or Richey as all his friends called him, lived within a mile of all the other Manics, in a bungalow at the foot of a steep cul-de-sac, which his family had owned for over nine generations. His pre-teen years were a model of tranquillity – at school he was very quickly noted as a high achiever, he loved to play football, mess about with his mates, or fuss his dog Snoopy. His mother and father treated him well, and the only parental rule he disliked was being made to go to chapel every Sunday. His parents both worked full-time as hairdressers, and his grandmother, who lived with them, would often be the one to look after him. In fact, Richey's childhood was no different from that of millions of children in Britain.

In the light of later events, much has been made of Richey Edwards being something of a depressed loner by the time he was thirteen. He once said, 'When I'm driving in my car and the traffic lights turn red I think it's because *I'm* in the car. I feel persecuted . . .' He also later admitted that even at primary school he believed everything and everyone was against him – he had bad skin for a while but his fears of ridicule were unjustified. To add to this, he was quite a fragile child. Once he had moved up to Oakdale Comprehensive School he had a girlfriend for two weeks but hated it, and after that he stuck to media figures like Clare Grogan, on whom he had a big crush. That same year, an energetically pubescent James thoroughly enjoyed watching a friend's porn movie every lunch time for a month, but the young Richey was made of different stuff. When his friend Brian Summers showed him some dirty magazines he had found under his brother's bed, Richey had to run home to be sick. So there was some evidence that he was very sensitive, but this should not be read as a clear precursor of Richey's later troubled life. Once the four friends, Wire, Edwards, Bradfield and Moore, had come together, they became inseparable. As their teenage associates turned their attention to drinking and sex, these four became voracious readers and television-watchers. Richey would later say to *Q* magazine, 'You go out and get pissed and have fights, or you stay in and get on with your boredom. We were happier to go along with the boredom.' He also said, 'It's no big deal, I didn't spend my teenage years wanting to fuck.' Whilst their school friends were out at the local Bierkeller club, they would go round to James's house, drink tea and watch videos, read books and listen to music. Their bedroom walls became veritable shrines to a myriad of twentieth-century icons: Marilyn Monroe, James Dean, Steve Ovett, Ian Botham, Brigitte Bardot, Cherokee Indians, some Edward Munch characters, Marvel comic heroes – an eclectic and varied mix. They watched hours of television: documentaries, popular culture programmes like *Pebble Mill At One*, and *Bullseye*, and dozens of quintessentially British black and white dramas from the sixties, like *A Taste Of Honey*. They all became insatiable readers, devouring the works of Shakespeare, William Burroughs, George Orwell and Philip Larkin, to name but a few. Orwell's *1984* and Aldous Huxley's *Brave New World* were said to be the only texts that Richey enjoyed at school. If they did wander out it would be to play football among themselves or hang around the 24-hour garage. This lifestyle encouraged an entrenched mentality, whereby they felt isolated from everyone else at school, and they deliberately cultivated this, mocking the wafer-thin moustaches that Blackwood teenagers struggled to grow, scorning their pissed peers and laughing at their inferior knowledge. Richey later claimed that they only ever read the predictable literary greats, and never anything genuinely avant garde, but at this young age they were still streets ahead of their peers in their knowledge.

One notable hero of a thirteen-year-old Richey was Bobby Sands, the IRA hunger striker. Sands was imprisoned for terrorist offences and began a hunger strike protest in early 1981 along with several other inmates. By 5 May of that year he had starved himself to death. Richey worryingly described Sands and the self-discipline he saw in him as 'beautiful'. Apart from this interest in terrorism, the foursome's adolescent years were decidedly uncontroversial. The wildest thing that any of them did was when Nicky got arrested for stealing a car while under the influence of alcohol. He had got drunk with a friend in a pub which was a long walk from home and then decided, in his inebriated wisdom, that it would be quicker to steal a car than walk. His friend hot-wired the chosen vehicle whilst Nicky passed out in the passenger seat. The car got no more than 100 yards down the road when it was stopped by the police. Nicky was conditionally discharged.

Despite their intense interest in the media and literature, they harboured many 'normal' teenage feelings – Nicky wanted to be a famous sportsman like Ian Botham or Ian Woosnam, while James had a passing interest in being in the SAS, after reading about their role in the Falklands War. But they never allowed themselves to be drawn into any laddish gangs other than their own. They were seen as, and deliberately cultivated, the epitome of teenage pretension; as Nicky told *Volume*, 'We've always got a kick out of goading people into thinking that we were complete tossers.'

Among the bedroom posters and clippings were increasing references to their growing interest in music. James's first record was Diana Ross's 'My Old Piano'. He saved up for it for over a week and finally had enough to wander into Woolworth's and get his copy. Unfortunately, an older heavy-metal-loving friend of his caught sight of the record when he met James on the way home, and, finding it most hilarious, proceeded to tell everyone. Nicky's first choice was a little more acceptable to these provincial metal-heads, Black Sabbath's 'Neon Nights', while Sean bought Queen's 'We Are The Champions' and Richey got 'It's Only Make Believe' by Child. Their formative years were filled with the sound of Darts, Queen, Mud and the one and only Shakin' Stevens, but it was not until the lengthy evenings and weekends entrenched in one another's bedrooms that they really started to become passionate about music.

Richey's earliest infatuation was with Joy Division, who took their name from the prostitution wing of a concentration camp. Ian Curtis's evocative, poetic words and oddly discordant vocals struck a real chord with Richey. Songs like 'She's Lost Control' and 'Transmission' were indicative of the emotional turmoil of their lead singer, who had suffered a seizure and blackouts onstage. When Curtis killed himself on the eve of a promising American tour, the music world was devastated. Ironically, the material released

'We've always got a kick out of goading people into thinking that we're complete tossers.'

posthumously that had Curtis's involvement, most notably the single 'Love Will Tear Us Apart' and the following album *Closer,* was the best that Joy Division had produced, and was a creative landmark for British alternative music. Curtis's death was Richey's first rock 'n' roll casualty:

'[He was] the only musician whose death I was saddened by,' he told
Kerrang!. 'I love music, but I couldn't give a fuck if anybody dropped dead
tomorrow, I wouldn't shed a tear.'

Another group they enjoyed was the Finnish glam rockers Hanoi Rocks,
whose 'Don't You Ever Leave Me' and 'Boulevard Of Broken Dreams' were
massive hits, made all the more popular by their over-the-top glam clothing
and extravagant live shows. Hanoi Rocks were massive in Blackwood, as
indeed they were in many provincial towns in the UK. At this stage the
Manics' musical preferences were largely apolitical, but that all changed after
the Miners' Strike of 1984–5. With the Kinnock household being so near,
they would often see the marches walk right past their front doors. Television
and newspaper reports featured the strike every day for a year, and with such
a highly charged political atmosphere, the four friends could not help but
become involved. James became so embroiled in events that he found himself
shouting 'scab' at the television screen when the Yorkshire miners were filmed
returning to work.

The major problem for these young music-lovers was the severe lack of
local music venues. The nearest gig was TJ's in Newport, but that only ever
managed to attract minor-status bands such as the Wedding Present and the
Close Lobsters. As a result, they had to experience their music through the
pages of the *NME* and *Melody Maker*, which gave them a window onto a
world that was otherwise completely out of reach. Each Wednesday morning
they would rush down to the newsagent and pore over these papers,
devouring the news stories, gossip and record and live reviews. They knew
every band, every journalist, and every argument that filled their pages.
One of the first bands they discovered in the music weeklies was McCarthy,
an Essex-based quartet who attended the same comprehensive school as the
Bard of Barking, Billy Bragg, of whom James was a fan. After releasing a
self-financed single in 1984, limited to just 485 copies, McCarthy's firebrand
songs were full of radical left-wing ideas and rough-hewn guitars, and first
came to national prominence on the *NME*'s highly influential *C86* cassette.
Their best-known single was 'Red Sleeping Beauty', a typically sharp and
incisive commentary on Thatcher's Britain. To the Manics, this was
genuinely exciting – a band who seemed to know all their own frustrations,
understood the Miners' Strike and anti-Thatcherite feelings, and, more
importantly, were able to transpose these ideas onto vinyl. McCarthy's first

two albums, *I Am A Wallet* and *The Enraged Will Inherit The Earth*, duly took their pride of place in the Manics' record collection. McCarthy's singer Tim Gane went on to form Stereolab in the 1990s and the Manics later recorded their version of McCarthy's 'Charles Windsor' for the B-side of their *Life Becoming A Landslide* EP.

The Manics were similarly inspired by an older band, the Leeds-based Gang Of Four. Again, they were an overtly political band whose music was harsh and guitar-based, as was clear in their debut album *Damaged Goods*. Another favourite was Big Flame, a Manchester trio who delivered an uncompromising combination of stabbing raw guitars and unusual rhythms, as best seen on their *Rigour* EP. They rigidly stuck to the 7" format when all around them were banging out formats by the dozen. Big Flame were also featured on the *C86* cassette but, like McCarthy, failed to capitalise on their critical acclaim and remained a left-field act. Richey remembers Big Flame well: 'We didn't really enjoy their music, it's such a disgusting noise, trying to fuse jazz with punk – but they were a brilliant band, easily the best of the whole *C86* bunch.' Indeed, the four friends spent much of 1986 writing letters to Big Flame (a hobby that soon became an obsession) who, of all those who received this attention, were the only band to regularly write back. Richey later told *Melody Maker*, 'The biggest argument we ever had was when we spent a whole summer arguing the merits of Big Flame and McCarthy against Guns N' Roses or any other major reference point. It went on every single day – we'd go down James's, by midday, get some fish and chips, practise our guitars, watch videos and then argue.'

Although it wasn't just alternative guitar bands the future Manics listened to – Simple Minds, Frank Sinatra, Ultramagnetic MCs and even Glen Campbell all found a place on their turntable – a pattern of taste was beginning to emerge. Perhaps most predictable of all their late teens influences was the Smiths. Morrissey, pop music's most famed miserabilist, struck a chord with the four friends and they went to see the band live many times, loving Mozzer's stage appearance and Johnny Marr's acclaimed guitar work. Richey was especially enamoured with Morrissey's words, scrutinising each line and learning every song off by heart. In a change of heart that was to become characteristic of their own band, this flirtation with the Smiths lasted only six months, after which they decided 'there was no point standing onstage saying that life hurts you'.

CHAPTER 2

'There's an awful lot of white British kids who have never really gone hungry, always had a roof to live under but at the same time are desperately unhappy. It's not total poverty, just a poverty of ideas.'

Richey

By 1985 Richey was coming towards the end of A levels. Having been a model pupil at Oakdale Comprehensive, he had graduated to Crosskeys Tertiary College and breezed through the A level classes. Nicky Wire was not quite as academically gifted as his close friend, but still proved a very capable student: 'We grew up very early. By the time I was sixteen, I'd read and studied the complete works of Philip Larkin, Shakespeare, all the beat generation, every film,' he told *Melody Maker*. 'I find it unbelievable, the intensity of us as people . . . everything came fast to us. It's just the way we are, we are modern people.' Sean and James were also at the college, but even with the new social circles available to them, the four friends remained an exclusive clique.

Apart from the handful of aforementioned groups, the foursome became utterly disillusioned with the mid-eighties musical climate, despairing of the latest 'Best New Bands' that were heralded each week in the music papers. The *C86* tape had given them a few bands they loved, but it also gave them many bands they hated: for example, the Wedding Present were loathed for their linear guitar attacks, emotional love songs and the downbeat dress sense of the enigmatic frontman David Gedge. This dissatisfaction with the current crop of musical offerings was reinforced by the Manics' early gig experiences. Initially, Richey's sister Rachel would travel to Cardiff's Bogie nightclub and return home in the small hours to tell her younger brother all about the evening's events, and he in turn would tell his three mates. When they were confident enough to go themselves, they were invariably disappointed. They attended dozens of gigs by music press darlings, more often than not in the Raffles Club in Cardiff. This would involve a lengthy trip by train to see bands that also disappointed them. Quite often the gig would go on until after the last train had left so they were forced to sleep under railway bridges until the morning services started, the inconvenience of their cramped and aching bodies made all the more annoying by the lack of musical inspiration the previous night. If the gig was at TJ's in Newport, only a one-hour bus ride was required, but the quality of acts here was usually even poorer.

Apart from the *C86* tape, 1986 was a big year in another way for the proto-Manics – it was the tenth anniversary of punk. Obviously, on its initial arrival in 1976, punk rock passed them by, as they were not even at secondary school. However, in the musical vacuum of the mid-eighties, the media retrospectives about this incendiary movement captured their imagination. Of particular importance was a Channel 4 documentary *So It Goes.* Presented by Factory Records supremo Tony Wilson, the show featured the Clash, the Sex Pistols and a whole host of punk's prime movers. This was the first time the foursome had heard or seen the Clash or the Pistols and they were completely bowled over. They loved Strummer's snarling irritation and confusion on 'Garageland' and 'What's My Name', and adored the stencilled sloganeering and politicised lyrics. The next day they bought the Clash's eponymous debut album, which included their favourite track 'Garageland', and a biography of them. The Pistols' more brutal approach fascinated them as well, and they watched the grisly documentary of their final explosive American tour, *DOA,* scores of times.

Punk rock appealed in general, but it was the Clash's career in particular that became a total obsession. Having recorded their debut album in a matter of days and allegedly not remembering much about it due to taking copious amounts of speed, the Clash became punk's most mainstream-friendly band. They signed to CBS, released five albums which achieved international acclaim, and even supported the Who at the gargantuan Shea Stadium in New York. To the foursome ensconced in their Blackwood bedrooms, grasping at anything to encapsulate their feelings, the Clash's debut album was like a slap round the face. As James remembers: 'At first I wanted to be someone like Napoleon, then I discovered music, or the Clash to be more precise, and that was it, my destiny was determined.' With this in mind, they began to ransack the musical archives for more of the same. The Rolling Stones and the Who were duly discovered, as well as early Beatles and scores of other punk bands. By the end of 1986, they were totally fascinated with music's past glories, a fixation made all the more extreme by their continued disillusionment with what the present had to offer.

With this conversion to the Clash and their interest in Hanoi Rocks, coupled also with a liking for the New York Dolls, the four friends started dressing in outrageously glam clothes, borrowing flouncy blouses from their sisters and wearing garish make-up, which needless to say brought howls of derision from the local metal-heads. When they started shaving they were gutted for weeks because of the detrimental effect the stubble had on their make-up. Being so insular, and looking as they did, the lads had almost no success with girls, as they were either too shy or assumed to be gay. Nicky even earned himself the nickname of 'Shirley' after Shirley Temple. But they were not bothered; as Nicky recalls, 'We made no effort to make other friends because we felt so happy with each other.'

The following year, one record was released which had an awesome impact on the formation of the Manics – the 1987 debut of Guns N' Roses, *Appetite For Destruction.* Guns N' Roses had received frantic

Early morning at their first London photo shoot, 1990

major record company interest and a subsequent multi-million-dollar deal with Geffen before they put out their debut long-player. Their extensive and wild tours had heightened their profile still further, but no one could have foreseen the colossal success of *Appetite.* The record was the biggest release of the year and went on to sell over twenty million copies worldwide, reaching Number 1 in America a year after its release date. The monumental single 'Welcome To The Jungle' was an international smash and was featured in the Clint Eastwood movie *Dead Pool.* The singles 'Sweet Child O' Mine' and 'Paradise City' were then followed by the eight-song album *G N' R Lies,* including another massive smash single, 'Patience', which increased their fame even more, as did the band's glamorous clothes and reputation as 'the most dangerous band in the world'.

The future Manics first saw Guns N' Roses on MTV's *Live At New York's The Ritz*, and they were instantly taken. 'It was the first time that we realised rock wasn't dead,' Richey said later to *Melody Maker*. 'We had the Stones, the Who, the Clash and we'd basically given up on hearing a new rock record that we'd really like. When we heard this it was just so instant and exciting.' Hanoi Rocks had briefly inspired them at the start of the decade, but that band's glamour was disproportionate to their musical and lyrical prowess. Even the Smiths had not visually appealed to the boys, but here at last was a band that seemed to have it all. Axl Rose was mouthy, political, glamorous and aggressive, and with his band he was taking on the world. Richey talked about his admiration for Axl to *Kerrang!*: '"Sweet Child O' Mine" is one of the most amazing love songs ever written and "Welcome To The Jungle" is one of the most hateful, but people just dismiss him [Axl] as a redneck. He's one of the few people I'd like to actually meet and talk to.' Guns N' Roses seemed to say more than all the dreary *C86* and *NME/Melody Maker* bands put together. The only weakness was that Guns N' Roses were not as politically confrontational as the boys preferred. Enter Public Enemy.

It Takes A Nation Of Millions To Hold Us Back had as much effect on the future Manics as Guns N' Roses' *Appetite For Destruction*. Initially put off by the sexist language in the lyrics, the four friends gradually began to see Public Enemy for what they were – the first rap act to have a massive impact, the aggressive, confrontational and academic antidote to everything that is white and mainstream about the industry and society. Up until now, the fledgling Manics were armchair achievers; they listened, read, watched and commented on each new cultural discovery without actually doing anything themselves. What Public Enemy did was to make them pro-active. They had enough influences: the glamour and rock of Guns N' Roses and Hanoi Rocks, the militant politics of Big Flame, McCarthy and Gang Of Four, the emotional intensity of the Smiths, and the pained exasperation of Joy Division, plus the best parts of all the myriad other favourites. Inspired by Public Enemy, instead of sitting in their bedrooms casting a judgmental eye across music and the world, and with some ability on musical instruments, the future Manics realised that it was time to form their own band.

By now, Richey had passed his A levels with three straight 'A' grades and opted to go to university in Swansea. It was the first time the gang had been separated for any length of time. All four friends wrote to each other three times a week and met up in Blackwood all the time – far from diluting their clique, the forced separation actually focused them still more. Unfortunately, Richey did not take to the student lifestyle, and either returned home or asked his friends to visit on most weekends. He was expecting to be surrounded by others who loved to study, wanted to talk and discuss all manner of subjects and generally spend three years learning. What he found was like any other university – several thousand kids, first time away from home, with little or no interest in study (at least not for the first year or two), drinking, drugging and shagging their way through their grants. Richey

Complete with spray-painted shirts, make-up and loud mouths, 1990

initially planned to be a teacher and found his political history degree very interesting. What's more he loved the facilities on offer, as he later told the *NME Student Guide*: 'It was going to a nice library and reading books all day. That was a pleasure and a privilege.' However, he watched in horror as the drinking games and pally student cliques formed around him:

'I never equated university with fun, I thought it was about reading and learning, but for most people it was about reading and getting laid. Big fucking deal! I found that really offensive.' Richey went to university a virgin and left it the same.

Apart from a prank for the first year's Rag Week, when he painted himself white and dressed up as a sperm, Richey had little or no involvement in the typical student lifestyle. Living in communal digs was claustrophobic: 'I think if I'd been able to have a flat of my own my memory would've been very different because I've never been very good with very many different people. I've always surrounded myself with just a very few people. To hole myself up in a tower block with hundreds of people I had nothing in common with was a really bad experience.' The one thing that Richey did start doing that was in keeping with many students was drinking. He wasn't drinking to be with the in-crowd, he was drinking because the in-crowd kept him awake at nights. While he wanted to get some sleep ready for more study the following morning, the corridors were full of shouting, pissed students, and Richey hated it. He tried sleeping tablets, but found they gave him a shallow, restless slumber. He could only find the pleasure of deep sleep in the oblivion of drink.

He told *The NME Student Guide* how his grant money had easily been enough to live on because all he ever did was read in his room and buy the odd CD and bottle of wine. The facts are that by his second year, Richey was drinking heavily. Of greater concern were the first signs of self-mutilation. James saw this during Richey's third year, when he visited him in the Easter just before his finals and was shocked by his friend's appearance. Richey would often slice into his arm with a compass, and his weight had dropped to less than seven stone. Approaching his finals he had realised he couldn't do them drunk, so his manner of exerting some self-control and dealing with his inner pain was to gouge himself instead. When he subsequently graduated with a higher second-class degree, one potential check on this self-mutilation was gone. He left university in June 1989, aged 22, five-foot-eight, and weighing just over six stone.

A common myth about the Manic Street Preachers is that they are self-educated; but in fact all four have good A levels and two have degrees. The second is Nicky, who went up a year after Richey. Nicky's time at university was nowhere near as traumatic as his friend's, although the first few months were somewhat unsettling. At first he went to Portsmouth Polytechnic, because poor mock A level results had discouraged him from applying to a university. After three weeks at Poly he hated it with a passion. Fortunately, his mother rang up Swansea University dozens of times, pestering them to accept her son, and after some initial resistance they conceded, letting Nicky transfer to their politics course. He took up residence in a student village in the hills with two other lads who were regular all-England sporty types. He lived here for his entire three-year course, although for the first year he too went home nearly every weekend. Over that period, Nicky became much more confident and more outspoken: 'What a dork . . . I was much more outwardly nervous then. I always had a kind of quiet arrogance and slight bitterness against the world, but I didn't have the guts to do anything about it.' He had little interest in student political circles, and didn't spend his grant in the Oxfam and thrift stores so frequented by his peers. Instead, he tended towards the 'nerd' look, with Pringle golf jumpers and slacks. He and Richey became much closer friends at the university, with neither of them ever going near the legendary Union building. Instead they would often go and play golf alone together.

Whilst his classmates were getting drunk or smoking dope, Nicky was sipping Diet Coke and playing fruit machines, a hobby that became an addiction which landed him with £3000 of debt by his graduation: 'I've never drunk or taken a single drug in my life so I guess fruit machines took their place.' Back at home, James was working in a bar and used to mail Nicky fivers and tenners to help with his mounting debt. Nicky also had little respect for his tutors, most of whom he felt had personal agendas for being there, either writing books or pursuing academic careers, with little interest in teaching. He found the study regimes tiresome and struggled to fit in with the workload expected. As a result he struggled to get a lower second, but was not remotely bothered. He had gone there for other reasons. Whereas Richey loved to study, Nicky was there because he wanted to please his parents, who had been good to him, plus 'it was three more years of not having to decide what you want to do in your life. I've literally never done a day's work in my life, not even a paper round, so I couldn't handle going to work in an office.' He did actually have a postman's round over one Christmas while at university, but hated it so much that his father came and helped him deliver the letters, and he quit after only three days.

CHAPTER 3

'We were a band before we even picked up guitars and we didn't even know how, but we knew that Richey had to be a part of it.'

Nicky

Interviewer: 'Who's the best – Paula Abdul or Kylie?'
MSP: 'We are the scum that remind people of misery.
When we jump onstage it is not rock 'n' roll
cliché but the geometry of contempt.'

The idea of forming a band was not a completely blind leap of faith. Whilst Nicky and Richey were studying, James became a fanatical guitar player, having got his first six-string aged seventeen. *Appetite For Destruction* was learned note for note behind drawn curtains when his parents went to work. When the landmark 'Sweet Child O' Mine' single was released, he put his mind to creating a song that would be as good. James, who now wore a skinhead haircut, had become a regular busker in Cardiff city centre, where he would spend many weekends screaming the Clash's 'Garageland' at passers-by and chasing after them for money. Nicky sometimes joined him on rhythm acoustic guitar, after which they would go back to James's father's house to play more songs.

Nicky had been scribbling words for a couple of years. His first 'song' had in fact been written in 1984; called 'The Aftermath', it was a vicious diatribe against Mrs Thatcher and the effects of the Miners' Strike. Richey was also always writing, but at this point he was not considered as a potential band member. Sean was roped in because he was the youngest trumpeter in the South Wales Jazz Band, was their only friend with a music A level and, most importantly, he had started playing drums. Each night when they rehearsed in James's house, his father would return home from work shattered and dirty, and the sight of him inspired the three friends to pursue their already lofty ambitions of rock 'n' roll greatness. Both James and Sean duly deferred places at university (for philosophy and music respectively) so that they could pursue their musical interests full-time.

They enrolled a mutual friend called Flicker to play the bass, and booked their first gig. With James's bedroom as their base, they started rehearsing. In the week before that debut gig, they named themselves first the Blue Generation, then Betty Blue, before finally settling on the Manic Street Preachers. One theory is that the name was inspired by a band called Jasmine Minks, whose album *All Good Preachers Go To Heaven* was a favourite of theirs. Some say James just thought of the name in his sleep, but it was more likely taken from a passing comment by an old man who was being harangued by a crew-cut James during a busking stint in Cardiff. More shambolic rehearsals followed, with Richey joining them from university for all of them, and, as the only one who had passed his driving test, offering his services as the band's driver.

The very first gig was at a pub in Blackwood, where the hardy locals were so offended by the dire racket and glamorous clothes of the pretty boys onstage that they showered the band with beer bottles and ashtrays. The infant Manics played one more local gig then decided it was time to record something, having now written a batch of their own material. In June 1988, a friend of theirs who owned a studio agreed to give them some cheap recording time, so they pooled their giro cheques and prepared for their ramshackle opening session. Four tracks were recorded, namely 'Suicide Alley', 'New Art Riot', 'Tennessee (I Feel So Low)' and 'Repeat'. Only 300 copies were pressed. The first 150 featured cover artwork with a photograph by Richey but dwindling finances meant that the remaining 150 were placed in a cheaper hand-made sleeve, which Richey again produced. This release is obviously exceptionally rare and by the mid-nineties had been known to exchange hands for over £100. Also, the producer-friend who recorded the sessions has had to fend off frequent calls from Manics-wannabes who are desperate for him to record their work.

Much can be made of the Manics' lengthy evolution into a sophisticated rock band, but at this stage, with the 'Suicide Alley' EP, the music was quite dreadful – retrospective rock, with a splash of minor punk. The drumming was out of time and guitars jaggedly annoying, whilst James's vocals were screamed out in haste, making them sound grating and the lyrics incomprehensible.

The Manics made no attempt to sell the EP and recoup their expenses. Instead, all 300 were sent out to record companies, managers, agents, journalists and other industry types. Almost no one replied and there were no gigs forthcoming from the release, let alone contracts – the major label WEA contacted them, but that was only to return the record. The only glimmer of light at the end of the tunnel was a remarkable review in the *NME* by Steven Wells, who made 'Suicide Alley' his Single Of The Week, and then in the subsequent interview with them sang their praises still further: 'They have more anger and intelligence than any band I have ever interviewed . . . they will be the most important rock band in the world.'

In the face of such apathy, tension within the band flared up. Flicker's recruitment was not working, and after some discussion he was sacked and the bassist's job taken over by Nicky Wire. The vacant rhythm guitarist slot was immediately offered to Richey, mostly because of his beautiful good looks and a brand new guitar he had bought (which he couldn't play). So by December 1989, the line-up was complete, with the official joining date for Richey being the eleventh of that month.

For a band brought up on a love of rock 'n' roll and punk, their first decision was not a very reckless one – up until now, their giros and brief stints by James in a bar and Sean in a civil service job had been paying for much of their expenses, but with Richey already graduated and Nicky in his final year, the time was approaching when they needed more money. So they booked a meeting with their local bank manager. Once inside the bank, they told the bemused, besuited man that they had formed a band and had come for a loan to help them take on the music world. They based their proposition on two key arguments: (a) they were brilliant, and (b) everyone else was useless. 'This country is dead musically,' they said. 'There's got to be room for an exciting rock band.' They then showed him the *NME* and *Melody Maker,* filled with page after page of what they saw as faceless bands, and said 'Anything good in there? Now look at us, we're really exciting.' He turned them down flat.

Their initial rehearsals were severely disrupted when James was badly beaten up in a McDonald's by some yokels who took exception to the way the band looked. (Their behaviour beforehand in a pub where they had extravagantly been drinking Babycham because 'it's better than a pint of Websters and it doesn't make you fat' hadn't helped their image with the locals.) They had been out to celebrate Richey's birthday, and when the yobs started picking on him, James stepped in and was promptly kicked to pieces, breaking his jaw and rendering him unable to sing for some time.

When they had first started they cherished visions of being like Public Enemy but rapidly went off this idea when they saw the appalling standard of most early British rap acts. Then they said they wanted to 'sound like the Sex Pistols and look like Duran Duran', largely because all the girls at school had fancied the Brummie New Romantics. By the time Richey joined, all four friends had evolved a very idiosyncratic dress code – they wore girls' blouses or flowery ladies' garments, usually bought from Oxfam, and would then stencil slogans across them in spray paint. Part of the inspiration for this was the Clash, part was the *Situationist Internationale* of Guy Debord and the Paris revolutionaries whose writings the Manics read fervently. The SI, as they were known, preached a surrealist and Dada-ist ethic of expanding the imagination and of people taking control of their lives. Through confrontational art and sloganeering, they wanted to provoke a revolution in everyday life. The Manics adored this school of thought. Their first gig saw them emblazoned with 'Kill Yourself' and 'Teenage Beat'. They also set certain band rules that were supposed to never be broken: no love songs, no girlfriends and no drugs. Plus, they saw no point in only playing around their hometown, so they duly booked a gig at the Horse and Groom in Great Portland Street, in London's West End. It was only their eighth gig ever.

'We realised that as individuals we were very limited as people, so we had to fabricate ourselves and took a very academic approach at being in a band. We were quite clinical. We were like magpies, collecting information, keeping dossiers on journalists and learning how to manipulate them.'

Nicky Wire

'We came together around Nick. I was Baldrick to his Blackadder. More than anything he talked about being great, being legends. Nick reckoned he would be a great sportsman, a great musician, a great politician. We started on the basis of those delusions of grandeur.'

James

SCUM ON FEEL THE NOISE

Before the media had a chance to hear the Manics' music, they were bombarded with an amazing selection of venom-filled letters. During their time in South Wales, the band had meticulously kept press files of all the name journalists, how they wrote, who they liked, disliked, reviewed and so on. With this database of names and attitudes, the Manics now started firing off ranting letters to them, as well as to managers, record company executives, and industry types in general. The handwritten tirades would often stretch to four or five pages, wherein the band would rail against all the evils of the world, and announce their own brilliance. At the start of 1990, the music media was awash with these highly articulate, expertly written manifestos which drew parallels with the bitingly provocative fanzines of the early eighties like *Attack Of Bzag!* The sheer intelligence that shone through the letters was reinforced by the quotes from all corners of

● Venting their delinquent spleen at any target that moves Summer Of Love terrorists MANIC STREET PREACHERS plan to obliterate the monarchy, House of Lords, boredom and probably themselves on their blitzkrieg ride to hell.

"We are the scum factor of the Mondays meets the guitar overload of Five Thirty/Ride while killing Birdland with politics." READ THIS!

One of the flood of early Manics clippings

literature, from Marx to Burroughs, and Orwell to Greil Marcus. Steven Wells of the *NME* received one such letter which declared: 'We look like nothing else on earth. A car bomb kiss-off to the *Face*. Politics and adolescent cheap sex. Fuck the rotten edifice of Manchester. Too safe in dressing like a bricklayer. Too boring. Too macho, males afraid of themselves.' In one letter to the *Melody Maker*'s Stud Brothers they bemoaned the lack of 'heroin tainted rock 'n' roll', while praying for violence and alienation, talked of the Romanian revolution, and said all they knew was 'destruction, sex and heroin'. Many of the letters ended with the tempting promise that they were sure to keep 'drugs supplied'.

Such intense, delinquent spleen-venting was bound to attract attention among the dull mass of formulaic PR-speak that the music press were daily bombarded with. After receiving reams of these letters, journalists would then be phoned up and, their curiosity heightened, invariably spoke to the Manics in person. In this fashion the band were able to attract quite a few media names to that first London gig in Great Portland Street. Privately, the Manics were somewhat less enamoured with the music press: 'At the time most journalists seemed to be public school drop-outs,' Nicky later told *NME*. 'You could pick them off one by one. They'd been put in public school and they'd fucked up because they weren't very intelligent. And we'd come along. We were very bright, we'd stress the fact that we were educated and they didn't want to know. They wanted to make us their playthings.'

The spring of 1989 had heralded the beginnings of 'Madchester' when the Mancunian corner of the music world once again provided a plethora of bands intent on revolutionising the rock and dance format, following in the tradition of Joy Division and New Order. The Stone Roses led the way with the Happy Mondays and Inspiral Carpets following closely behind, as 'baggy' music swept the nation up in a tide of flares, shirts with extra-long sleeves and Joe Bloggs clothing. There was a general air of apathy around these bands, the drugs, the inactivity and the apolitical and abstract dismay towards life which came with the innovative musical territory. By the end of the next year 'baggy' was creatively dead with its foremost proponents, the Stone Roses, locked in bitter courtroom struggles, spending all their time in court rather than the charts. For now though, 1990 was theirs, and Madchester was a genuine and far-reaching phenomenon.

For those journalists attending that first London gig of the Manic Street Preachers, the whole baggy culture might as well have been from another planet. Everyone was saying, 'Chill out, spliff up,' and here came this new band handing out calling cards saying 'Anxiety is freedom'. By coincidence, as well as the writers who had specifically come to see the Welsh band, there were several other music journalists in the pub, who were enjoying a quiet pint before the Wonder Stuff gig down the road later that night. The tiny room where they were to play had no stage and no PA, but they strode out confidently in their hand-stencilled shirts and thick black eye-liner, with their skinny legs crushed into vein-burstingly tight white jeans. The immediate visual impact of the Manics was one of overt androgyny which made them as far from the 'bloke down the pub' look of Shaun Ryder as possible. Even their name was a verbose two-fingered salute to the hordes of monosyllabic bands around like Blur, Lush and Moose.

The gig itself was a bizarre pastiche of early Clash/punk concerts.

Richey and Nicky minced around provocatively with their pouting lips and high cheek bones, and all three guitarists reeled out all the clichéd punk rock poses, including whirlwind guitars, pogo-ing and scissor kicking. Had the onlookers been deaf, the gig might have actually been quite entertaining. However, at this stage, the Manics' live performance was diabolical. On 'Suicide Alley' they had offered a fractured and poorly recorded debut, and their live set did nothing to improve on this. Any power that might have been found in the raucous guitars was lost in the frenzied aural attack, and James's still weak voice was all but unintelligible. That night, several A&R men scoffed and laughed at the band they had expected so much from, with more than one voice mumbling something about a 'poor SLF cover band'.

Their furrowed brows were eased somewhat by an interview the next week in *Melody Maker* by Bob Stanley, who had seen the gig and loved it. Bob Stanley was so impressed by the Horse and Groom gig and his subsequent interview that he put out a flexi-disc of the Manics on the front of his excellent *Hopelessly Devoted* fanzine, which cost just 50 pence. The songs included were 'UK Channel Boredom' with a flip side of 'I Don't Know Why The Trouble Is' by another new band, the Laurens. The flexi-disc contained the words on the label 'This record is not to be sold to anyone who was ten or more in 1977.'

After this gig, the Manics became convinced that if they were to succeed, they had to play much more in London. They laughed at the local bands in Gwent who ploughed the same old tired furrow of small-town pubs and clubs, hundreds of miles from the capital, hoping that a talent scout from Sony would just happen to be in the Dog and Duck in Newport and sign them up. The Manics always had more vision than this, as Richey explained to the *Toronto Star*: 'Once we got set in our minds what we were doing, we didn't play a single gig in Blackwood. It was straight to London and scrounging money to get on the pay-for-play circuit. Y' know, 50 for fifteen minutes. Next thing was getting the press out to the shows. This is extremely difficult in England because the music press wields the power to make or destroy taste and they don't like anything they don't discover themselves.'

The Manics got round this with their tirade of letters and glam photos, and when journalists did attend a gig, the band would corner them for hours. When the men from the press could take no more, the Manics would duly pack up their gear, jump in the van for the four-hour drive back to Blackwood, sleep for a few hours and then get up to watch that day's episode of *Neighbours*. Any gigs that were near to London were considered worthwhile – in February 1990, they played a social club in Oxford during a severe snow storm. With the roads thick with snow and many curious local punters unable to make it because of the weather, it was highly unlikely that the band would complete the treacherous journey from South Wales. But eventually they did, after six hours in a freezing, skidding van. They finally took to the stage at 10.30pm, played for 25 blisteringly short minutes (no encore), packed up and drove back home.

On these treks up and down the M4 to the capital, the four provincial lads were shocked to see how the music industry worked close-up. Having spent their adolescent years dreaming of this ideal place where grandiose schemes and perfect bands were formed, they faced the harsh truth one night in trendy, sycophantic Camden. As Richey told the *Guardian*, 'We went down to the Underworld club one night. It was unbelievable. There were, like, five bands and loads of journalists, all drinking at the same tables. We were naive, but we never thought there would be that really close level of friendship.' He continued: 'It was a sad time when we came up here and realized how small and ghetto-ised everything is. There wasn't one figure who was larger than life.' Other revered venues in Camden, the so-called music capital of London, equally failed to impress. As Richey told *Lime Lizard*: 'We went to the Camden Falcon, we'd grown up with this idea of a seminal venue, this brilliant place where all these really interesting people go. You go there and it's worse than any pub gig in our town. There are bands playing at home that are twice as good as anything that goes on at the Falcon, and they never get noticed.'

However, their London-oriented plan paid off when shortly after a gig at the Bull and Gate in Kentish Town they agreed an informal record deal with Damaged Goods Records, run by Ian Ballard. He had seen the Horse and Groom gig as well and, on a handshake in Walthamstow, agreed to put out their 'debut' EP. Damaged Goods was perfect for the Manic Street Preachers. Ballard was a massive record collector and music fan who ran this one-man operation from a very small office on an industrial estate in east London. In the early days, he printed a large range of posters and postcards of primarily punk bands, most of which were hand-made by Ballard himself.

At their first London gig, he had been immediately impressed by the intelligence and passion of the four Welsh boys, particularly Richey, of whom he said to *Select* magazine: 'He must have read books from day one while the rest of us were watching telly. He's very intelligent. I think he finds it difficult talking to people who aren't similarly educated. He'd sit there quoting things and I'd be nodding thinking, "I don't know what you are talking about."'

Circa 'Suicide Alley', 1990

What Ballard did know about was releasing records. So while the band were piling up and down the motorway, Damaged Goods released the Manics' second EP in June 1990. Due to the scarcity of 'Suicide Alley' this was to be the first chance that most people had to hear them. The informal deal was that in exchange for Ballard releasing the record, he could put those tracks out forever, in whatever format he chose, and however many times. Consequently, the initial EP was black vinyl but has since appeared in numerous re-pressings of 1000 a time in various lurid shades as well as a picture disc. It featured four tracks: 'New Art Riot', 'Strip It Down', 'Last Exit On Yesterday' and 'Teenage 20/20'. Musically there was still not much sophistication or apparent potential. In many ways, the Manics sounded more akin to the Senseless Things and Mega City Four than the Clash, with James's unusually high vocals reminiscent of the Mega's brilliant lead singer Wiz. The record was a throwback to 1977, but at least it was a refreshing change from the dance-based, lackadaisical hedonism of Madchester. For many kids, it was the first punk rock record they had ever bought.

With this release under their belts, the Manics started to attract more attention, but as yet were still without a manager, an agent or a long-term record deal. Into the fray stepped Philip Hall of Hall or Nothing PR. After the band had got his phone number from *NME* journalist Steve Lamacq, Hall had been hounded by calls from them. Then he received his copy of the *New Art Riot* EP and a photograph of them in their full attire. So taken was he by the noise that greeted him from his sound system that he arranged to go and see them in Wales. He did not even wait for a gig, but instead dropped in on a rehearsal at Newbridge School. When he arrived the band were still mostly unsure of what he could do for them, but they knew he was an important figure in the business.

They were not wrong. Philip Hall was currently in the midst of splashing the Stone Roses over every music magazine in the UK. The Mancunian band were perhaps the flagship name on the roster of his PR company, which would also look after the publicity work for bands such as Radiohead, the Beautiful South, James, the Pogues and the Sundays. Hall himself had an impressive pedigree. Born in Ealing in 1959, he went to school in Wimbledon before moving on to the London College of Printing where he graduated in journalism. He immediately joined *Record Mirror*, then moved onto the record company side with a job at EMI, before taking over as Head of Press for Stiff Records. He worked at Stiff until its sad demise in 1985, whereupon he set up Hall or Nothing, behind which he very rapidly established an enviable reputation as one of the finest PR men in the business. This expertise was rewarded in the late eighties when he twice won *Music Week*'s PR Award Of The Year, firstly for his work with the Pogues and then with the Stone Roses. As well as being instrumental in revitalising Reading Festival, the Fleadhs and Finsbury Park gigs, he also set up his own record label, Sacred Heart, one of whose first signings was the momentarily fashionable three-piece from Hull, Kingmaker.

Despite this experience, he had never seen anything like the band he found in that classroom rehearsal. Covered in eyeliner as usual, and wearing their spray-painted slogan shirts he had heard so much about, the Manics were indeed a sight to behold. Nicky was covered in blood, although only from something as innocent as accidentally hitting himself in the face with his own bass. Philip Hall and his younger brother and partner Martin were so impressed by what they heard that they signed up as managers of the band within three months (partly urged on by the band's claim that 'we will die of boredom if you don't help us'). At a time when the Manics were being ridiculed and dismissed in the music press, this was a typically fractious thing for Hall to do, and the continued attacks on his new charges in the media only strengthened his resolve to help them. They had played fewer than a dozen gigs to date.

Having just recently got married, Hall could have been forgiven for wanting to enjoy some domestic bliss at home with his wife for a while. Instead, he offered the Manics the floor of his Shepherd's Bush flat to sleep on while they moved to London and looked for a permanent roof over their heads. They took him up on his offer and ended up staying for over a year.

In keeping with the paradoxical nature of the band, Hall found the Manics to be mouthy firebrands in the press but quietly spoken gentlemen in real life. They kept Hall's house spotlessly clean while he and his new wife were out at work. Each night they would have dinner ready on the table when they came home and very quickly became like family – because of this Hall would often tell bemused Manics-haters that the band were in fact 'sweet'. The only bad development during this exciting time was when Richey occasionally cut himself. He would be sitting in the living room absent-mindedly opening a wound on his arm until someone would cough or nod and he would stop.

Hall also started sinking his own money into the band's future, so much so that by the time they signed their major label record deal he had remortgaged his house and was owed £45,000. Even when the band developed a habit of going onstage and smashing up their expensive gear he never said a word – indeed, he encouraged it, being the ever-opportunistic publicity expert he was. His faith was returned by their unbelievable drive and vision; he had never seen another band with so many ideas and such a focus on what they wanted to achieve, represented by the steady stream of proposals and plans they drew up for him. Richey summed up how crucial Philip Hall was to the band's career and lives at this point when he told *Melody Maker*, 'He had a big impact on our lives, he was the first person that ever believed in our music, the first to respond to all the stupidly long letters we would send out to anyone we could think of.'

CHAPTER 4

'Whatever anyone thinks of us, whatever happens to us, at least we'll know that we always tried to be a brilliant band. We've set ourselves up to be compared with the greatest rock bands ever. We've always set out to be something worthwhile that meant something real and valuable, to make records about ideas and attitudes that are important and real, and that no one else is doing, to be the band that we never had when we were growing up.'

Richey

With *New Art Riot* selling over 4500 copies, things were beginning to look up for the Manics. During the summer and autumn of 1990 their impact on the music press was nothing short of astonishing. There were three key factors to this impressive arrival – their image, their sexuality, and their so-called masterplan.

Their image was a stark contrast to virtually every other band around at the time. When the vogue was for scruffy baggy trousers and brand-name designer labels, the Manics were walking around in skin-tight white jeans and home-made shirts or their sisters' borrowed blouses. In the bloke's world of Madchester, stubble was the order of the day – the Manics had to shave religiously so they could put their make-up on properly. While the floppy bowl haircut was the national trend, the Manics were piling their locks high, plastering them with gel and dying them jet black, more reminiscent of Izzy Stradlin of Guns N' Roses (who were infinitely unfashionable in alternative circles at the time) and Keith Richards than the Stone Roses or Inspiral Carpets. While the Madchester ethic was general apathy, the Manics forced their issues down the public's throat, harking back to Paul Simonon and Mick Jones of the Clash. James often wore a salmon pink pyjama top (only Sean refrained from blouses) which once belonged to his auntie, although it probably did not bear the legend 'I Am A Slut' when she owned it. Richey also remarked to *Sounds*, 'You can maybe ignore our songs but when we walk down the street and you see our song titles on our chests you've got to think something.'

For the Manics, this glamour was essential to their ideas. It referred back to the basic appeal of frontmen like Mike Monroe of Hanoi Rocks or Axl Rose of Guns N' Roses. They claimed that people, especially in the provinces, enjoyed coming back from work, taking a bath and dressing up to go out. The Manics scoffed at the scruffy likes of Happy Mondays, the Stone Roses and the dozens of lesser Madchester bands such as Inspiral Carpets, and the Farm. Richey once told *Melody Maker*, 'They can't understand any band who has pretension, who thinks of rock 'n' roll as power, who wants to dress up. You can tell they're middle-class poseurs because they wanna dress down like scummy people. The working-class tradition has always been to want to be clean and dress up.'

At the same time, these trashy, almost Warholian-style pouting poseurs from the Valleys made it clear their image was not reflective of their general frame of mind. Nicky told *Melody Maker*, 'If you're hopelessly depressed like me, the ultimate escape is dressing up.' He also said to *NME*, 'If we looked like we felt then we would have come onstage like Joy Division. We had to make a massive effort to be a glamorous band, because inside we know we're not particularly glamorous really.' Even so, it was a positive depression, if there can be such a thing, and part of that was to rid the music business of so much of the rubbish that filled its shelves, as this classic quote from an increasingly rent-a-gob Nicky showed: 'We want to be the perfect mix between politics and beauty . . .' he told *Sounds*. 'The Bridewell Taxis, the Paris Angels – it's just so obscene that fat people are allowed in bands.'

Instrumental to this image was the second key aspect of the early Manics – their peculiar, ambiguous sex appeal. Against a backdrop of South Wales rugby-playing, beer-drinking, women-shagging 'blokes', the Manics were androgynous with a passion. Obviously the make-up and blouses were a focal point, but the band were also openly honest about their personal lives. Nicky said he had once had a girlfriend but only briefly as 'it was too scary'. Richey had still had had no relationship, despite now being 23, and openly admitted he was a virgin until the middle of 1990, and even then he showed little interest in sex, saying to *Melody Maker*, 'Personally, though, sex is just another way of blocking out the boredom.' James admitted they were always

useless at getting girls at school and were now too self-obsessed to bother – it was only Sean again who was the exception, as he had been 'going steady' with someone. They quite deliberately left their sexuality ambivalent, such as at one live show when James said, 'If there's any pretty boys out there who want to bugger me, I'll see you all after the show.' Nicky was even more direct, saying, 'When I go onstage I feel like everybody wants to kill me or fuck me. It's as simple as that.' He continued, 'Sex is crucial to this group. It's the most subversive thing in Wales because everybody fucks all the time. You come to London and no one seems to fuck at all, unless they're paying for it in some way.'

The Manics attacked Happy Mondays' reinforcement of gender barriers, with their all-male bravado which was making lager louts fashionable – the Manics clearly appealed to both sexes. As for their only loosely applied rule never to have girlfriends, Richey told *Melody Maker*, 'Once you fall in love or get your girlfriend pregnant or fall into credit, you've got no chance. You've got responsibilities. There's no way you can ever do anything. Once you're reduced to a couple, alone, together between your four walls with your TV set, you're cut off.' They thought that emotional ties would impair their single-mindedness and focus and hence impede their third and most crucial factor – 'the masterplan'.

With a panache that was quite simply astounding, the Manics informed the public and media of this plan during a barrage of press interviews in the latter part of 1990 and most of 1991, in a campaign for media domination. If the band's music was still somewhat stunted, their ability to manipulate and work the press was without equal. Their arrogant and often outrageous statements of intent ensured that by the end of that period they were one of Britain's most loved and most hated bands. With a venom that was fascinating to watch, the Manics poured forth their own plans, what they saw as the useless nature of their peers, their alienation from their own generation and even the future of society, and in the process enjoyed more coverage and press column inches than perhaps any band since the Smiths.

The 'masterplan' was nothing if not simple. First, release a debut double album of 30 tracks, on a major label, that will be so monumental it will provide the reference point for all other rock albums thereafter. Second, sell sixteen million copies of said debut album. Third, tour the world, conquering America on the way and filling stadium shows worldwide.

Fourth, introduce a new revolution through their music, which would incorporate Leninist and Stalinist principles, abolish the monarchy and House Of Lords and revert Britain back to a grassroots socialism. Fifth, denounce all other bands. Sixth, denounce their own generation. Seventh, do all of the above in one year and then split up. And last but not least, look fantastic while doing it.

Despite currently being on an informal handshake with Damaged Goods for one single only, the Manics seemed to think this preposterous ambition was not a problem. Also, the fact that their music to date was little more than clumsy retrospective dirges did not deter them. The sixteen million copies sold looked rather unlikely as *New Art Riot* had not struggled up to 5000, and the stadium-filling concerts seemed a tad ambitious when they were playing the likes of Exeter University to 300 disinterested students who were only there for the cheap beer. The social revolution seemed a small order by comparison. However, these fairly serious flaws in their plan never once bothered the Manics.

While the multi-platinum sales and worldwide domination were not instantly achievable, they set about one of their more immediate aims with a vengeance – verbalising their

In Hall or Nothing's offices, Fulham, 1991

apparent utter hatred of all other bands. They never acknowledged any influences, and even the obvious early comparison with the Clash was denied with venom. Apart from a passing reference to liking the Gang Of Four, no one was sacrosanct. The Manchester scene was abhorred because it retreated from any kind of action or class politics into a cosy world of Ecstasy and apathy. The forthcoming so-called 'Scene That Celebrates Itself' was not spared either. Loosely based around a batch of bands including the Boo Radleys, Slowdive, Ride, Chapterhouse and Moose, the guitar effects and sumptuous sonic perfectionism of these bands was coupled with almost completely static live shows and seemingly non-existent opinions. Richey had no time for this, telling *Melody Maker*, 'All those bands are educated and

Soho, London, summer 1991

middle-class but all they have to say is "We don't want to say anything."' Nicky agreed: 'It's nullifying. There's nowhere you can go with it but into your bedroom. We've done that all our lives, that's the last thing we wanna do. It's an aesthetic of blanking out everything.'

The highly popular fraggle/grebo/Stourbridge band scene that had emerged at the end of the eighties was also attacked. The Wonder Stuff, Pop Will Eat Itself and Ned's Atomic Dustbin all hailed from the same West Midlands town of Stourbridge, and along with other bands from around the provinces such as Mega City Four, Senseless Things, Carter the Unstoppable Sex Machine and the Levellers, had brought a new style of indie culture to the fore. Lurid T-shirt and surf-short-wearing kids bought their records in the thousands and succeeded in putting many of the major proponents on *Top Of The Pops* and into the higher echelons of the charts – indeed, the Wonder Stuff enjoyed a Number 1 hit with Vic Reeves's cover version of 'Dizzy'. This success had little clout with the Manics: 'We want to destroy all the subcultures that have been around for so long – like gothic, anarcho, that Wonder Stuff/Stourbridge scene, Carter. It's so terrible, so unclean,' said Richey to *Sounds*. When it was pointed out that the Neds were selling hundreds of thousands of records, Richey was unmoved. He told *Vox*, 'We never said it was a crime to come from Stourbridge, but if you do . . . perhaps you should reflect that more in your lyrics.' They attacked the Mega City Four's alleged lack of ambition, as that band were renowned for their lengthy Transit van capers, yet neglected to mention the begging letters which all these bands received from the Manics pleading for support slots (the Megas duly gave them one in Newport).

Acknowledged classic bands were also seen as fair game, hence Sonic Youth were 'the biggest pile of art wank' and David Bowie was 'a sad old cunt'. Richey later said, 'I like the PM Dawn title but you can't allow yourself to listen to records by fat people,' and of Bob Mould and PJ Harvey's critically acclaimed work Nicky said, 'I find this endless catharsis of modern life really depressing.' On the subject of the much-heralded guitar work of the Stone Roses' John Squire, they claimed Richey could play his music with his hands behind his back (in fact Richey could barely play a note).

When their interviews turned to subjects other than crucifying your entire peer group, it was clear that here was a band with an intellect far superior to the norm – quotes from people such as Lenin, Camus, Nietzsche,

Marx, and Kierkegaard, mixed with highly informed discussions on all manner of subjects including situationism, modern art, socialism and revolution. While the band were happy to dwell on lengthy conversations about deep philosophical matters, they also emerged as the masters of the soundbite, which in the nineties media is quite a skill. In their first eighteen months in the public eye, the Manics delivered more classic one-liners than most bands manage in a lifetime, including 'We'll always hate Slowdive more than Hitler,' 'Today I would rather fall in love with a washing machine than a woman,' 'We'll do one brilliant album then disappear, gain everything then give it away, create this franchise then scrap it,' 'We promise to die young and leave good-looking corpses,' and 'The only time it will all be worthwhile is if we go Top Ten in the national charts . . . and the government's trying to stop us.'

The music press thought all their Christmases had come at once. The controversies of Madchester, Happy Mondays' apparent homophobic comments, the gun culture at the Hacienda, the drugs and the rock 'n' roll now seemed like small fry. Richey Edwards and Nicky Wire, the glamour twins and self-proclaimed mouthpieces of the band, looked and sounded unbelievable. The magazines were queuing up to speak to these four mouthy revolutionaries and the Manics were more than happy to oblige – they never turned down an interview, including fanzine articles and even two school magazine pieces.

If the Manics had been producing groundbreaking music when they slagged off every band in the country, then people might have been a little more understanding of their distaste. As it was, all people had to go on so far were their two tatty EPs, so it was understandable that their criticisms were met with either contempt, or hoots of laughter. More often than not, their attacks were parried with the observation that they were little more than Clash revivalists. For many of their detractors, it was highly ironic that a band with so much hate for their peers were apparently touting a tired 1977 formula that was far less original than those bands they criticised. Indeed, many thought the Clash comparison flattered the Manics, and felt a poor SLF/Ruts/999 parallel was more accurate. The obvious comparisons with Hanoi Rocks and glam rock were usually ignored, so although the Manics would often play Alice Cooper's 'Under My Wheels' or Guns N' Roses' 'It's So Easy' at gigs the review the next week would invariably ramble on and on about Joe Strummer.

Not everyone saw the Clash comparison as derogatory. There were always people who were anxious to herald the return of punk rock, and consequently an array of bands such as GBH, Anti-Pasti, the Exploited, the Oi! Movement and even the farcical pantomime of Sigue Sigue Sputnik had been lumbered with that burden. For these retro fans, the Manics were the latest torch-bearers. They were never going to be as linear as this, however – musically their songs were direct enough, but the lyrical content and intellectual background were far too complex. Plus, the Clash were often criticised for being a narrow-minded 'male' band (like the latter-day Happy Mondays, Flowered Up and MC Tunes, they were often accused of homophobia and sexism), whereas the Manics' feminine side was always paramount.

However, many of the same people who criticised the Manics for stealing from 1977 were hailing great new dance bands who were openly plundering the sixties. It was okay to steal a Byrds riff or a Stones hook line, but not to do the same with punk rock. This contradiction was especially apparent at a spring 1991 gig the band performed with Flowered Up at Manchester International. (The festive tour included the Manics' first date in Europe, at the Locomotive Club in Paris, for which the opinionated foursome had to get their first passports.) In many ways, the Manchester date crystallised the degree to which the Manics and the dance craze were poles apart. Hordes of baggy-trousered kids on Ecstasy watched in total bemusement as their very antithesis, the Manics, in their tight jeans and slogan-painted shirts, screamed highly charged political lyrics over their sub-two-minute blasts of punk while windmilling their guitar arms frantically. For many kids in the crowd, this was the most aggressive band they had ever seen – they were in a chemically induced state of love and here came the Manics pouring bile and hatred all over them. When they finished their set and a man dressed up as a flower came onstage, it suddenly made sense why the Manics claimed they were radical. The Manics' retro-isms were certainly no more overt than Flowered Up's Woodstock plundering, but the fashion dictated that one was acceptable and the other wasn't. Most of the people watching thought the Manics were the worst band in the world. Just a few thought they were the best. Who was right?

CHAPTER 5

'The only perfect circle on a human body is the eye. When a baby is born it's so perfect, but when it opens its eyes it's just blinded by the corruption and everything else is a downward spiral.'

Richey

This tour with Flowered Up was the result of the band's first record contract, with music publicist Jeff Barrett's Heavenly Records. Barrett had first seen one of their typically vitriolic interviews in the energetic fanzine *Hungry Bear*. Then he received one of their infamous letters: 'I was handed this letter and told "Read this",' Barrett recalled to *Volume*. 'It was passionate, it was on fire, it wanted to change the world and it really excited me. Unfortunately their demo tape didn't do as much for me.' However, the Manics pestered Barrett ceaselessly until after much persuasion he gave in and signed them to a two-single deal. At the time, Heavenly was a very hip label to be on, with bands like Flowered Up, St Etienne and East Village on the roster.

The first fruit of this deal was the new single in January 1991, called 'Motown Junk'. Although Nicky said, '"Motown Junk" was the starting point for us really. That was the first time we ever felt like a band, the first time we created a record we could live with,' the record itself was devoid of anything that placed it beyond 1978, other than the Public Enemy sample that kicked things off. It was a trite love song that contained an undercurrent of rebellion masked in a heavy layer of white noise, with Richey's lyrics delivered in an unintelligible, shrill voice. 'Motown Junk' was indeed their best offering yet, but remained way short of being the revolutionary manifesto they had talked up so strongly. The punk lyrics and tinny guitars were appealing but not quite convincing enough. The overall sound did little to deter the continuing Clash snipes, and even the B-side of 'We Her Majesty's Prisoners' was a faint echo of the Pistols' 'God Save The Queen'.

Even so, the media were gobbling it up – the *NME* made 'Motown

Junk' their Single Of The Week and the band were invited on to *Snub TV*, *Rapido* and BBC Radio One's *Mark Goodier Session* off the back of the release. A planned eleven-date tour to support the single had to be lengthened by another twelve dates due to sheer demand. Amidst all this, the band won their first ever music weekly front cover, when *Sounds* slapped them across the nation's newsstands, complete with Richey in a self-styled 'Kill Yourself' shirt and the legend 'Generation Terrorists' scrawled on the wall above them. Ironically, the first few dates had to be cancelled after Nicky was taken to hospital for emergency surgery on a thyroid cyst in his neck. The cyst was removed and he received twelve stitches, but as a result of the operation the band was unable to fulfil the Reading, Southampton, Leicester and Coventry gigs (the fact they were playing venues like the Joiners Arms in Southampton and the Stoke Wheatsheaf thrilled their detractors). A comment from an apparent 'specialist' said the injury arose out of 'boredom and physical inertia due to a lifestyle of force-fed TV, no sleep and a diet of Coke and chips'.

With the next single, the Manics continued their controversial rise to fame. The artwork for 'You Love Us' was the subject of multiple writs over the allegedly unauthorised use in a collage of images of Beatrice Dalle from the film *Betty Blue*, Robert De Niro in *Taxi Driver*, and stills of Marilyn Monroe, Bob Marley, the Who, the Clash, Travis Bickle, Robert Johnson and Aleister Crowley. They had in fact originally wanted to use a picture of the boxer Chris Eubank also, because, in their words, 'everyone hates him as well'. Intended as a sarcastic Valentine to their detractors, the song was their ultimate live number, but again was filled with tired old riffs and dull metal guitars. The sentiment, however, was brilliantly aggressive and this track came to be a core Manics song.

The tour to promote this single showed the growing support for the band. Each of the gigs was packed with punters while lengthy queues formed outside of those unable to get in. This did not stop the Manics getting their usual share of abuse – James was punched on the nose in Scotland and over 100 bottles and cans were picked off the stage at the Brighton University gig. During this tour, they enjoyed a front cover feature in the *NME*, when journalist James Brown wrote an excellent article following them around Britain. The cover shot showed Richey lying seductively across his bandmates with the word HIV scratched in reverse into his upper chest, whilst Nicky bore the legend 'Culture Slut' in lipstick on his stomach. The article within offered a revealing insight into life on the road with the Manics. Richey and Nicky shared rooms in the cheap B&B's they used, but Richey frequently went sleep-walking. He constantly scribbled notes and ideas on a pad, and at one point offered Brown over six pages of writing, saying that he would like to go through them with him later if possible. The band were being paid only £5 a day at this point and it was revealing what they each spent that on: Richey bought a cheesecake and some deodorant, James got a set of darts, Sean a music magazine and Nicky purchased a cocktail that made him sick.

Some of the dates were in Northern Ireland, where Richey was clearly moved and concerned by what he saw. His notes said, 'London expresses nothing more than its desire to sleep. Belfast expresses nothing more than its desire to kill. Recognised censorship. Berlin Wall gone. Belfast Wall still exists. We're caught, tourists in the war zone.' On the tour bus he read Guy Debord, while the band would all watch videos from their huge collection, a sample of which was kept in an old leather suitcase under the back seat of the van with the words 'Street Preacher' written on it. In the case for this journey were *Taxi Driver*, *Rude Boy*, *Naked Gun*, *Heavy Metal Heaven*, *The Song Remains The Same*, and a Guns N' Roses live video. Sega games were very popular, although there was little credence given to the freshly held belief that such computer games were the new rock 'n' roll. This was clearly something Richey, at least, had put much thought into. He told Melody *Maker* , 'Where we come from, to see any band you like, you normally have to travel quite a way. Faced with a choice between doing that, or staying home and blowing up planet after planet, then I know what most people would do. But the idea that video games are killing rock 'n' roll is misleading. They exist with each other. They're different mediums.' This did not stop him spending eight to ten hours a day playing Sonic The Hedgehog.

One of the gigs on this tour was in Cambridge at the Downing College May Ball. The band's reputation for being aggressive and controversial preceded them and the rather formal college decided to book them, hoping for a wild gig. With the Manics' gear-smashing reputation in mind, the Student Union hired an array of security guards to protect their rather expensive PA system. The band were unsure about the gig but were offered a substantial fee – enough money, in fact, to pay off the mountain of debts they had acquired from their pile of broken instruments (£26,000). When the band walked out to perform, there were only two people in the crowd, but even so the specially recruited bouncers immediately circled the stage. When the Manics launched into their first blast of punk energy, the previously empty 1000-capacity marquee filled almost immediately. Nicky (at least) was absolutely blind drunk and this showed in his performance – at one point he knelt down before James in a mock blow-job, getting nearer and nearer whilst unzipping the singer's jeans, until James could risk no more and said, 'One step nearer and you're dead!' Nicky started to worry the security by kicking the microphone stand around, then four songs in he harmlessly put his foot on the monitor. All hell broke loose. The Union staff feared imminent and expensive damage was about to be done so they immediately pulled the plugs, at which point the crowd went mad. Nicky dropped his bass and screamed at the crowd. The band started to smash the gear up, thinking they may as well live up to the over-reaction. Sean virtually demolished the drum kit while James punched a student before the bouncers chased the group offstage.

The college rugby team were called in to sort out the Welsh boys but James somehow flattened the biggest one who approached him. Then a crowd of angry soundmen gathered around the band's tour manager and tried to bundle him back into the marquee for a good beating, but were dissuaded from doing so by the music press photographers present. When the band's road crew tried to empty the dressing room of their belongings, they were man-handled by the burly security guards. By now the local police had been alerted and the Manics were eventually escorted by police dog handlers through the front gates, which were only normally opened for ceremonial occasions. Two pages in the *Daily Star* followed and the May Ball committee refused to pay the band, saying they had not fulfilled their commitment to play, even though the band offered to pay for any damage done. Richey was suitably unimpressed, as indeed he had been while at university himself: 'Students are just brain-dead – they deserve Carter and Kingmaker.'

If this gig was controversial it was nothing compared to events at their Norwich date, which, in short, saw the creation of music legend. The actual gig itself was poorly attended and the band were disillusioned and disheartened backstage afterwards. To make matters worse, they knew the gig was being reviewed by the notable *NME* journalist and future Radio One DJ

Steve Lamacq, who had made no secret of his dislike for the Manics. During the interview, Lamacq was surprised to find the four Welsh revolutionaries very affable and quietly spoken, but no matter how much they discussed things, he would not accept that the band were sincere. Eventually they agreed to disagree, and went their separate ways.

At that point, Richey, resplendent in his 'Spectators Of Suicide' self-painted shirt, took Lamacq to one side and said, 'Have you got five minutes?' While the other three conducted a fanzine interview, Richey and Lamacq continued their discussion. Richey had been chatty and enthusiastic all night, and tried desperately to convince Lamacq of their sincerity. He said, 'I know you don't like us but we are for real. When I was a teenager I never had a band who said anything about my life. That's why we're doing this. Where we came from we had nothing.' As Lamacq listened, he noticed Richey take a razor blade out from somewhere (Lamacq doesn't know to this day if it was on the floor or, as is more likely, if Richey already carried it with him) and proceed to cut the words '4 Real' in deep gash marks along his left forearm. Lamacq was slightly distracted by Richey's hand movements but it wasn't until he saw blood dripping onto the floor that he realised the damage he may well have done to himself. As the blood drained out of the horrific wound Richey stared Lamacq straight in the eyes and said, 'We do mean what we do.' Once Lamacq saw the extent of the open wound, which on the spine of the letter 'R' cut through to the bone, he found Philip Hall and told him, 'I think you should go and see Richey, he's a bit shaken up,' before retreating outside to drag on a cigarette.

Having been driven to Norwich General Hospital, Richey felt terribly guilty for wasting the staff's time with a self-inflicted wound and insisted on waiting for all the serious injuries to be treated first before he was seen to. The young nurse who treated him knew of the Manics and was very friendly, probably only increasing his embarrassment still further. When it was time to have the seventeen stitches removed, he arranged to come when the hospital was quiet and free of emergencies. The next gig at Birmingham's Barrel Organ was cancelled.

Lamacq received a phone call from Richey the very next day apologising for causing him any distress, but Richey's motivations for doing it remained the same. He said to *NME*, 'I tried talking to Steve for an hour to explain ourselves. He saw us as four hero-worshipping kids trying to replicate our favourite bands. There was no way I could change his mind. I didn't abuse him or insult him. I just cut myself. To show that we are no gimmick, that we are pissed off, that we're for real.' As for any regrets, he said, 'No, because at least now people might believe that we're not in this for personal entertainment. We aren't wallowing in any musical nostalgia like the music papers' Clash/Dylan freaks. We might sound like the last 30 years of rock 'n' roll but our lyrics address the same issues as Public Enemy.'

Lamacq was unsure at first of what to make of this deed. He called it 'an act of stupid spontaneity' and refused to acknowledge that this made the Manics anymore '4 Real' than they had been before. He seemed shocked most of all by Richey's demeanour at the time: 'He was so frighteningly calm. He didn't look in any pain whatsoever. He could almost have been writing in biro.' Once the wound had healed, it did in fact look like someone had written on his arm in a thick, dull felt-tip pen. The rest of the band admitted their shock; as Sean told *Q* magazine, 'It shook us all up. We stood in disbelief. I think that was the beginning. Richey had always been very straight and normal through school and university. He was no one you'd point a finger at and say "He's strange."'

Looking back on the incident later, Richey's attitude towards Lamacq, if anything, hardened. He called him 'a writer who should be in fanzines', and told *Melody Maker*, 'I sliced up my arm because it was the only way I could get through to a 24-year-old who thinks like a 45-year-old. I wasn't doing it to be like Iggy or Sid. I couldn't give a fuck for those people . . . Anyway, the fucker was asking for it.' He also denied he had cheap motives, telling *Raw* magazine: 'It wasn't a shameless publicity stunt . . . the argument descended so low that it was the only thing I could do. I've never hit anybody in my life. I never would, and the only way I could make a point was by hurting myself . . . it's something that I've done since I was a teenager.' What was perhaps more shocking was that when Richey went home to his parents in Blackwood, which he admitted was 'a little awkward', teenagers began walking up to him and displaying their own self-inflicted wounds, made in honour of him, many of which also read '4 Real'.

For a band so well known for shameless publicity-seeking, it was perhaps inevitable that they were slated for this episode. It was no coincidence, said their detractors, that a cameraman was there, and indeed the pictures in *NME* appear to show Richey almost proud of his work. It certainly gave the band a higher profile – shortly afterwards, Richey was caricatured in his own favourite magazine *2000 AD*, when a character called Clarence from a band called the Crazy Sked Moaners sliced '4 Rael' into his forehead with a laser. Plus, the timing was surely revealing, the incident coming as it did just four days after the band had signed an eight-album deal with Sony. By all accounts, at the time most people were convinced it was a cheap publicity stunt. In retrospect, it is now seen as the first public display of Richey Edwards's deteriorating condition.

The aforementioned deal with Sony was a major step in realising one element of the Manics' masterplan. They had always said they had no time for indie ethics, for small labels with poor distribution, and wanted to be on a major, sold by a major and succeed with a major. Plus, they always argued that the level of corruption on an indie label was the same, just on a smaller scale. Although there had been a debut album pencilled in on Heavenly Records after the success of the 'Motown Junk' and 'You Love Us' singles, the band never hesitated when the major contract was shoved under their noses.

Obviously this caused some ill-feeling with Jeff Barrett but the Manics were very single-minded: 'You don't have a dream so you can cut off little faded pieces from fanzines all your life,' Nicky said to *NME*. 'Signing to a major record company is the price of an education, we don't care what they do to us. The credibility of indie labels is shit.' However, they later gave Barrett a cut from their debut album's profits.

After a frantic four-way race, it was Rob Shreeves of Sony/Columbia who won their signatures on 21 May 1991. One of the companies who lost out had patronisingly invited the Manics to smash up their offices during the meeting. Sony seemed to be more aware of where the band were coming from, and besides, they had signed the Clash. Tim Bowen, MD of Sony/Columbia, was determined to have the band once he had seen them: 'I signed the Manics,' he told *NME*, 'I suppose, because I went to see a gig in Guildford and I thought they were the most exciting thing I'd seen since the Clash in 1977 . . . who I also signed. I just thought they were amazing, it's refreshing all the way through, even for an old fart like me.' He went on to say, 'They're no more anarchistic than anyone else of their age, or my age come to that. They have something to say, they're pissed off about where they live, they're pissed off about unemployment but they're not so pissed off that they can't enjoy themselves and express themselves. And that's what young people are meant to do.' Bowen was obviously serious – on signing the band he also handed over a cheque for £250,000 with a guarantee of at least £400,000 to record their debut album. They had played just 30 concerts to date.

Inevitably in these childish, indie-fixated times, there were mumblings about the band selling out. As ever, when a small relatively unknown act starts to go mainstream, the indie fascists who treasure that band as their own feel betrayed and accuse their heroes of 'working for the man'. With the Manics, such a view was clearly myopic: there were no signs that signing to Sony had changed them one iota. All they bought with their substantial advance was a portable CD player each and a few Game Boys, apart from James, who also bought the Gibson Les Paul he had always wanted. He was to smash it a few weeks later onstage, and then felt ashamed when he realised it was worth four weeks' wages for his dad. That aside, things were falling into place for the Manics, who could now pursue their Guns N' Roses-style world domination

Backstage on the debut album tour

Photo session, later used on the 'Turning Rebellion Into Money' bootleg

plan to fruition, with Sony willing to be the pimp to their tart.

First up on Sony was the single 'Stay Beautiful'. It was originally titled 'Generation Terrorists', but the name was instead reserved for the forthcoming debut album. Produced by ex-Wham! producer Steve Brown, 'Stay Beautiful' was not a huge advance musically for the band, but it did at least show they had not gone soft with corporate money. The title itself reflected the Manics' vanity and was to become a one-liner forever associated with these early days of the band. The single was backed with two, more interesting, new songs. The first, the semi-acoustic 'R.P. McMurphy', was a homesick lament drawing on the Jack Nicholson character in one of the band's favourite films, *One Flew Over The Cuckoo's Nest*, being particularly inspired by the scene when Nicholson tries in vain to lift up a wash basin. 'Contamination' was harder and more old-school Manics. With a video featuring all-night poetry readings from Ginsberg and Aleister Crowley, the record was a solid release, and another Single Of The Week in the *NME*, but many people felt it was not as good as 'Motown Junk'. Even so, the release was the first single of theirs to go anywhere near the Top 40 (albeit Number

40 itself), but it still failed to win them their coveted *Top Of The Pops* debut.

During the subsequent mini tour in August, there were no signs that major label life had diluted the Manics' passion at all. The T-shirt stall carried the usual array of slogan-bearing merchandise, including 'Destroy Work' and 'London Death Sentence', while onstage Richey wore the message 'Waste '91'. The band took to the stage to a taped reading from Allen Ginsberg's 'Howl', written in honour of the poet's friends who couldn't cope with the establishment and many of whom were suicidal and/or self-mutilators. This poem was specifically dedicated to New Yorker Carl Solomon, a teenage prodigy who had travelled to Europe to meet intellectuals, but cracked up after his twenty-first birthday and returned to America, where he shaved his hair off and asked a West Coast psychiatrist to lobotomise him.

Once onstage the Manics launched into a biting set of punk-rock adrenalin salvos, their venomous live set perhaps starting to make complete sense for the first time. The only indication of major-label money came at the end of the show, when balloons advertising the 'Stay Beautiful' single drifted down from the ceiling. If the Manics were to achieve their world domination in one year, the clock was ticking away. Their concerts were still played to no more than 500 people on average and their radio airplay was minimal; for most people they existed only in the pages of the music press.

By the second half of 1991, the Manic Street Preachers' thoughts were turning to recording the debut album that was meant to be the reference point for all other rock albums. Utterly undaunted, they began work in late autumn at a £1000-a-day studio, Black Barn Studios in Ripley, Surrey. It was an ivy-covered cottage in a small Tudor hamlet – in typically paradoxical fashion, the four Welsh insurrectionists were to record what was meant to be their once-only masterpiece in a quiet leafy Middle England village. Notable previous clients of the studio were Black Sabbath and Procul Harum. The working title for the debut was 'Culture, Alienation, Boredom and Despair'. The sessions very quickly began to over-run, with deadline after deadline missed and Sony soon pulling their hair out in frustration.

Steve Brown was again in the producer's chair, but James and Sean were also heavily involved in the production of the album, while Nicky and Richey worked on the lyrics. This unusual dual structure was the Manics' normal songwriting method and it worked perfectly. As Nicky said to *Melody Maker*, 'We decided all that from the start. We can't write music but we can write lyrics and look pretty tarty. Richey's the spirit of the band, he's totally what we're about.' Apparently, Richey could just about manage to play live, but found the clinical environment of the studio too demanding, so opted out altogether, leaving James to play all his guitar parts. (The only addition to the group was Spike Edney, keyboard-player and orchestrator of much of Queen's work, who was used on some tracks.) At one point, Richey told a member of the technically talented band the High about his inability to play, and the man said, 'There should be a Union to stop people like you!'

In fact, Richey was almost completely uninvolved in the musical side. While the rest of the band slaved over the mixing desk, he would jump in the record company limousine and drive down to Soho, where he would wander alone around the dark neon-lit streets for hours. He would spend money on his Sony AmEx card in strip joints and only returned to the studio if it rained, often covered in lovebites. Nicky told the press he was proud of Richey for this, although Richey himself admitted he felt a bit undignified and sad. When he was at the studio, his behaviour gave some cause for concern. He ate lightly, usually only cheese and tomato, drinking Highland Spring mineral water and copious amounts of Glengettie tea. He would either watch videos or television, play Nintendo or table tennis and collect clippings which he stuck to his studio room wall. He constantly wore eyeliner, and when that ran out he walked around indoors with his Vauranet sunglasses on. There were rumours that he was drinking a lot and crying often. He told James that if the band ever split up he would have nothing left.

When mixing began at the Hit Factory in London, Richey was no more involved. Progress was equally slow, and when the record was finally completed it had taken 24 weeks in total and was £250,000 over budget. Despite his disengagement, Richey was devastated when the process was finished. He tore down all his clippings and posters from the wall, which had included the likes of Stalin, Flavour Flav and Liz Taylor, and burnt them all on a small fire along with some cut-up books, while he played 'Don't You Ever Leave Me' by Hanoi Rocks on full volume and repeat.

Even with the album finished, the Manics could not keep things simple. For the artwork, they ploughed through dozens of ideas, all of which were unsuitable or posed a problem with clearing copyrights and approvals. Their first key idea was to use 'Piss Christ' by Andres Serrano, a notorious and highly controversial image of a crucifix suspended in the artist's urine. Permission was not forthcoming. Then they wanted a Marilyn Monroe picture by Bert Stern, taken from one of the last sessions he ever shot with her. Monroe herself hated the pictures, claiming she didn't look any good, and had scratched

● The Dutch auction surrounding the **MANIC STREET PREACHERS** finally ended on Monday May 21st when they signed, for an undisclosed sum, to Columbia Records at the company's offices in London. Our picture shows the Manics with (left) Paul Russell, chairman of Sony UK and Tim Bowen, Sony's MD. The band immediately start work on their next single, 'Generation Terrorist', due for July release.

Signing to Sony

the film and thrown paint over the prints. Permission was again refused. Next was 'Death Mask', which was a mould of an artist's face filled with his own blood, but Charles Saatchi had bought it for his own massive private collection before the Manics could get hold of it, and demanded a gigantic reproduction fee. Eventually, they had to plumb for a doctored photograph of Richey's tattooed left arm, which actually said 'Useless Generation' but was changed to 'Generation Terrorists'. When asked how the album had turned out and whether they might have to carry on if it wasn't the record-breaking success they had been predicting for so long, Richey was suddenly resolute and confident: 'This LP will be perfect for us. That situation won't happen.' Nicky was predictably more blunt: 'With the confidence we have in this album we wouldn't be happy unless it sold sixteen million.'

CHAPTER 6

'Coming up to London thinking we could sell sixteen million records within six months is absolutely fucking insane.'

Richey

While they had been entrenched in the Black Barn, another single had been released by Sony, the inflammatory 'Repeat', a live favourite with its five-line denouncement of royalty, including the none-too-subtle closing line 'Fuck Queen and country'. Unfortunately, it made a pretty dire single. Backed with 'Love's Sweet Exile' and 'Democracy Coma' the release was, by any standards of musical measurement, not a good product. The lead track had a certain punk rush that grabbed the attention, but the adolescent riffing, pubescent royalty target and contrived feel of the record made it meat for their critics, who claimed they were clearly a short-term band who had already been swallowed up by their own hype. One reviewer claimed it was crass 'Sun-speak' and the Manics agreed, saying that was exactly the point. Richey continued to *NME:* 'Everyone used to go, "Oh, the Queen is Dead, what a brilliant statement." Well, the Queen's not dead, she still exists. And covering it up in high art or sartorial elegance is not a good way of dealing with these issues.'

The next single just prior to the album's release was the re-release of the by-now highly ironic 'You Love Us'. Only 3000 copies had originally been pressed, and they were getting lots of letters from fans who couldn't get hold of it. Plus, with opinion on the Manics now more divided than ever, the song was a classic riposte to their many critics, and put out with Sony clout gave them their first *Top Of The Pops* appearance, albeit with a video which had cost them £38,000. The track itself was a re-recording, and – where the original had been completed in less than two days, this new version took over twelve, using the far better facilities available to Steve Brown.

I wouldn't want them

On 10 February 1992, the Manic Street Preachers' debut album, *Generation Terrorists*, was finally unveiled – the record that was to be a testament of greatness that future bands would struggle to compete with.

Well, perhaps not. The double album ended up being a monstrous eighteen tracks, and was priced as a single album, with a gatefold sleeve. All formats contained lyric sheets. As well as the three Top 40 singles – 'You Love Us', 'Stay Beautiful' and 'Repeat' – the album also contained a track from the soundtrack to the movie *Times Square* called 'Damn Dog'. The opening line was 'You need your stars' and the Manic Street Preachers did at least try to deliver that throughout the album. The opening track 'Slash 'N' Burn' was pure Rolling Stones, although a little stunted. It was followed by the clumsily titled 'Nat West-Barclays-Midlands-Lloyds', which was like a sixth-form effort. The first real classic of the album was the epic 'Motorcycle Emptiness', a grandiose track that James had written when inspired by Slash's legendary track 'Sweet Child O' Mine'. It had been written three years previously, but as yet they were unable to play it live. It was very probably their greatest moment so far, a eulogy to the clichéd motorcycle culture of the West Coast of America, where Harley Davidsons and leather jackets are so pathetically revered by bands like Poison. As Richey put it to *NME*: 'We were never interested in moving to LA, buying a Harley, cruising up and down singing songs about girls and sniffing cocaine off beautiful models.'

Another key track was 'Little Baby Nothing', which points out the dichotomy that women are in fact stronger than men yet somehow are still exploited by them. The band originally wanted Kylie Minogue, who was enjoying a sexy renaissance after her squeaky clean days as Charlene in *Neighbours*, to sing the vocals, but the Australian singer-actress asked for a huge amount of money. With Sony already deeply in debt, that was never an option, so instead they recruited Traci Lords. She had become the most notorious porn star in the world when it was discovered that 39 of the 42 adult films she had appeared in were actually filmed when she was only fifteen. The resulting furore almost brought down the American porn industry. Traci Lords appealed as much as Kylie, because the band saw both women as people who were perceived to be puppets in a male-dominated industry, yet were actually very much in control of their lives. Lords flew to

London and saw a Manics gig, then met the band backstage, by which time Nicky was convinced, saying, 'She's the nicest American I've ever met.' Her vocals, which oddly aped James's own style, were added the next day.

The rather juvenile 'Repeat' was salvaged by its Public Enemy treatment – from day one, the band had expressed their wish to work with Public Enemy and originally wanted them to produce the entire debut album. That was never a realistic possibility, but the Public Enemy engineers and remixers Hank Shocklee, Nicholas Sansano, Frank Rivaleau and Dan Wood worked on 'Repeat'. They delivered four versions from which the delighted Manics picked one. Nicky later said: 'Actually, I'm really glad that Public Enemy wouldn't work with us. I wouldn't want them to be wasting time on a poxy white band like us. They're way above anything we could ever do.'

Elsewhere, the Manics had moments of unusual reflection, such as 'Spectators Of Suicide', but as promised, there were no love songs. The album was a strange and not always efficient mix of slogans, snapshot ideas and lyrical brilliance, which was generally let down by the rather derivative and uninspirational musical accompaniment. The gesture of releasing a double album was a ridiculously pompous and brilliant one, but unfortunately, that was the best thing about *Generation Terrorists.*

Media responses were mixed. Due to the band's own preposterous predictions and rantings, and their love–hate relationship with the press, it was perhaps bound to be panned. Critics talked of the over-obvious targets: the Royal Family, the government, institutions like banks, male chauvinists, and so on. The project was clearly not worth a double album, something that even the Beatles had struggled to pull off. There was justifiable disdain at the musically limited palette, which made the album hard listening, and accusations that the Manics' lyrics were still being poorly misrepresented by the music. These complex and at times highly articulate lyrics were often forced into shape by James, who frequently struggled to fit the verbose writings of Nicky and Richey into any melodic form. Some critics hated the lyrics as well, saying they were just sloganeering scissors-and-paste jobs thrown together with chunks of pretension and little subtlety. On this point at least, they could not have been more wrong.

The album sometimes slipped from punk to heavy rock – at which point, said the critics, could you stop calling them the Clash and start naming them AC/DC? One writer said the much-lauded collaboration with

with Sony needing to sell four million copies just to

break even, the band were in no position to argue

Traci Lords was supposed to be an important statement but actually sounded 'like Tiffany with REO Speedwagon'. The Public Enemy re-mix was dismissed as no better than Killing Joke ten years on. The album was ridiculed as hopelessly derivative, with obvious reference points to any number of bands including the Stones, the Sex Pistols, Public Enemy, Billy Idol, Guns N' Roses, Dead Kennedys, Queen, Bon Jovi, Aerosmith, the Velvet Underground, Led Zepellin, the Ruts, Poison, REM, Elvis Costello, Europe, Meatloaf and so on and so on. Also, they criticised the Manics' penchant for obvious iconography – their heroes were all very famous, with little to surprise anyone. They said that their music should match their words and be groundbreaking and provocative, whereas, far from being revolutionary, this was merely average, listenable nineties punk. *EP* magazine said, 'It's an okay album for now but in years to come it might seem like a misguided teenage tattoo.' Some of the writers were even less charitable, such as Andy Gill for the *Independent*: '[This album is] a protracted bout of sullen huffing and puffing desperately trying to fan the flames of a punk revival. Except there's no punk revival happening, as far as I can tell, and I suspect it will take rather more than this tired collection of glam-punk tat and hand-me-down hard rock stylings to create one.'

In the band's favour, the point about their heroes was completely irrelevant – the band themselves had always claimed that they had no time for obscure writers and artists, that they loved the big name icons such as Monroe and Karl Marx. That was the whole point. As for the accusations of derivativeness, the band quoted the anarchist ethic that 'originality is a myth', and acclaimed all their influences openly now, admitting their appropriation of major rock bands like the Stones and the Who. Besides, how pointless and futile is it to expect a band in the nineties not to sound like its predecessors – the sheer weight of history dictated that reference points were unavoidable. Many people criticised the way James's words were virtually unintelligible, but the band supplied a lyric sheet for that exact reason. Each song had a brilliant title, and a quote from one of their favourite icons to back up its lyrics – in this way they exposed Manics' fans to the likes of Philip Larkin, William Burroughs, Sylvia Plath, Nietzsche, Rimbaud, Chuck D, Camus, Kierkegaard, Allen Ginsberg, Henry Miller, George Orwell and Van Gogh. Critics even picked nits here, one, for example, claiming that Plath was a poet famous for taking her own life rather than a famous poet who took her own life.

The world domination plan was further complicated by difficulties with the US release. Initially, the signs were hopeful, as Steve Brown's production gave the album an epic feel and the tracks were decidedly aimed at the USA market (which occasionally slipped into dire blandness). However, things soon started to turn sour. For a start 'Nat West-Barclays-Midlands-Lloyds' meant nothing to the American public, and the record company also wanted 'Condemned To Rock 'N' Roll' dropped from the American release. Furthermore, certain tracks were 'beefed up' to be more suitable for the rock-oriented US market, including 'You Love Us', 'Stay Beautiful' and 'Love's Sweet Exile', and were only put on the album once they were considered FM-friendly. The final insult was the reduction to a single album format rather than a double. With such a massive debt to recoup from the overdue recording sessions, and with Sony needing to sell four million copies just to break even, the band were in no position to argue.

In the light of all these difficulties, the Manics asked people to look at the whole package, the hours of contemplation they had done over the artwork, the quotes carefully plucked from a vast array of classic work, the images, the photos, everything. In that one sleeve, the Manics had put more aesthetic worth than most bands do in their careers. At least, their debut album was to be an event.

Generation Terrorists was released in a year when so-called 'grunge' took over the world. The brutal thrashings of Sub Pop and Seattle had turned the American record industry on its head and Nirvana's *Nevermind* had sold nine million copies. Slacker culture was everywhere. Seattle, grunge, Eddie, Kurt, Hole and Sub Pop were the words on everybody's lips. To millions of disenchanted kids enlivened with the new teen spirit, the Manics' retro-isms and glam clothes were complete anathema.

With the debut album selling only modestly, the rest of 1992 was spent touring the record. Their trek around the globe did not get off to a good start when the proposed single sleeve version of the album was scrapped due to low sales. On the road, the Manics looked like a classic heavy rock band, with rows of Marshal stacks and retina-burning lights, a smoke machine and a drum kit raised at least four feet above the stage. Needless to say, during the course of that year on the road, they created their fair share of controversy. It started as early as late February in a gig at London's Astoria. The band were

Astoria, 1992

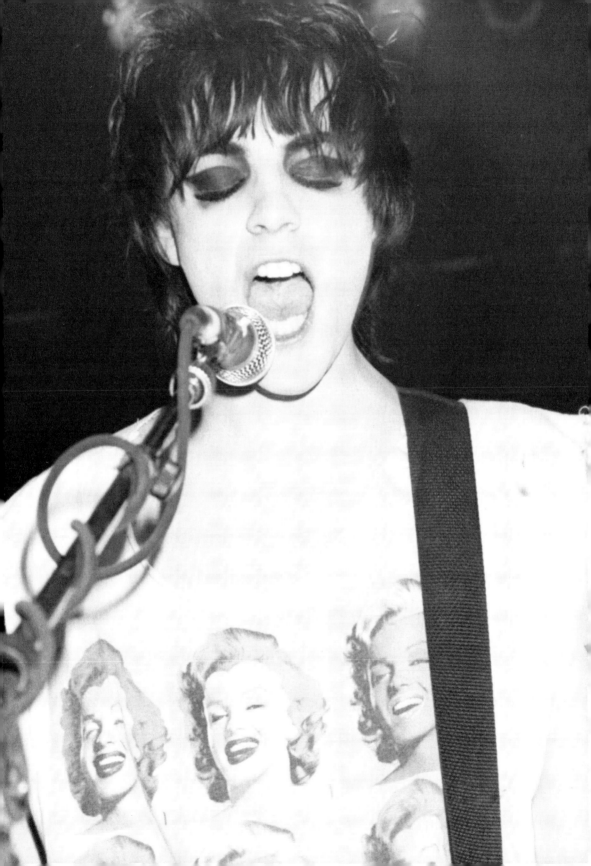

First trip to Japan, for the 'Motorcycle Emptiness' video shoot

halfway through the second song, 'Nat West-Barclays-Midlands-Lloyds', when Nicky took exception to a cameraman who was filming the show for a Japanese television station, unhooked his bass and swung it wildly at him. Fortunately, the cameraman ducked out of the guitar's way, but it did crash into the £20,000 camera, knocking it to the ground and causing considerable damage. At the end of the month Nicky also had to be dragged away from a fight with a bouncer in Cardiff. They then cancelled a scheduled appearance at Piccadilly Circus's Tower Records 'due to unforeseen circumstances'. Shortly after, Richey did an interview for the teenage bible *Smash Hits* in which he said, 'Don't do it kids, never get past the age of thirteen,' a comment that caused outrage as some parents felt he was urging teenagers to kill themselves.

In March, they were invited to perform at the Irish Music Awards ceremony, filling in for the last-minute withdrawal of AOR king Seal. This Irish equivalent of the Brit Awards was very prestigious and was some accolade for the Manics, who were being touted as the show's 'new talent'. They took to the stage to perform 'You Love Us' heavily under the influence of Guinness. As the song progressed, their state of inebriation became increasingly clear, and by the end they began kicking over the amplifiers while James dived into the crowd and then climbed up the lighting rig. Despite the fact they were the only band doing live vocals and that the performance was nothing if not energetic, the show's presenters were scathing in their distaste, particularly Gerry Ryan, who said sarcastically, 'How anarchic! I bet that performance will go down in rock history.'

At the black-tie dinner (they weren't in dinner jackets, of course) they proceeded to drink even more Guinness and Jameson's before starting a food fight. Eventually, the organisers had had enough and the band were thrown out. After this, Sean went to a rave in Dublin with 2 Unlimited and the Pasadenas, James passed out in his hotel room, Richey had a massive public argument with a businessman about Catholicism, and Nicky was thrown out of the hotel bar after trying to get a drink wearing only his boxer shorts. Even the record company executive from Sony called them 'scum'. Martin Hall, their co-manager, told the press, 'It was just high spirits from a bunch of young lads not used to the Irish way of drinking.'

In April 1992 they headed out to America and Canada for a brief tour, starting in New York, where, bizarrely, they had a US manager who also looked after Billy Joel. The tour kicked off with an American 'coming out party' at the Limelight, where the band didn't go onstage until well after 2am, by which time the local record company executives and media types were long since in bed. So the next New York show, some two weeks later, at the legendary CBGB's, was far better attended – as potential guardians of the spirit of '76, they could not have picked a better venue. This time they were reeled out at only 9.30pm to play a 30-minute set that perfectly captured what the Manics were about. The high-point was when Nicky, frustrated at the inactivity of the crowd, said, 'The only good thing about New York is that it killed John Lennon.' Richey later told a journalist, 'You know, we can only really make basic straightforward white rock music, 'cause we're not patronising people to pretend we understand the street, that we understand New York City. We live in a crap little town in Britain.'

There were grave doubts about whether the Manics would ever translate across the Atlantic, not least because of the complex lyrics, but the fans that did turn up were entranced. Having said that, on this American tour they only ever played very small venues, and there was no media. This was most apparent in Los Angeles, where they did the rounds of alternative rock radio stations, even some television, but were generally met with muted applause. They were not helped by arriving in the City of Angels just as it was erupting into the riots sparked off by the Rodney King trial, and so there were far more distractions than a parochial punk band from Wales ('that cute city in England'). As a comment on the violent situation, the Manics inserted a verse from the Dead Kennedys' 'California Über Alles' into their live version of 'Repeat'. They also turned down the *NME*'s offer of a photo shoot in the riot zone, instead opting for a trip to Disneyland.

At least the Los Angeles gig went well. The set had been ended when the band ripped up loads of pillows and threw the feathers across the venue, producing a bizarre snow-like effect in the sweltering heat of LA. In the urinals for that gig, Sony had *Generation Terrorists* splash mats and Manic Street Preachers napkins portraying Richey's tattoo, and even a Manic Street Preacher bumper sticker featuring the Prague Crucifix. There were various luminaries in the crowd, including Jon Bon Jovi and his producer Bob Rock, as well as Gilby Clarke from Guns N' Roses. The next day, Flea from the Red Hot Chili Peppers called their hotel to say how much he enjoyed the show. By now, it was clear that Richey was not right. At one Los Angeles television studio, the presenter had been talking inanely about how wonderful the band was and how much everyone in LA loved them, whereupon Richey took out a paper clip, unwound it and started to drag it across his skin, causing large red abrasions and scratches across his forearm. The day before had been the Disneyland trip and he had thoroughly enjoyed it, but he then complained that he could not understand why, and that he thought it ideologically unsound of himself. And while the rest of the band seemed to have had no difficulty in dropping their original commitment to celibacy, he still seemed anxious about his sexuality. The *NME* journalist with the band recorded how intense he seemed to be: 'It's really fucked me up. People just seem to want so much over here, they're not content with anything. I've been completely celibate on this tour. We could have fucked every night – in Europe and Britain we did – and in America I just haven't slept with anybody. It just doesn't interest me. Everything just seems for sale.' Amongst the things that disturbed him were the fact that the well-known LA alternative radio station KROQ played 'Slash 'N' Burn' alongside Fabulous's 'There's A Riot Goin' On' to commemorate the South Central disturbances, when in fact the Manics' track was about the deforestation policies in the third world and poor non-Western economies. Another time, a record shop keeper whipped out a copy of 'Suicide Alley' for them to sign, no mean feat as there were only those 300 original copies sent out to the UK media and record industry. Rather than being surprised and flattered, Richey panicked and ran out of the shop.

Sean was particularly introverted on this tour, and spent most of his time alone, hating all the bullshit of the American record industry. All the band were tired and hankered after what they called 'the golden era' of the *Generation Terrorists* sessions in the Black Barn. During their Transit van days, they would travel to each gig arguing and talking about all manner of subjects, whereas now they just sat quietly with their own Walkmans playing at the back of the tour bus. Nicky hated it, and told *NME*, 'It's made me much more inward. I haven't gone out at all. I've been reading more than I've done in the last three years. Every gig we've done girls have brought us books, and I've become really insular – I've gone back to the days when I used to love Morrissey.' Whilst some UK fans had hoped the Manics' controversial rock 'n' roll touring would spill over into America and provide a 1990s 'Hammer of the Gods' experience, Nicky spent much of his time in bed,

Sean was like a hermit and James and Richey were constantly miserable. Nicky summed it all up when he described them all as 'poxy British white kids in the heart of this grim nation of corporation'. He also said, 'I still think that at the end of the day we will tour America properly and at the end of it we will split up, because I am getting really bored. The only sensation I get is three minutes a day if a song goes really well.'

While the band had been on the road, two more singles from the album *Generation Terrorists* had been released. The first of these was the poor 'Slash 'N' Burn', a rather turgid rock affair, filled with naff riffing and a weak metal rhythm, plus the usual references to icons like Madonna and God. Some dates were arranged to promote the single, and it was during these, on a day when they were playing at the Northampton Roadmenders, that the anniversary came up of the day when they predicted that they would be playing Wembley Stadium within twelve months. When Nicky was reminded of this by *Melody Maker* he remained defiant: 'Our ego has always been way ahead of our bounds. We have no sense of proportion at all. But we still think it will happen . . . we're not afraid to say that anything short of all-out success is worthless.'

The second single of the year was far, far superior to 'Slash 'N' Burn'. The brilliant 'Motorcycle Emptiness' was the Manic Street Preachers' first epic record. Easily the strongest track on the debut album, the CD format came backed with a live version of Alice Cooper's 'Under My Wheels' taken from a Tommy Vance radio session, and the band recorded the promo video for it in Japan. They even debuted the song live at a July Town and Country Club gig in London, finally feeling able to do it some justice in performance. The success of this latest single, making it to the lower reaches of the Top Twenty, meant the Manics were now regulars in the charts, reflected in an a capella performance for the mainstream *Steve Wright Show*.

It had been a while since Nicky delivered one of his caustic attacks on someone or something (who were usually completely undeserving). He made up for his silence around the release of 'Motorcycle Emptiness' when he denounced the travelling community in an *NME* interview. He lambasted the 'crusties' knee jerk' hatred of all things in a suit, which he claimed ignored the likes of genuine folk heroes like Aneurin Bevan, the Welsh politician who founded the NHS. When asked whether he thought the authorities were treating these communities too harshly, Nicky said, 'I think they should be

Always deeply self-conscious, Richey applies make-up backstage

treated more harshly, actually. As far as I'm concerned, I wouldn't care if they were rounded up and put on an island. I don't think they do any good. I don't think they perform any worthwhile role in society. You know this idea that the land is ours – that's a very obscure, pathetic notion. We live in a twentieth-century democracy where people buy land . . . what the fuck have they done to earn it? I think they deserve total hatred and contempt.'

His comments provoked outrage from travellers and their supporters, and the *NME* postbag bulged with attacks on him and the Manics. Richey tried to defuse the situation by saying they were argumentative types, and that is what they did all day just to entertain themselves when they were sitting in their bedrooms. However, the New Gypsy Council Chairman, Charlie Smith, was not amused and said 'Uninformed rubbish . . . What a sad bunch of people. Basically they are just cretins. People like this are not even worth entering into a conversation with. Who are they anyway? They can't be a very good band, I've never heard of them. And do they really need to say things like this to get publicity?' Jenny Smith, the Travellers Officer for Shelter, pointed out that many travellers are not on the road through choice, and that there are 'multiple reasons [for homelessness] caused by government legislation'.

In typically defiant mood, Nicky did not retract his statement, but instead warmed to the idea that people still hated them, as this comment from *NME* shows: 'I welcome it. Our audience has become far too reverent over the last two tours, so to have an antagonistic section of the audience will be a blessing. We'll thrive on it. Too many of the people who come to see us just want to get pissed and do nothing.'

Nicky remained in the news at the Reading Festival, where he seriously injured two security guards who were watching the crowd as the Manics performed. Towards the end of the set, Nicky took his bass off, smashed it against the amplifiers then threw it into the crowd. Unfortunately, the guitar fell badly short and crashed into two bouncers, fracturing the arm of one and giving the other a head wound which concussed him and required eight stitches. Nicky apologised and claimed that he was more feeble than he thought and couldn't throw the bass far enough. Fortunately for him, the owner of the security company, George Cameron, was in an amicable mood and laughed off suggestions that he should sue the band: 'You can't really hold someone responsible for something that happens in 30 seconds of an hour-long performance,' he told *Melody Maker*. 'That said, next time I do the Manics I'll have a couple of guys facing the stage as well!'

The Reading Festival happened in the same month as the release of the Manics' most successful single so far. The Manics were asked to submit a track to the *NME*'s *Ruby Trax* album, which was being compiled to raise funds for the Spastics Society and at the same time to celebrate the magazine's fortieth anniversary. Richey wanted to cover a Bay City Rollers' song, and they also considered 'Geno' by Dexy's Midnight Runners, a song which they had often covered in their early days. 'School's Out' by Alice Cooper was also a possibility, but that was deemed too obvious as they had already done Cooper's 'Under My Wheels' for the B-side of 'Motorcycle Emptiness'. In the end, they opted for Nicky's suggestion of 'Suicide Is Painless', the theme from the monumentally successful television programme about the Korean war, *M*A*S*H*. The song reminded them of a grim period in their childhood when the Musicians' Union was on strike and so *Top Of The Pops* was not shown, thus removing the only visual contact they had with their beloved music world.

The song was recorded in its entirety in one day for £80 in a cheap studio in Cardiff, but this did not stop it becoming the Manics' first Top Ten hit. It was backed with the Fatima Mansions' version of Bryan Adams's record-breaking Number 1 hit 'Everything I Do (I Do It For You)' from 1991. The song could have been written for the Manics, and its popularity was such that in its second week after their *Top Of The Pops* performance it actually went further up the charts, a rare occurrence during the early 1990s.

The dates for this single were frantic, especially with the newfound fame of the Top Ten. The Manics crowd was now a peculiar thing, with die-hard slogan-wearing fanatics (the band had now stopped wearing these stencilled shirts themselves), indie kids on a night off from Ned's Atomic Dustbin or Mega City Four, as well as the odd Guns N' Roses fan and even a sprinkling of old-school punks. They hung a huge hammer and sickle emblem behind them for these gigs and lit the stage with a manic red strobe throughout. For 'Little Baby Nothing', female fans were often asked onstage to fill in for Traci Lords. It became increasingly apparent that the musical heart of the band was James, who frequently held the whole show together.

The weary band finished 1992 off by flying to Japan for a small sell-out tour there, where the debut album had gone Top Twenty. The Japanese record company had heard about their antics on the road in Britain, and faxed their management before they flew out saying, 'Please ask the Manic Street Preachers to be obnoxious and spit on people.' As it was, the band were too tired. It had been a good world tour, with a disappointing time in America balanced out by solid gigs in Europe and a fast-developing support in the UK.

Generation Terrorists did not sell sixteen million copies. It did not even get close to one million. Eventually it shifted 300,000 copies, over a third of which were in the UK. It did yield six Top 40 singles, but apart from that there was no sign of the global impact the Manics had so ludicrously talked of, and Sony were massively out of pocket. The average Manics venue was no more than 500 or 600, usually in university halls of residence. Having once threatened to retire and go play with dolphins as triumphant millionaires, the self-confessed 'useless sluts' now had to stay together to soldier on.

Although admirably aware of its failings, the Manics were justifiably proud of their opening volley. 'The thing about *Generation Terrorists*,' said Richey to *Raw* magazine, 'was that the title was misunderstood. At the age of ten or twelve everybody is full of some kind of optimism, yet by the time they leave school they've given up on everything. In those five or six years your life has been dramatically changed and pretty much destroyed. That's what the title meant.' He went on to say, 'The whole point was to be hypocritical, to be false. All we wanted to do was to write better songs and find a better economy with words. We are improving all the time. Everybody knows the first album would've been better if we'd left out all the crap but we wanted it to be a double, so nothing was left out.'

Nicky was similarly candid as he told Jon Savage, 'It would be wrong to say we regretted it. We could have sold a lot more records if we'd done a debut album that was ten songs just like 'Motown Junk' and played the game a bit more carefully, but I prefer bands when they're messy and sprawling and epic, and they make mistakes.' He also felt the Manics had re-focused their peer group: 'We've made indie bands realise – even on the smallest level – that you can be stars again . . . that's all down to us. Musically and lyrically they're not gonna take anything from us. I know that – they're too scared.' However, Richey was clearly quite saddened by the band's failure to capture the imagination of the public: 'In terms of something explosive, I don't think it will happen. People just aren't interested anymore. They're too selfish.'

CHAPTER 7

'A typical rock band drink Jack Daniel's and get fucked up because they have this romantic glamorous Jack Kerouac vision of the world. When I sit in my bedroom with a book and a bottle of vodka, I do it because I'm sad, not because I think it's cool. I do it because I want to forget what I am thinking about.'

Richey

The first half of 1993 was a relatively quiet period for the Manics – quiet, that is, apart from a Yuletide outburst from Nicky that sparked a new level of hatred for the band. Rumours in the record industry were rife that the lead singer of R.E.M., Michael Stipe, was suffering from HIV, although the gossip was to prove unfounded. Despite the delicate nature of the subject, during a Christmas headline show at the Kilburn National, Nicky walked up to his microphone and said, 'In the season of goodwill, let's hope Michael Stipe goes the same way as Freddie Mercury pretty soon.'

The remark understandably caused widespread outrage. Any celebrity with a phone or a pen wrote or called the music papers to express their disgust at Nicky's words, and the letters pages were filled with the anger of furious, disappointed music fans, such as from Kevin in Kent in the *Melody Maker*: 'Your ignorance is dangerous. Maybe you should think about these things before spouting off just for the sake of saying something. Wishing people dead is not hard. It's not rock 'n' roll. It's not even controversial enough to be worthwhile. It's just crap, clichéd and very unfunny.' Even the band's associates and friends were hard pushed to pass over this outburst. Aids charities like the Terence Higgins Trust denounced his comments, but what was more worrying was the handful of letters from neo-Nazis who saw something anti-gay in Nicky's words and consequently wrote bizarre letters of support.

Nicky stood by his comments. Although he later said the outburst was down to 'too much vodka and too much adrenalin', he reiterated the point he had been trying to make, that the disproportionate 'reverence held up to rock stars and the liberal argument about Aids' unfairly focused on Stipe and other celebrities, whereas had he not been a megastar, no one would have been interested. The band backed him. The public and media saw this as a thin excuse and as desperate back-tracking by Nicky, and it was certainly not the ideal way of making his point.

The Manics were probably more media-literate than any of their contemporaries, and in their adolescence had read a thousand times how small incidents could be blown up into major controversies. In a world where the soundbite rules and mud sticks, Nicky should have known that this one-liner would cause a massive furore, and should also have known it would always be remembered, regardless of the context. Years later, Nicky said, 'The Stipe comment is the one I could be pushed into showing a morsel of regret about,' but for a time afterwards he felt the whole episode had even been positive, as he told *NME*: 'It was at a time when I think we'd become too close to the press. There were too many people in love with us. It was too pally, we needed to distance ourselves again, to be treated objectively.'

Once the scandal had died down, the Manics retreated into the media wilderness for nearly six months, not to lick their wounds but to record their second album. Obviously, before they even started the record they had to answer the pedants who pointed out they should have split up after *Generation Terrorists*. The Manics, as ever, were difficult to argue with, not least because they were constantly changing their minds. So when this accusation was thrown in their faces, they had no problem justifying themselves. Richey told *Lime Lizard*, 'We knew the hypocritical nature of that statement as soon as we made it, and any decent journalist knew it as well. We knew that there'd be all these precious people going around saying, "But you said you'd never make another record." No band would ever sell sixteen million copies of their first record. It never happens does it?' The band claimed that the masterplan was a self-confidence thing – that when they were driving to London to play shitty little gigs in front of a handful of pretentious Londoners, the only way they could keep going was to dream in such a fashion. After each poorly attended gig, the gruelling return van journey would be eased by saying, 'Never mind, next time someone will sign us and we'll sell millions of records.' They needed that blind optimism to survive. Besides, they enjoyed the impossible standards they had set themselves, as Nicky continued: 'The more you achieve, the more blasé most bands get . . . *Generation Terrorists* went gold in Britain, sold 100,000, but that wasn't an achievement to us because we said we were going to sell sixteen million. It does make a better band by putting that continual pressure on yourselves. We're always striving for something more.'

During the recording of the Manics' second album, which would be called *Gold Against The Soul*, further signs of Richey's long-term mental problems started to appear. There had been comments for some time in the music business about the amount he was drinking, and during these lengthy recording sessions this became more apparent. The environment of the album itself hardly helped – they spent five months in one of the most luxurious studios, using an additional three studios along the way. At the helm this time was Dave Eringa, who had first worked with the band on the Heavenly Records singles 'Motown Junk' and 'You Love Us', where he had engineered and added some Hammond organ. Rehearsals for the album had taken place during the summer and autumn of 1992, overseen by Eringa, so just before the recording began, the band asked him to produce the entire album.

Eringa first heard the demos when James played him some tapes in December 1992. The band began demo-ing the new material at Impact Studios in Kent and a gothic residential studio in Surrey called House in the Woods. They worked quickly, demo-ing an average of one track per day. Actual recording began at Hook End Manor, another plush residential studio near Reading that came complete with swimming pool, a gymnasium, and live-in caterers. There was a stone room for the drums and a special dry room for vocals – in short, no expense was spared.

The general atmosphere was one of extravagance. For a start the studio cost £2000 a day. For the drums on the track 'Life Becoming A Landslide' they used 25 microphones. On several tracks they started again from scratch just as they seemed to be nearing the finish. Ian Kewley, formerly of Paul Young's Q Tips, was drafted in to play keyboards, and they even brought in a percussionist called Shovel who played on all tracks except 'Gold Against The Soul'. Experimentation was openly encouraged – for example the strange sound on 'Nostalgic Pushead' was achieved by dropping a pool ball into a frying pan. James as usual was very intense, and this time Richey actually recorded a guitar part, for the track 'La Tristesse Durera'. He was understandably nervous doing this, as Eringa recalled in his diary in *Melody Maker*. 'We cleared everyone out and it was just me and Richey and he did pretty well. He was nervous and he was like "Oh we're going to be here all night, Dave," but he just played it. No one laughed at him at all. Except Richey at himself, of course.'

Once the lengthy recording was complete, mixing began at the equally expensive Olympic Studios in Barnes, west London. In fact, the album was to be finished under budget and within schedule. Of more concern than the studio bills was Richey's frame of mind. His mood swings were unpredictable and frequent, and when he was low he was utterly dejected. He walked around soaked in Cacharel perfume and seemed to be constantly carrying a bottle of vodka, which was usually half-empty. While James took advantage of the facilities to keep in shape, satisfying his long-time fanatical love of running and fitness, Richey's use of the set-up was more like self-abuse. He would often get up and have no breakfast, go to the gym for hours then have a swim, before eating maybe a jacket potato and some grapes. This would be all he ate all day; the rest of the time he drank. When Andrew Collins went to the sessions for *NME* he remarked how differently the four members spent their day: James was heavily involved in the production of the album, Nicky was busy with the artwork, Sean was generally playing Nintendo, watching sport on the television or helping James with the mix, and Richey drank. The rumours said he was getting through a bottle and a half of vodka a day.

While they had been recording the second album, they released a parting shot from the first. 'Little Baby Nothing' was put out on the B-side of a re-release of 'Suicide Alley', due to a huge belated demand for their 300-copies-only debut vinyl. The advert for this release caused yet more controversy, featuring a naked woman in a Stetson hat marked into the prime cuts of meat like a butcher's carcass, under the title 'Break The Dull Steak Habit'. Feminists were outraged and complaints flooded in, with one complaint to the Advertising Standards Authority saying the artwork portrayed 'woman as a piece of meat'. This completely missed the point. The song, after all, featured Traci Lords on vocals and was about the strength of women in the face of men's exploitation. Sony Music replied on behalf of

Gold Against The Soul *tour*

the band by saying that the image was 'intended to draw attention to sexism (as addressed on the record), rather than to promote a degrading view of women'. Sony also pointed out that the image was actually designed by American feminists in the seventies. Despite this, Advertising Standards 'concluded that the approach was nonetheless offensive', upheld the complaint and ordered the withdrawal of the image.

As a precursor to the new album in June, the Manics released yet another single, on the first day of the month. 'From Despair To Where' looked at the misery of many people who are materially well off, and the mundanity of much of Western life. The track itself was a straight rock tune, with uneventful drums and rather plain metal guitars, smothered in a heavy corporate production. For the video, the band wanted to mimic a scene from the film *Exterminating Angel*, which involved a lot of sheep, but because of the obvious comic connections between the animals and the Welsh, the Manics decided against it and used albino alsatians instead. The press were not overly impressed, despite the blistering small tour to support the release, complaining that 'From Despair To Where' was a chugging MOR rock sound, and fears were expressed that this taster for the second album suggested the band may have left their punk-rock roots behind and dived headfirst into adult rock.

Such concerns were heightened when the Manics appeared in the press just prior to the album's release, hailing the merits of all sorts of bands: Rage Against The Machine, the new Britpop leaders Suede, Happy Mondays, the Beatles, Dinosaur Jr, even the dire and short-lived Riot Grrrl. Concern was increased still more when Richey was interviewed talking about his chord progressions, when previously he would have proudly announced he couldn't play a note. The stencilled blouses were gone, the make-up was decidedly subtler, and even the references to literature were more muted. The mouthy foursome the media had grown to love and hate in equal measure were far more reserved now, and even their infamous androgyny was nowhere to be seen – they said that at 24, they were 'too old for that now'.

In fact, 'From Despair To Where' and these interviews were correct in indicating a move away from their more brash beginnings, and early industry rumours that the album would see a return to raw punk rock were way off the mark. For obvious reasons, *Gold Against The Soul* was considerably less ambitious than *Generation Terrorists*. But musically, the record was infinitely

Gold Against The Soul-era Sean

more polished. Kicking off with the Black Sabbath guitars of 'Sleepflower', with its heavy metal riffing and pained power, the album moved the Manics nearer to stadium-filling, radio-friendly rock. Next up were the straighter beats of the trudging 'From Despair To Where', but then came the album's first great record, 'La Tristesse Durera (Scream To A Sigh)'. The title was taken from a book on Van Gogh and referenced the painter's last words, 'the sadness goes on'. The first minute was a subdued acoustic lament, drawing in the listener to the lines about war veterans, admonishing those who use personal tragedies to win pity and sympathy from people. Then the rock monster crashed in, with a crescendo of pianos, strings and crashing drums. It had that epic sound that the Manics were to cultivate so well in the future. James sounded oddly American on this track, as indeed he did on many Manics songs, which lent even more credence to their AOR sound. One line in the song about stubbing cigarettes out on one's arm to find a solution was a direct and revealing Richey lyric. Of this track, James told *Melody Maker* (in an excellent interview, quoted often here), 'It's always a beautiful image every year when the war veterans turn out at the Cenotaph, and everyone pretends to care about them – but then they're shuffled off again and forgotten. I'm much more sympathetic towards older people than towards my generation – I think they have a lot more dignity, and seem to be able to take care of their problems themselves. People of my generation seem to be so selfish. I'm no exception, because you can't escape from the culture that surrounds you.'

'Yourself' was about being dissatisfied with yourself, and was a study in bleak dejection, again soundtracked by a solid rock backing. 'Life Becoming A Landslide' continued the Manics' core theme of femininity, a sequel to 'Little Baby Nothing' in effect, discussing the confusion between pornography and love, the horrors that young children are faced with and the rejection of the onset of adulthood. 'Drug Drug Druggy' points out that everyone has their own little obsession, or vice, and the ambivalent attitude to drugs that some people have – that it was okay to brag about smoking a joint yet doing the same about alcohol was now unfashionable. This track was probably the most upbeat song on the album.

Future single 'Roses In The Hospital' was another Richey lyric. Despite the infectious seventies rock feel and polished Bowie quality, the track was the album's first truly disturbing song. Richey's search for beauty in the

horror that he sees in hospitals is fruitless and upsetting, and the narration of this search is filled with his desperation. He told *Melody Maker*: 'It's just about the idea of something beautiful in a decaying place. It's about people who hurt themselves in order to concentrate, or just to feel something.' The rather second-rate and tiresome record-company-slagging of 'Nostalgic Pushead' was a weak point before the fascinating 'Symphony Of Tourette'. The soft metal sound hides a disturbing description of Tourette's syndrome, whereby a sufferer lapses into involuntary abusive profanities, and mimics the speech of those around them. Involuntary spitting is also a common symptom.

Last up was the title track, 'Gold Against The Soul', with its depressing vision of Britain since the Thatcher days, complete with condemnation of the selfish eighties. A rather dull musical backdrop soundtracked a criticism of what Richey saw as a patronising view of the lower classes; he said to *Melody Maker*: 'If you're working-class, you've got to be one of two stereotypes – either tipping your cap to your employer, or a drug fiend permanently bombed out your skull. You've got to be a lager lout, or an effete Morrissey fan who never does anything. But working-class people can be violent and sensitive.'

Gold Against The Soul was much less dangerous than its predecessor. At its low points it strayed worryingly near to seventies shock-rockers Styx or a poor Thin Lizzy tribute band, and, despite moments of elegance and sadness, rarely rose above the suffocating gloss of the plush recording environment it had been created in. Sony were hoping to move the Manics on to stadium rock in the future and this album, with its soaring guitar solos, big choruses and massive harmonising riffs and vocals, certainly opened that door up for them, but at the same time seemed to exclude the very venom and mistake-ridden rough edges that had made the band so exciting in the first place.

Fans and critics were divided when the album was released in June 1993. To those who were in love with the Manics' punk manifesto and raging guitar attack, it was a grave disappointment. Many complained they had already ripped up their early ideas and trashed them in exchange for American rock blandness. The over-worked songs and less political lyrics saddened those who wanted more of the band's anger and confrontational rhetoric. Others welcomed the rounder sound and the less 'cock-rock' approach, which had been replaced by the Manics' increasingly feminine side. Plus, the record was still filled with despondence – the Manics' sound may have become more corporate, but signing to a major and touring to filled halls had clearly not cheered them up – the album was still wracked with lyrics about the brutality of life, self-pity, anger, bitterness and self-loathing. Some also welcomed the move away from politics, fascinated by the Manics' deeper more personal side, and were glad that the baton of political music had been passed on to other up-and-coming bands.

Reviews were mixed, with the music weeklies unsure of the corporate sound, but the broadsheets predictably liked it. In the near future, the band themselves would dismiss *Gold Against The Soul* and came to regret the way it was made. For now, it was admittedly not the greatest second album, but it did not hold back the Manics' ceaseless progression one iota.

The album was supported by a rash of festival shows, which was rather ironic because in many ways the Manics were the ultimate anti-festival band, not least due to their anti-traveller comments. They once called Reading Festival a 'cultural Chernobyl', and James openly disliked the festival concept, telling *Melody Maker*, 'It stands for the worst punk ideal, that anyone can get up onstage and do it. And seeing a band in daylight, without all their masking effects, is the biggest myth-blower.' They slagged off the cultural stalls set up at festivals and generally stayed in the backstage bar avoiding anything to do with the punters. Perhaps their view of festivals had been tainted when they played on the same bill as Ringo Starr's All Stars in Belgium and the stage collapsed.

First up was the relatively new Phoenix Festival, which was most notable for Nicky's appearance in a floral dress, complete with head scarf, white nylons and NHS spectacles, an outfit which over the coming months would become his trademark. Anyone who felt the Manics had indeed gone soft were in for a shock – the first thing Nicky shouted as he walked out onstage was, 'The whole history of society is the history of class struggle!' Shortly after, James grew tired of some annoying female hecklers and blasted 'Shut up you fat little cunts!' The actual performance was rather muted, made worse by a poor PA system, and at the end of the set, in reference to a forthcoming stadium support slot, Nicky shouted, 'Bon Jovi'll be better than this fucking shit!'

Next they had to travel down to Swansea's Singleton Park for a free festival they had offered to headline. Support came from Pele, the Tansads, Lovecraft, Asher Man, Captain Scarlet and the Big Pink, and there was a smaller stage for showcasing local talent. The Manics were the biggest band on the bill by far, and it was a genuine gesture of goodwill to their native area from the four South Wales boys, but this did not impress the drunken local crowd. Previous bands had been plagued with a shower of bottles, and this continued when the Manics took to the stage, with cans and bottles hailing down while fights broke out in the crowd. Halfway through the set, as they were playing 'Drug Drug Druggy', a bottle of Liebfraumilch hit Nicky full on the head and he went down, a rather peculiar sight as he was dressed in full drag, this time with a leopard skin head scarf and white shades. Seconds later, when another bottle smashed at the feet of one of their road crew, James ordered the band off the stage, leaving with the parting shot of 'One concussed, three to go you brainless wankers!' While Nicky was attended to backstage, the organisers appealed for calm but that did little to dissipate the tension. After ten minutes the band returned to finish the set and almost immediately another bottle narrowly missed a roadie's head. James growled, 'We don't fucking need this . . . just one more . . .'

Oddly enough, that seemed to stop the violence, and the band started to turn the afternoon around. By the end of their set, the bottles had stopped and the Manics had produced a triumphant gig, the concluding rendition of 'You Love Us' rattling with even more irony than usual. The highlight was when Richey climbed a high speaker stack, and held a Jesus Christ pose for a few seconds before diving into the swarming crowd below. Despite seeming okay straight after the bottle hit him, Nicky felt unwell shortly after the show and was rushed to the City's Singleton Hospital where he was treated for concussion.

Richey was disgusted at the attitude of the Welsh crowd, especially as it was a free gig, but was unsurprised by this aggression: 'Most bands look forward to their homecoming gig. I don't expect roses and petals at my feet but the amount of grief we get here is non-stop. Anything from Welsh bands complaining about us not singing in Welsh to gangs of blokes pouring lager over me and saying, "What are you gonna do about that?" Tom Jones doesn't get this!' The band spokesman was a little more conciliatory: 'They walked off because they were concerned about the welfare of the road crew.

Supporting Bon Jovi, Milton Keynes Bowl, September 1993

But overall I think they quite enjoyed it – they've been getting too much of an easy ride at their own shows.'

Unfortunately, they did not receive such an easy ride in the press over their gigs. There was widespread criticism of their new FM-friendly sound. In a harsh but nonetheless rather funny review Chris Roberts said the Manics were nothing more than Dot Cotton on bass, Gazza on vocals and Hattie Jacques on drums. Quite apart from the manifest injustice to a far-from-fat Sean, this was clearly not an opinion among their fellow bands, as it became increasingly difficult for organisers to find bands willing to go onstage after the Manics – at Glastonbury they were offered a joint headline slot with Suede, but they allegedly refused to follow the Manics, so the Welsh outfit ended up below Teenage Fanclub and Belly, despite outselling both these bands considerably. Some also criticised the amount of festivals they were doing, and particularly the forthcoming Bon Jovi date, as too commercial. James was happy to answer: 'We thought we were bound for an explosion but that explosion never happened. So now we're trying to force ourselves on the audience,' he told *Melody Maker*. 'It's a sad fact of our existence. We do it for purely mercenary reasons.'

The band warmed up for a series of summer dates with a secret gig at London's Marquee on 23 July. Advertising themselves in the press as a band called Generation Terrorists, they allowed fan club members to buy most of the tickets in advance. Shortly after, they began a tour to promote *Gold Against The Soul* which provided one of the most interesting and diverse alternative bills to play in the UK for some years. The Manics had a plethora of nice safe indie bands to choose from for their support acts, but as ever they wanted to challenge people and make them think. So, they chose to go on the road with Credit To The Nation and Blaggers ITA. Credit were the brainchild of the prodigious Matty Hanson, aka MC Fusion, a black teenager from Coventry and son of a Pentecostal minister, whose brand of highly politicised lyrics and ultra-cool hip hop had him earmarked as potentially the greatest rapper to come out of the UK so far. His infamous and brilliant sampling of Nirvana's 'Teen Spirit' on 'Call It What You Want' was a fantastic opening volley, and he spearheaded an onslaught of talented British hip hop acts like Collapsed Lung, Gunshot and Katch 22. Blaggers ITA, meanwhile, had first gained prominence with their aggressive ska-punk-political rantings on the inspired single 'Stress'. Their lead singer, also called Matty, joined the

Gold Against The Soul-*era James*

British Movement at age fourteen, went to Borstal for drinking and fighting, and on his release turned his experiences around to become an ardent and knowledgeable anti-fascist. These were two seriously opinionated young bands.

The Manics first saw Blaggers on the 'United Colours Of Frustration Tour' and the impact was immediate. James told *NME*, 'I actually felt isolated watching them, there was this imposing almost violent threat coming from the stage . . .' And Credit had blown them away with their debut single 'Call It . . .' Despite the potential for being upstaged, the Manics booked both bands anyway: 'We're prepared to admit that our live show has a limited shelf life,' James continued. 'It can only be interesting for so long. This tour is a way of keeping us away from being complacent, from being workmanlike.' Many people agreed – with the Manics' new milder approach, several onlookers doubted if they could keep pace with this fresh new talent.

The tour was during a summer when music was becoming re-politicised by a batch of new young bands who put the venom back in where grunge had left it out. Cornershop's 'England's Dreaming', Blaggers ITA's 'Stress' and Fun-Da-Mental's 'The Wrath Of The Black Man' had re-opened the political agenda for music once again. The gigs themselves were impressively diverse, mixing Credit's articulate and rhythmical onslaught, Blaggers' more blunt and brutal approach and the Manics' noticeably more fragile, but no less stunning, offerings. However, the musical and political aspects were totally overshadowed by events on the tour, which for once did not centre around the Manics. The Blaggers ITA frontman, Matty, was accused of assaulting journalist Dave Simpson, who was reported to have sustained a broken bone beneath his eye and severe haemorrhaging. The alleged unprovoked attack was reported to the police who immediately started to investigate, and Simpson was still receiving treatment a week or more after the apparent incident.

The music business was horrified. Fun-Da-Mental immediately cancelled some forthcoming dates with Blaggers ITA. Scores of letters poured into the music press condemning the alleged attack. Matty meanwhile laid low and denied all the allegations. The Manics were disgusted, as Richey told Stuart Clark: 'I can't think of anything more fascist than using physical violence to intimidate people whose viewpoint differs from yours.' James was equally adamant: 'I just don't believe in bullying full stop. I don't agree with their means to an end at all.' He told *Melody Maker*, 'No matter what they think, this is a different kind of fascism, it shows such a lack of foresight. I've been a connoisseur of violence in my younger days and I know that if I had indulged in it much more than I did then I would get to enjoy it . . . in the end this is the worst thing they could have done. It's probably the single biggest mistake they'll ever make.' He was right. When the furore died down, the Blaggers ITA career was in tatters. At the time, the Manics considered sacking them from the tour, but decided against it, since this could have been construed as censorship as well. Instead, they stopped the Blaggers' intimidating entourage coming on the road with them.

Most interesting of all these album dates was the support slot to Bon Jovi at the Milton Keynes Bowl. The Manics always said they would support anybody when they first started, so when they were offered a spot on Bon Jovi's Milton Keynes Bowl bill, they duly accepted, despite rumblings of discontent from their hordes of indie fascist fans. Alongside them on the bill were Billy Idol and the Little Angels, so the day was a decidedly middle-of-the-road rock affair. James was quite realistic about the daunting task ahead. 'We're not going to win over any of those fans,' he told *Melody Maker*. 'We're gonna sound worse that day than we ever have in our lives! We know that now.' When the day arrived it was to be an abject lesson in success for the band – having fronted countless music magazines and been feted as a great alternative British rock band, they realised, as Bon Jovi took to the stage, that in the big wide world of the mainstream which they had so aspired to, they actually meant very little. 'We were surprised at the scale of things that day. . . we find it hard to be with people we haven't known for a long time,' Richey told *Raw* magazine 'We've only got a crew of four or five people and it's taken us two years to trust them.' The band's sound was stadium-friendly enough but their complex and despondent lyrics were completely lost on the mega-size crowd. They performed well, but there was none of their usual crowd abuse, no venom, no real spirit. By the time they packed up their gear that night, they already regretted playing on the bill.

The anti-Manics tendency in the press was pleased to see this rather humiliating display with Bon Jovi, and when they played more dates in Ireland, the critics did not let up, as this vicious piece by Kevin Courtney from the *Irish Times* shows: 'We've seen it all before. Last Friday night's gig in McGonagles mixed the worst excesses of trash/noise with a disturbing sense of irrelevance, and the punters must have wondered, as I did, what the hell this band was even trying to rebel against. In an age where everything gets recycled before it even becomes stale, the Manic Street Preachers are trapped in a vacuum of punk revivalism, without a "movement" to support them, without a frame of reference to validate them. They're reliving a time they never knew themselves, a time when all you had to do was kick your heels against the system and the public made you into demi-gods. The Manics make the same motions, but all they get are bemused looks and perfunctory applause. It doesn't matter how often Richey slashes his arms, he'll never knock Johnny Rotten, Sid Vicious, or even Joey Ramone off their pedestals, because these people have already passed into punk history. The Manic Street Preachers are desperately trying to create their own history, but haven't even got the bottle to become martyrs.'

During the long hot summer of festivals, the Manics rattled out two singles from the album, first 'La Tristesse Durera' then 'Roses In The Hospital'. Both did reasonably well, adding to the list of the Manics' Top 40 hits. The B-side of 'La Tristesse', 'Patrick Bateman', was based on the bloodthirsty character in Bret Easton Ellis's highly controversial novel *American Psycho*. The lyrics were inspired, but unfortunately the musical accompaniment was turgid, trudging soft metal, and James was quick to acknowledge this. The second single came out just as Nicky Wire got married to his long-time sweetheart, Rachel, at a small family ceremony in Blackwood. A sell-out tour of Japan reinforced that market as their second best behind the UK, and despite the critical knocks the band were taking, they were perhaps in a healthier position now than they had ever been. Ironically, the next year was to be their worst ever.

CHAPTER 8

'I'm weak, all my life I've felt weak compared to other
people, if they want to crush me they can. But I know
I can do things that other people can't.'

Richey

On 24 January 1994, the Manics released another single, their last from *Gold Against The Soul*, 'Life Becoming A Landslide'. Little did they know how accurate that would be for the coming twelve months.

The events of the year were pre-empted in the worst possible way. Just before Christmas 1993, Philip Hall lost a battle with cancer which had appeared at the end of 1992, and died aged 34. Having been diagnosed as having terminal lung cancer, Hall had continued to work in between sessions of painful chemotherapy at the Cromwell Hospital in London. If he was in too much pain he worked from home. He had been a very popular man, respected in business and with a wide circle of close friends. The Manics cancelled their Christmas gig at Brixton at the last minute, and issued the following statement: 'Philip was not a businessman in the background, he was a very close member of our family. It would be impossible to give a performance of any quality. We hope our fans understand these reasons.' Hall had cared for the band rather than just managed them, and they could never forget the belief he placed in them right from the start; as the Manics told *Melody Maker*, 'Philip was the first person who understood us. He was more than a manager and his input into the band was invaluable. Without his help, motivation and generosity, it is doubtful whether we as a band would have carried on.'

In the aftermath of this tragedy, the band struggled. Nicky was worried about the amount both James and Richey were drinking: '. . . [in the last eighteen months] there hasn't been a single day when Richey hasn't had at least half a bottle of vodka. Neither him nor James can go to sleep at night without drinking that much. It's pretty depressing.'

Ironically, from a career point of view the New Year started off reasonably well. The release of 'Life Becoming A Landslide' saw yet another Top 40 hit. The live dates around this time showed a harsher Manics, heading back to their punk roots. Gone were all the glamour costumes, replaced by combat gear and balaclava masks. The live set was much faster, harder and aggressive, and it was as if the radio-friendly rock of the second album had never happened. This was the case at a gig they played in the first week of March, at Clapham Grand, in aid of Cancer Research and in memory of the late Philip Hall. Towards the end of the set, Bernard Butler of Suede joined them onstage for an excellent cover of his band's 'The Drowners', then they finished the night with the Faces' 'Stay With Me', which provided some light relief from the otherwise fairly harsh set. Unbelievably, they were receiving grossly insensitive flack for their eleventh-hour cancellation of their Christmas show at Brixton. Richey was furious about this, as he told *Indie-cator* magazine. 'The thing that really pisses me off about these charity appearances by top stars is that the minute they come offstage they're counting their record sales, pissing off to Browns and snorting cocaine out of some six-year-old boy's backside.'

The Manics' harder new approach was clearly visible on the two singles that preceded the next album. The May release of the double A-side 'PCP/Faster' was a white heat blur of punk, trashing the fashionable evil of political correctness on one hand and the voyeuristic apathy of the new generation on the other. Richey discussed the latter song's scathingly intellectual lyrics in a rather worrying way: 'It's about people who take their frustration out on everyone around them. I never raise my voice. Cutting myself or hurting myself is the way I deal with anger.' As if to reinforce the return to their more brutal origins, a live version of 'New Art Riot' was put on the flipside of some formats.

Behind this latest success however, the Manics were falling apart, and this began to show during a tour of Thailand in the spring of 1994. The Far East gigs were to raise funds for Cancer Research, and had been arranged after *Gold Against The Soul* sold over 50,000 copies in Thailand, making the record platinum and the Manics the premier alternative Western band in that country. Their popularity owed much to Wasana Wirachartplee, an alternative DJ who had played 'Motorcycle Emptiness' endlessly on her radio show. She also opened up her own indie music shop, where the Manics' records took pride of place. There was even a glossy national magazine called

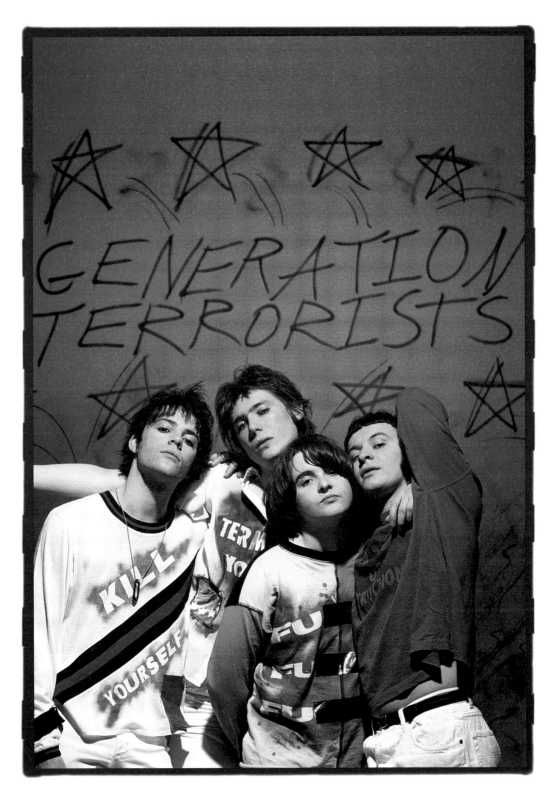

Manic Street Preachers 1991

'We are the sad victims of 20th-century culture.' – Richey Edwards, 1992

Dot Cotton on bass

Richey mid-1994

Gold Against The Soul- *era*

Generation Terrorists, run by the organiser of the Manics' Thailand fan club. Just before the gigs, the band did a shopping mall signing session and an amazing 3000 people turned up.

Backstage with Philip Hall

The gigs were booked for the MBK Hall, which was a cavernous venue on the fourth floor of a massive Bangkok shopping complex. Both gigs were sold out in hours, quite an achievement considering that the tickets cost 440 bahts each in a country where the average monthly wage was around 2500 bahts. Consequently, many in the crowd were affluent, middle-class young people. Their dress sense ranged from oddly retro bondage punk to yuppie type to Manics diehard with home-made T-shirts, one of which said 'Fuck Me and Leave'. Instead of burly T-shirted bouncers, the crowd was controlled by armed police, who shone torches into their faces and kept the front rows in order with cattle prods. Neither this, nor the suffocating heat, stopped the fans going absolutely mental when the band came onstage, and their fanaticism was such that one fan had his leg broken in the madness.

The electric atmosphere was muted slightly by Nicky shouting, 'Long live the king, may he reign in hell!' In Thailand, the Royal Family were revered almost universally, and, with severe penalties for such treacherous statements, Nicky was pushing his luck. When the band had been given their platinum disc by Sony Thailand before the gig, the MD gave a gushing speech about how they owed it all to the King and Queen, which obviously made the four anti-royalists squirm. Despite the band's popularity, the ardent fans at the gig could not understand why they chose to disrespect their Royal Family in this way. Their conservative reaction surprised Nicky, who told *NME*, 'It makes you realise how free Britain is. For all its supposed oppression it's not really, it's probably one of the freest democracies in the world. That's the truth, unfortunately.'

This clash of cultures did not stop the fans loving every minute of the hour-and-a-half gig. The venue was directly above a very exclusive restaurant, and on that first night the impact of 4000 people jumping up and down in unison caused cracks to appear in the ceiling and plaster to fall in the laps of the worried diners below. As a result, the second night's show was put on hold, and the next day the city's engineers and various structural experts met with the police to discuss if another night's concert should be allowed. The band were formally asked if they could play more quietly, but refused. Fortunately, after much discussion, a permit was granted anyway.

The second night reinforced the obsessive loyalty the band commanded in the country. Before the gig they had hordes of fans waiting for them in the hotel lobby, and others in the street screaming at the band's van as it drove past. Amongst the bags of presents they received was a huge Snoopy cuddly toy, which Richey held on to lovingly – his beloved dog at home had the same name. The actual performances themselves were angry and biting sets, the only respite coming when the band left James alone onstage to perform some acoustic numbers, most notably a mellow rendition of 'Raindrops Keep Falling On My Head', a Burt Bacharach classic used on the soundtrack of the film *Butch Cassidy And The Sundance Kid*. After this, Nicky returned to the stage in his floral dress, which completely threw the Thai onlookers, and after a few numbers ripped it off and played the rest of the gig in his pants only, his gangly, anaemic body there for all to see.

Photo session for NME *interview, with Richey about to enter The Priory*

The gigs themselves were an important chapter in the Manics' lives. However, their activities around the concerts were of far greater significance. Trailed by excellent *NME* writer Barbara Ellen, the band reached depths of despondency they had never touched before. They were very low when they arrived in Bangkok, and the city's rampant sex industry and social degradation fuelled their despair further. Many of the girls on offer were underage and often forced into the sex industry by their own drug-addicted parents, who knew the money was far better than their own meagre peasant wages. Many of the girls (who were often actually young boys) preferred the lifestyle in the city, deeming the choice of sex with seedy Western businessmen over extreme poverty in a provincial farm a fair swap. One in a hundred of the population carried HIV, making the notorious Pat Pong red light area of Bangkok, where the Russian roulette sequence from the *Deer Hunter* was shot, little more than a supermarket of death.

Sean, as ever, was withdrawn, reserved and seemingly unphased by the whole experience. Nicky walked around with the words 'I'm so modern that everything is pointless' scrawled onto his back. He detested the whole Pat Pong experience and stayed in most nights, fuelled by his paranoid hypochondriac fears that he might catch some dreadful tropical disease. 'Perhaps I am xenophobic,' he told Ellen, 'in that I find it very hard to fit into other countries. Then again, I find it equally hard to fit into Wales sometimes.' James was more pro-active, taking in the sights, observing the repulsively fat businessmen at play, yet completely able to sleep well at night, due to the amount of alcohol he was now drinking. 'Nicky and Sean are still true to the way we were, true to the spirit of the Manics, whereas Richey and I are tending to lose the plot a bit.'

Richey, in fact, was losing the plot a lot. When Barbara Ellen asked him his views on the rampant sex trade around him, Richey was quick to pontificate, saying, 'All developing economies abuse their young. When Britain was a developing economy we sent our children up chimneys and down coal mines and out into the street to steal. This is just abuse on a wider scale.' Moreover, he was the only Manic to take advantage of the sexual services on offer, wandering off alone one night into a hardcore area away from the more tourist-based Pat Pong, where he bought himself a hand-job in a brothel. Ellen understandably had difficulty understanding this and quizzed him about it on his return. Richey was unmoved: 'Perhaps I did it because I knew that I'd be talking to the press . . . perhaps I wanted to make a point about my sexuality.'

The incident led to a lengthy conversation about sex, where Richey's state of mind was revealingly exposed. He talked of his emotionless encounters with groupies, and how he hated it when they hung around after sex for kisses and cuddles – 'There's no passion involved for me so it would be immoral to pretend there was.' He said sex with groupies made him feel dirty afterwards, and that it was merely a small change from wanking, and that furthermore, he was not a sexual person. He talked of his fear of relationships – 'I've seen so many people get left or hurt, it looks terrifying' – and was deeply offended when the interviewer asked him if he would still have had the hand-job had the hooker been underage.

Richey's fragile state of mind was far more visible at the actual gigs. His celebrity in Thailand was far greater than that of any of the other band members, and his reserved, calm manner was very Thai-like. The 4 Real arm wound was legendary; one fan-club organiser had even said, 'If Steve Lamacq comes here, we will kill him!' In the hotel foyer, girls would ask him to sign photographs of his arm and then burn the print with a cigarette, while some fans even displayed their own duplicate mutilations. Onstage, most people watched Richey, and his frail body seemed unable to take the load of the thousands of pairs of eyes bearing down on him. Before the second gig, a girl who had never seen the band play live before walked up to Richey and handed him an expensive and razor-sharp set of ceremonial knives. As she gave him the present she said, 'Look at me while you cut yourself . . .'

Richey seemed grossly offended, replying, 'I'm not going to be anyone's circus sideshow freak!' He then walked off, taking the knives with him and neglecting to thank the girl. He played most of the gig that night seemingly unperturbed by this bizarre incident, but when James took the stage alone for his acoustic slot, Richey went into a dressing room on his own, took out the knives and slashed several deep horizontal wounds across his upper chest. When he returned to the stage, the blood was running freely down his torso. Richey was not drunk, and did not appear to feel any pain.

Although the band were aware of their difficulties, they did not seem capable of changing things: 'In Thailand, definitely for Richey and me, something just snapped,' Nicky told *Select*. 'It isn't that we weren't getting on . . . from then on, that summer, it got worse.'

Holy Bible *tour*

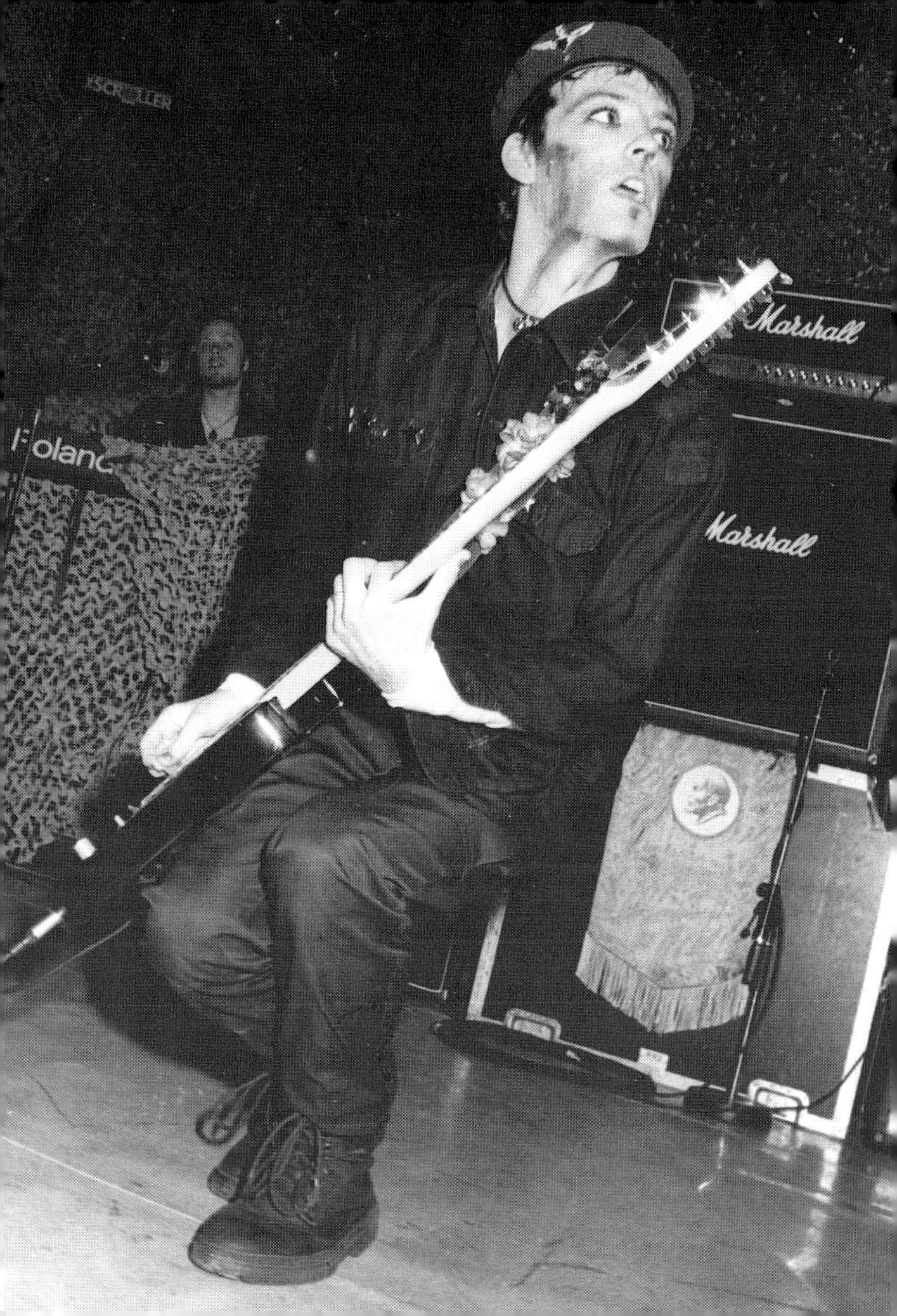
Roland
Marshall
Marshall

CHAPTEЯ 9

'I think he feels deep down it would have come to this whether he'd been a teacher or a bank clerk or anything, but I personally think being in a band has accelerated it.'

Nicky

The band continued to court controversy at Glastonbury, where their performance was screened on Channel 4. At a festival where communal goodwill and a generally relaxed atmosphere prevails, the incendiary Manics could be relied upon to upset things. Sure enough, halfway through their otherwise well-received set, Nicky said, 'They should build some more bypasses over this shithole.' Despite this, the Manics' set was almost universally hailed by the media as the highlight of the weekend. Ironically, though, James hated the show: 'It just seemed like the worst gig we'd ever done, it was like cabaret for post-degree students.' Glastonbury was to be the first of a string of festival dates through the summer of 1994, including Reading, Dublin, Glasgow's T in the Park, the Pop Com Showcase in Cologne and Park Pop in Amsterdam.

The next single was put out just before the third album, in early August, and was entitled 'Revol'. Again it was a punk affair. At this time there had been a spate of anti-government singles, including the Family Cat's 'Bring Me The Head Of Michael Portillo' and S*M*A*S*H's '(I Want To Kill) Somebody', but although 'Revol' was indeed a militant song, the band were publicly unhappy about being lumped in with these newer, far more one-dimensional groups.

After the studio excess of *Gold Against The Soul*, the band wanted to record their third album in altogether different surroundings. Where the previous album's studio had cost £2000 a day, the tiny, sparse Sound Space studio in Cardiff they chose for the next project was a mere £50 a day. They had been asked by Sony if they wanted to fly to Barbados for the album sessions, but flatly refused. By now, the band regretted the soft metal sound of *Gold*, feeling they had become distracted by the bloated Primal Scream decadence on offer: 'That was a time when we'd been working really hard for two years, we'd started reaping the rewards money-wise,' said Nicky to *Kerrang!*, 'and we were working in this studio that was costing us two grand a day, with swimming pools and all the rest of it. We got sucked into MTV land for a while, all we did was sit on our arses all day.'

Just before the sessions, Richey saw a flat he liked and bought it the next day with his share of the proceeds from the band's growing record sales. (The others had already got their own places.) Aged 25, it was probably about time that he moved out from his parents' bungalow. For a person so wracked with self-doubt and emotional pain, Richey felt surprisingly unconcerned about his newfound financial security. Indeed, he admired those people who were forced to face everyday difficulties through lack of money. It is a sign of the complexity of the man that his superior intelligence was not enough for him to work out the washing machine in his new Cardiff flat, and he continued to take his dirty laundry home for his mother to wash.

Soundtracked by a batch of Joy Division records, the band deliberately set strict working codes for the new album: they were picked up by Richey in his car at set times and driven to the studio, where they recorded for seven or eight hours, before returning home, commuter-like, to Blackwood. Sometimes, Sean would get the train in separately, drum for six hours then return home. The studio was in a red light district of Cardiff, and each day on their way to 'work' in the pouring rain, they would see businessmen and kerb crawlers in shady encounters with prostitutes. The studio itself had a simple fifteen-track mixing desk and few technological extravagances. The entire sessions took four weeks, and some of that included rehearsing. The Manics self-produced the whole record, and the atmosphere was fairly relaxed. Even Richey seemed mellow, and although he was still drinking copious amounts, he was full of enthusiasm for his lyric writing. This was an album for the band themselves, rather than for the record company or MTV. After Thailand, the band had endured a terrible tour of Portugal, where no one was happy and Richey was constantly drinking and regularly cutting himself. The first time the band had visited that country, a few months earlier, they had heard that Philip Hall had died. This second visit was no more relaxing. Richey was crying all the time and was desperately unhappy. Nicky felt ravaged by the whole experience: 'We had to put him to bed one night 'cause he just burst out crying in the car,' he told *NME*. 'And then he phoned me up at about half-three in the morning and – you know those terrible commercial presentations you get? Some American twat showing you how to flatten your stomach or summat – he phoned me up – and we were watching that together, and it seemed so bleak and nondescript. We didn't have a row or anything, but he kept yapping and I was really tired. The next morning, he comes up to me and he says, "Here you are, Wire." And he gave me a fucking Mars Bar, as a little present.'

Around this time, Richey did an interview for *Select* magazine in which he expressed his admiration for the controversial author J. G. Ballard, whose novel *Crash* portrayed characters getting sexual arousal from being involved in or watching car crashes. Richey said the book was 'very sexual all the way through' and went on, 'Sex and death are very closely linked. Sado-masochistic imagery, bleeding . . . [cutting himself] I find it attractive . . . I find it . . . sexual.'

Richey's troubled mind was exacerbated when he heard that his only friend at university apart from Nicky had hung himself. He didn't take the news well, although rumours that he threatened to quit the band on hearing of the death were swiftly denied. He became morose and extremely depressed, and even told his management that he perhaps needed professional help. With such a backdrop to the new album, it was to be expected that it would be a fairly despondent affair, at least thematically. As it turned out, no one could have guessed just how desperate, hopeless and brutally despairing the Manics' third album was to be. Before the album's release, however, the situation got worse still.

Throughout early 1994, Richey Edwards grew increasingly unstable. Philip Hall's death and the suicide of his university friend added to the terrible anxieties that ravaged his mind. Industry rumours claimed he went missing for a few days after the Glastonbury festival and eventually turned up in a terrible state. His drinking was out of control and his eating problems were grave. Richey had openly discussed his accelerating problems in several interviews. For example, he told *NME*, 'When I cut myself I feel so much better. All the little things that might have been annoying me suddenly seem so trivial because I'm concentrating on the pain . . . I'm not a person who can scream and shout so this is my only outlet. It's all done very logically.'

He denied he was an alcoholic but his comments suggested to the contrary: 'I'm the sort of person who wakes up in the morning and needs to pour a bottle down my throat . . . I'm paranoid about not being able to sleep, and if by about eight o' clock at night I haven't had a drink I get massive panic attacks and I'll be awake all night and that's my biggest nightmare. I can't stomach that thought. That's why I drink. It's a very simple choice. I know that until one in the afternoon I'm going to be shaky and have cold sweats. By six o' clock I feel good but by eight it starts coming round again, the thought of not sleeping. And that's when I start drinking.' He went on, '[An alcoholic] is someone who wakes up and needs a drink straight away. My need is more functional. By about midday I need a drink to stabilise me but I've got to drive the group to rehearsal, so I can't have that drink. But on tour I drink all day, just so I don't have to think about going onstage . . . that's why as a live band we fuck up so many times . . .'

It was with little surprise to the media that the news broke in July 1994 that Richey had been committed to a mental hospital. The band had taken him to health farms in the past, but he had reverted back to his self-destructive ways as soon as each session was finished. This time, more drastic measures were needed – Richey's weight was down to six stone. It was therefore decided that professional medical attention was needed as a matter of urgency.

Matters had come to a head early that month with a damaging two-day self-mutilation session. The night before, Richey said a few strange things that preyed on Nicky's mind all night, and when the bassist couldn't get in touch with him at his flat he began to worry. There were rumours of a desperate dash down to Wales by the management company to help Richey out. When they found him, he was locked in his bedroom, badly lacerated and mentally in shreds. Rumours of an apparent suicide attempt were denied at the time, but unnamed sources said the management explanation of 'nervous exhaustion' was a cover-up. Richey was rushed to hospital as a result of his self-inflicted wounds. Another lurid rumour reported in *Melody Maker* alleged he had slashed his wrists in the bath but had then awoken confused the next morning and phoned a friend to say, 'I've done a stupid thing.' At first, the band had hoped to keep Richey's problems a secret, but the over-heating rumour mill soon made this impossible.

The NHS hospital in Whitchurch where he was first taken did little to

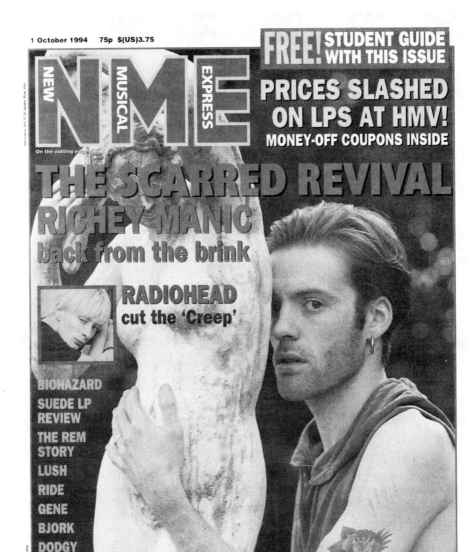

1 October 1994   75p $(US)3.75

NME
NEW MUSICAL EXPRESS

On the cutting edge

THE SCARRED REVIVAL
RICHEY MANIC
back from the brink

RADIOHEAD
cut the 'Creep'

BIOHAZARD

SUEDE LP
REVIEW

THE REM
STORY

LUSH

RIDE

GENE

BJORK

DODGY

SEBADOH

Germany Dm 5.20 Spain Pts 200

Richey Edwards photographed by Kevin Cummins

9 770028 636048

39>

**EXCLUSIVE OFFER! SPEND £10 MILLION
AND BUY YOUR OWN BAND IN 'NME SUPER GROUPS'**

ease his troubled mind. He shared a ward with twelve other very sick men and there was a definite *One Flew Over The Cuckoo's Nest* atmosphere about the place. In the eight days he was there, he saw a doctor only once, and was heavily sedated for his entire stay, mumbling incoherently under the effects of librium and other heavy drugs. His celebrity meant nothing to the staff, and the noisy, unstable inmates he lived with made his problems with sleeping worse than ever. When the band visited him there they knew immediately he had to be moved somewhere else, and he was duly booked into the £300-a-day Priory Clinic in Roehampton, in the outer suburbs of south London. The Priory, a 92-bed hospital with specialist units for alcoholism and eating disorders, had previously successfully treated Shaun Ryder, Elton John and Michael Barrymore. One of the first things Richey did while he was in there was to join Alcoholics Anonymous. Then he embarked on the 'Twelve Step Recovery Programme' used at Roehampton. Step One is where the patient has to admit they are powerless over their addiction and that because of this impotence their lives are unmanageable, and will remain so until that power is taken back.

The band visited him nearly every day, and at first his progress seemed rather good. With the expert medical attention and psychiatric skills on hand, Richey began to put a little weight back on and seemed enthusiastic and attentive in the therapy sessions. This was not to say he didn't have problems with the recovery. In Step Three the patient has to reconcile himself with a god of his understanding, whether that be the Christian or Jewish God, a family member or even an animal, whatever. Shaun Ryder had admitted that at this phase he used an image of his grandmother to help him through. Richey could find no such crutch, saying, 'Everything in my life has let me down.' When it was suggested he use a cat or dog, he said that was useless as either could die at any time.

Meanwhile, with the guitarist in hospital and the album about to be released, the media were having a field day with the dramatic news. The music weeklies were the most sensitive to the situation, reporting the events fairly and frowning on the dozens of rumours that abounded. Statements from the band's management were given plenty of space: 'There were contributing factors to his decline,' said Martin Hall. 'The death of Phil was one of them. But now Richey says he would have probably have ended up the same way regardless . . . the thing is he doesn't see anything wrong with cutting himself. It makes him feel better, it's his way of releasing the pain, and his argument is it doesn't harm anyone else. It's almost like a badge to show he's emotionally strong enough to deal with his problems in his own way. He was at the point though where no one – not even himself – knew how far he might go. If he had carried on without any help he might have ended up killing himself.'

The band members were also given room to air their concerns and views. James told *Melody Maker*, 'It's strange. Richey never had as many setbacks as a kid as me. He's more acutely intelligent than me, he's more beautiful than me, and yet he has more problems. Problems that I'd just snip off with fucking scissors in two seconds flat really get to Richey. But he has a very acute perception of things . . . we all saw Richey's problems getting to a stage where things were gonna get very nasty, and now he's going to see a psychiatrist and try to nip that in the bud. That's the true story. Those are the facts.' Ironically, James did not feel this period was any more difficult than any other, at first. 'I was probably much more worried about Richey at other points than this year. Like when we recorded the first album, he was royally fucked-up then, in terms of every kind of abuse. He would cry a lot. But it always got back on an even keel quite easily. Then this last Christmas I felt he was the oldest and yet the youngest of us all . . . he was quite immature in terms of what he'd experienced in life, never been in a relationship, things like that . . . No matter what I said there was nothing I could say to make him feel better.' Sean simply had this to say: 'The only people who are disturbed by Richey cutting himself are those who don't know him. They don't understand . . . we do know him, we do understand.'

Nicky had this to say to *Max* magazine: 'Richey always saw himself as a weak person. He tried to cover that up with either drink or mutilation. It happens to a lot of people in bands but the more sensitive crumble. It's a question of how you deal with it . . . it's hard to separate walking up to the abyss and falling into it.' He went on, 'I think he just feels things so fucking intensely. He always had this vision of purity, or perfection, a kind of child-like vision, that became completely obliterated. A misprint on a lyric sheet, or whatever would just upset him so much.' And finally in *Melody Maker*: 'Richey just reached a point where something clicked. His self-abuse has just escalated so fucking badly – he's drinking, he's mutilating himself, he's on the verge of anorexia.'

Unfortunately, not all of the media were as charitable as the weeklies. Various tabloids circulated rumours – he had found God, he was a rampant atheist, and so on. The main one which kept returning was that he was to leave the band, suggestions which were denied vehemently by their management: 'Speculation that Richey is leaving the band is completely unfounded. Even from the clinic he is still very much involved with the artwork design and other marketing aspects for the forthcoming album, which everybody feels is the band's greatest release to date.' Other papers claimed Richey had tried to kill himself again while in hospital, and again Martin Hall had to issue a clarifying statement: 'Richey is still active in the band and he's getting better. He is, however, very ill at the moment and things have now developed to the point where the band, but more importantly Richey, have decided that he needs to seek out professional psychiatric help to deal with what is basically a sickness.' One tabloid stooped so low as to criticise the Manics for sending Richey to a private clinic when, they claimed, as 'Left Wing Ravers' they should have left him in the NHS ward. Some sick people even said it was all a fake publicity stunt. His management tried to make sure Richey did not see the press while he was recovering.

As the Manics were probably the most written-about band of the previous ten years in the music weeklies' letters pages, Richey's condition provoked a huge response. The *NME* and *Melody Maker* were swamped with messages of support, which heavily outweighed the criticism from unsympathetic quarters. Richey's illness and public discussion of eating disorders and self-mutilation gave a profile to problems that had previously been taboo – other stars had suffered from anorexia, for example Karen Carpenter, but it had never been discussed so openly before. Drinking and drugging were age-old rock 'n' roll problems, but never before had an alternative musician so openly admitted to these particular difficulties. When Richey had cut 4 Real into his arm, the response in the letters pages from people who felt the same as him was frightening. Now again, many people, particularly girls, wrote in to say they acted or felt similar. Others said Richey should not feel guilty about his over-active mind and that this was the sign of a great poet. Richey himself held little sympathy for this view: 'Fucking bullshit. When you're in the places I've been in, the first place especially, it's just any job, any occupation, housewife, bricklayer, plumber

Richey, Blackwood, 1994

. . . whatever. It doesn't pick or choose people who pick up a pen . . . it's very romantic to think I'm a tortured writer but mental institutions are not full of people in bands.' Despite his concern, the canonisation of Richey Manic was already under way.

While Richey was in Roehampton, the rest of the band gave a revealing interview to *Sky* magazine. James said, 'He doesn't have a second skin; he absorbs everything too easily. He has a mental illness. It's not schizophrenia or anything like that, but he's mentally ill. Manic depression.' He also said, 'If you knew him you'd say he was functioning normally now but if you didn't know him you'd think he was pretty weird.' Nicky also answered the burning question of whether the Manics would continue if Richey never made enough of a recovery to rejoin the band: 'No, not in any shape or form. The thing with Richey is that he's never seen his own worth in the band – you can tell him his worth a million times and he thinks it's all down to his guitar playing or something.'

In the immediate future, the band had certain gig commitments to meet. Richey was far short of being able to rejoin, so after much debate they agreed to play the forthcoming T in the Park and Reading festivals without him. No stand-in would be employed and no replacement auditioned. The only other time the band had ever performed without a complete line-up was when Nicky took time off to get married, and his place on the *Top Of The Pops* stage for their rendition of 'Slash 'N' Burn' was taken up by their tour manager Rory wearing a Minnie Mouse mask. Nicky calmed down fans' fears before the two summer festivals by saying, 'We haven't turned into one of those power trios like the fucking Jam or anyone like that,' but he hated the whole experience: 'When we played in Glasgow without him it was horrendous. It just felt like a massive fucking spiritual betrayal . . . we thought of just doing nothing, not doing press, cancelling gigs, but we talked it over and decided that we were duty-bound to fulfil certain responsibilities.' Although the band's sound was hardly affected – after all Richey had made no secret of his lack of playing input – the void left onstage was cavernous, and both shows seemed a muted memorial for the missing Manic, with the crowd asking after Richey constantly. The Reading festival slot was even more emotional as it would have been Philip Hall's birthday.

Richey had always been a very professional band member. He was never late for rehearsal, and always turned up for gigs on time, priding himself on his punctuality. He admitted that part of the reason for this was that the discipline helped to give him some structure in his life. So when he missed the Reading Festival he was desperately unhappy. As a result, his ambition to return in time for the forthcoming French tour with Therapy? and then Suede was very strong.

While this was going on, the Manics' third album, *The Holy Bible*, was released. Understandably, with the background of Richey's hospitalisation, the album was the subject of unusually intense discussion. With the depths of depression expressed on *The Holy Bible*, 70 per cent of whose lyrics Richey had written, reviewers did not have to look far to unearth the demons inside Richey's head. Put simply, *The Holy Bible* was an album of massive paradox. On the one hand it was incredibly hard listening, the barren, harsh musical landscapes making it a record that would rarely get played. On the other hand, the lyrics were a masterpiece, far surpassing anything the band had written before, and it made for compelling reading. Musically, the record varied very little – Nicky described it in the press as 'gothic with a small g', but it was much darker than that. The entire album was washed in clashing, abrasive guitars, stripped-down production and screamed, forced vocals. James told *Sky* magazine, 'We were sucked into the stupid fucking new eclectic age were supposed to be in [with *Gold Against The Soul*]. I just feel really thick for allowing ourselves to be subconsciously compromised. So I've gone back to the original point.'

The album was unusual in that it was formed around the lyrics completely. Richey and Nicky sat down with structures and written plans for the songs, and then when James was given the words, he found the music was easy: 'This time we seemed to be capable of saying everything we wanted to say,' Nicky told *Melody Maker*. 'We weren't shoe-horning the lyrics in this time, the lyrics suggested the melodies, these beautiful melodies – James is so happy with this record, and he's not a man who's easily pleased.'

With the brilliance of the lyrics far outweighing the musical accompaniment, any analysis of the album has to focus on Richey's words more than anything else. The opening 'Yes' was relatively tame, talking about the hypocrisy of society's views about prostitutes, when people often do little more than whore themselves everyday at work (the Manics felt they had done this already, and hence called themselves 'media sluts' and 'the band that likes to say "Yes"'). Richey talked of how Marlene Dietrich complained of being 'photographed to death' and compared this to the Red Indian belief that each photograph takes away a little of the soul. The bizarrely titled 'Ifwhiteamericatoldthetruthforonedayit'sworldwouldfallapart' compared British imperialism with US consumerism, and mocked the gun laws in America and its belief that it is a civilised nation. The political angle deepened with the focus of 'Of Walking Abortion', which lambasted the pre-Second World War Hungarian fascist ruler Nicholas Horthy. Of the simple song 'She Is Suffering' Richey said in the tour book to accompany *The Holy Bible* dates, '"She" is desire. In other Bibles and Holy Books no truth is possible until you empty yourself of desire. All commitment otherwise is fake/lies/economic convenience. "Salvation is purity."'

'Archives Of Pain' was the album's most worked and re-written lyric, with both Richey and Nicky changing it endlessly. It denounced the fashion for glorifying serial killers in films such as *Silence Of The Lambs* and the media coverage of Jeffrey Dahmer's appalling crimes. Boris Yeltsin is also mentioned as a figure of hate. 'Revol' compares relationships in politics and in personal lives and says that both are ultimately failures. This was Richey despairing of love, bereft of optimism.

The next track was Richey's finest-ever work and a high point in modern lyrics. '4st 7lbs' was also perhaps that harrowing album's most harrowing track. The weight is said to be the point where an anorexic is faced with death. Describing the feelings of a young woman in this condition, Richey's words were poetry of a high calibre. Their obviously autobiographical slant and Richey's current predicament made the song even more disturbing. It is a sign of *The Holy Bible*'s mood that its most triumphant and celebratory moment is when the girl expresses delight at her emaciation.

Further tracks provide additional evidence both of Richey's brilliance and of his terrible state of mind. 'Mausoleum' and 'The Intense Humming Of Evil' were inspired by the band's trip the previous year to the Dachau and Belsen concentration camps and to Hiroshima. At Dachau, the knowledge that 700,000 bodies were buried underfoot, and the total absence of noise, without even birds singing, completely devastated Richey. Having studied the Holocaust at university, he knew all about the horrors already, but the trip to Dachau seemed to have left an indelible impression on him. His frail mind simply could not cope with what he was seeing. When he returned home and read some revisionist historian's work claiming the Holocaust never happened, he fell into a terrible depression.

'PCP' talked about the right to freedom of speech and the monster that is political correctness. 'Faster' was a joint effort, but strangely one that Nicky didn't understand himself. Richey told *Melody Maker* it was about 'Strength through weakness. All morality sown in the soil of the ruling caste. Self-abuse is anti-social, aggression still natural. Society speeding up – finds worth in failure.' 'This Is Yesterday' was a sad glance back at the glorious childhood that Richey had never recaptured. The album included another deeply harrowing song, 'Die In The Summertime'. With Richey's illness, this lyric was seen as completely autobiographical, a track that even Nicky found unnerving. Yet Richey said it was actually about the condition of old age, and describes a pensioner's desire to die with his favourite teenage memory in his mind.

Of Richey's achievement on *The Holy Bible*, Nicky later recalled to *Melody Maker* how they knew at the time he was writing his best work: 'He just kept handing us lyrics that were absolutely perfect, absolutely beautiful, and yeah, very personal. I mean, he's not here to speak for himself, but I think he's explained himself pretty fucking perfectly in those songs.' Even the title itself represented Richey's impossible burden: 'You're talking about a guy here,' James told *Raw* magazine, 'who wanted to call the album *The Holy Bible* because he believes that everything on there has to be perfection: the music, the words, the artwork, everything. Richey has always been in love with rose-tinted perfection, so he was always in danger of being let down.'

The artwork for the album showed a triptych of a colossally obese woman in white bra and knickers. The picture was by Jenny Saville and hung in the Saatchi gallery. When the band had previously asked to use another Saatchi-owned piece in a piece of artwork they had been asked for £30,000, so Richey asked to meet Saville and proceeded to talk her through the album, explaining every line. She immediately agreed to let the band use the image for free.

The public and media reacted in the only way possible to this album. While acknowledging the genius of the lyrics and expressing some reservations about the inaccessibility of the music, the general consensus was one of concern for Richey. Amazingly, the record reached Number 6 in the album charts, despite its bleak nature, and despite the torrent of swear words that necessitated a 'Parental Advisory' sticker and eliminated the possibility of any substantial radio airplay. Somehow, this all seemed irrelevant, for with *The Holy Bible* the Manic Street Preachers had delivered one of the finest albums of the decade.

In the light of later events, this album has been seen as Richey's suicide note. At the time the despair of the words led to comparisons with Kurt Cobain and Nirvana's third album, *In Utero*. That record is now seen as Cobain's epitaph – a record that was barely listenable at times, and which had borne the working title 'I Hate Myself And I Want To Die'. The production was also harsher than the relatively polished sound of its immediate predecessor. Unlike Cobain, Richey had publicly and very famously denounced the option of killing himself: 'In terms of the "s" word: that does not enter my mind. And it never has done. In terms of an attempt. Because I am stronger than that. I might be a weak person, but I can take pain.' He did not seem able to actually say the word 'suicide', however. Richey and Kurt were both now part of rock mythology, and these similar records, which opened up each writer's respective spiritual abyss, rightfully take their place as two of the bleakest yet most accomplished albums in alternative music history.

In the autumn of 1993, two *NME* journalists had listened to the likes of S*M*A*S*H, Blessed Ethel, and These Animal Men and announced that here was British music's saving force: 'The concept is New Wave of New Wave. The reality is a lumping together of (at times) vaguely like-minded fresh British bands with ants in their pants and vocabularies laced with shrapnel.' The two key players, S*M*A*S*H and These Animal Men, were lyrically astute and articulate in their call to rebellion, and their energetic and vibrant live shows initially seemed to offer the injection of energy that British music so needed. Then in the New Year of 1994, the New Wave of New Wave went overground with magazine covers and packed gigs, and a whole host of other bands were included in the 'movement', such as Done Lying Down, Action Painting and even Elastica. But it was to turn out that the movement's significance was sartorial as much as it was musical, with rather one-dimensional, speed-fuelled songs that harked back to the Jam and the

Clash, and the NWONW's days were numbered. By the end of 1994, many of the NWONW bands had split up and barely any long-term success was achieved. In retrospect, the movement had no more cultural significance than shoe-gazing.

For the Manics, this latest scene was rather old hat. They had been saying and doing these things with far more style for years and could not avoid a wry smile when it was suddenly flavour of the month. It was particularly ironic that New Wave of New Wave was so fashionable at a time when the Manics' own work was more apolitical and personal than ever before. Even more ironic was that some of the journalists renowned for hating the Manics hailed the New Wave of New Wave as revolutionary. 1994 was a notable year for music in other, darker ways. Most obviously it was the year that Kurt Cobain took his life, sending the industry into a lengthy period of mourning. Hole's bassist was found dead from an alleged heroin overdose, Sinéad O'Connor suffered a nervous breakdown after an apparent suicide attempt, and the American rock scene was riddled with hard-drug abuse. Many big-name bands split up as well, with the Wonder Stuff going, and Bernard Butler leaving Suede. The entire year was shrouded in gloom.

The Holy Bible did nothing to lift the spirits. With Richey's difficulties still not resolved, the strain started to show on Nicky. He told *Melody Maker*, 'Right now I don't wanna go out, I don't wanna make friends, at the moment all I want to do is make enemies. I've never felt so much fucking contempt for everyone and everything in my entire fucking life. I don't feel the need for anyone to like me anymore. Jesus, it's hard enough to like myself.' The band admitted that they now felt cheapened by their earlier desperation to succeed: 'Basically we've reached the point where we feel as if we've prostituted ourselves so fucking much,' Nicky said, 'just given and given and given, that we've given everything away, and we've got absolutely fucking nothing left of our own.' Nicky now lived in Blackwood with his wife and became increasingly withdrawn and even domesticated. He had stopped drinking, and now resided in a small terraced house in the valleys. 'I've always believed in marriage,' he told *Sky* magazine. 'It's about the only thing I do believe in and it's very un-Manics I agree. My mum and dad always seemed really happy and I had a good childhood, so perhaps I looked up to it subconsciously. It's strange but it's something I actually wanted to do. From the first moment I met her. Fuck knows why.'

James meanwhile had gone the opposite way. Just before Christmas 1993 he had split up with a long-term girlfriend and moved to a smart flat in London's Bayswater to enjoy a change of scene. Over the coming months, he became what Nicky called Seventies Man – 'steak-eating, fag-puffing, whisky-slewing, currently vogue-ish superlad'. The rest of the media saw this lifestyle as a 'new lad', a phenomenon represented by the huge success of the magazine *Loaded*. He drank at all the right pubs, hung out in all the right clubs, and generally had a great time in the capital. His appearance in the gossip columns of the music papers on a regular basis reinforced this new image, but James shrugged it off, saying, 'I just like a fucking drink.' He had other reasons for moving: 'Because Richey bought a flat in Cardiff, Nick lives with his wife, Sean lives with his girlfriend and I started feeling like Ronnie Corbett in *Sorry!*' he told *Select*. 'I was comfortable living at home with my parents. I was 25 and I couldn't put a plug on, I couldn't change lightbulbs or sew. Now I'm educated domestically. Although I can't get rid of the bachelor smell in the flat.' He continued, 'I discovered the art of switching off. Which I do by enjoying myself. I know that's at odds with our image, the conspiracy theory that getting out of it is just a way to get you down, but . . . I only go out and get blasted when I've finished work. I'm more professional now.'

Richey had eyed the planned October tour as the motivation for his recovery and this goal seemed to speed up his improvement. He had begun eating properly again, was taking a pride in his appearance and was even practising his guitar. By late September he was considered well enough to check out of the Priory. That he was keen to rejoin the others was a good sign: at one point during his illness, he had suggested to the band that maybe he should retire from playing live and just write lyrics for them. They said they would think about it, but as soon as they left Richey had burst into tears and phoned them to say he had changed his mind: 'I kind of think I'd be cheating on them,' he explained to *NME*, ''cause the touring part is the worst bit – the bit that no band really enjoys. It's the thing that makes it feel like a job.'

Understandably, when Richey finally left Roehampton, the media focus on him intensified. To his credit he was prepared to face the spotlight and was candid about his recent problems: 'Basically I wasn't in a very good frame of mind. My mind wasn't functioning very well, and my mind was stronger than my body. My mind subjected my body to things that it couldn't cope

with. Which meant I was ill. For the first time I was a bit scared, because I always thought I could handle it.' He gave some examples: 'I couldn't understand *Prisoner Cell Block H*. It was doing my head in. And then I realised that I'm not stupid. I had to convince myself that I'm not stupid. It was just a silly little thing. The little things, you see, are the worry, that put me in a mood that I can't really control . . . It can be anything, just a line in a film or a book and I've lost it. The last one that happened when I was hospitalised was just a dainty little thing on the *Big Breakfast* from Lee Marvin singing that stupid song "I Was Born Under A Wandering Star". There's a line in that, "Hell is in hello", and for two days I couldn't do fucking anything . . . what are they trying to say . . . "Hell is in hello"?'

With Richey now back in the fold, the Manics started rehearsing again for the tour in a Pembrokeshire studio which Take That had vacated only two weeks previously. Richey still looked ill, with sunken eyes and a painfully gaunt face. When the *NME* came along to interview them all, he was reluctant to be photographed alone, not wanting anyone to think the band might try to capitalise on his illness. But eventually he was persuaded, and, predictably, the picture was used for the next week's front cover. During the interview with journalist Stuart Bailie, the band diverted questions away from the subject of Richey when they became uncomfortable. Bailie nevertheless felt Richey was not quite right, a feeling later confirmed by Nicky, who blamed the sterilising effect of the Priory: 'They loved him in there, because he's so intelligent and sharp-witted, and he got into it, played along with them. But they ripped the soul out of him. The person I knew was kind of slowly ebbing away. I think he knew that too.'

If the Manics hoped for a turnaround after a traumatic nine months, they were soon to be disappointed. At first things went well: their short British tour supported by Sleeper and Dub War in October went reasonably well, with the media and public treating the band with kid gloves. The new single 'She Is Suffering' was also well received, although it was probably over-scrutinised for insights into Richey's frame of mind. The CD version had a live bonus of two tracks recorded at the Clapham Grand with Bernard Butler, 'The Drowners' and 'Stay Beautiful'. Some critics only half-jokingly remarked how James's shrill vocal was oddly reminiscent of Noddy Holder of Slade on this track.

Then in November they flew out to begin a large European tour with

Suede and Therapy? which saw the bill alternating each night. In theory it should have been a breakthrough tour for the Manics, and a positive experience, but it proved to be fraught with tension and unhappiness. This tension showed at the gigs. Richey was gaunt and frail and took up his slot stage left as always, but he was a reserved and odd presence, mouthing the songs silently. All eyes seemed to be on him, analysing how he looked, how he reacted, how he played. Yet he did very little, just standing there in combat trousers and a tight pink T-shirt with the word 'Fairy' written across his chest. Sean kept himself to himself behind his kit and Nicky was noticeably subdued. The band's sound was clean enough, but there was something missing. With Richey and Nicky, his two sidekicks, so muted, James came to the fore even more than usual. Despite the modest performances, the press seemed unwilling to lay into the Manics as they had so often done before, clearly because of Richey's illness. It was a little sad that it took a prolonged bout of mental illness to finally silence the doubters that this band were for real.

Behind the scenes, the Manics were stretched out. Richey was walking around reading from material he had been given at the Priory, weird stuff that embarrassed and unsettled the others. For the other band members, the presence of their apparently recovered friend was strangely unnerving: 'The first day I was really nervous,' James told the *Times*. 'I was so on edge about Richey, in case he started cutting himself again. I kept thinking, "If you cut yourself now son, everything will be wasted."' At first Richey managed to control himself: 'He has wanted to cut himself on this tour already but he hasn't, and that's a first. We're taking things slowly. He knows he can leave the band whenever he wants, whenever it gets too much. From the first time we knew Richey we knew he wanted to be in the band. If he left the band would probably be over. I can't imagine the Manics without him.'

It was not just on Richey that the strain was showing. Nicky was desperately homesick, had lost his suitcase and clothes and was physically unwell. He flew back to Britain for a week to see a specialist, and enjoyed the

were five of the best

break as he was missing his wife. James was constantly on edge about his friend's welfare, and was drinking all day alone and wouldn't show his face until just before show time. Sean was miserable and unsociable. All four of them hated the entire experience, and couldn't wait to get back home.

The extent of Richey's continuing illness soon became apparent. Many recovering anorexics hide their frailty in huge baggy clothes, but Richey turned up for the first show in a skin-tight pair of girl's leggings, fully revealing the painfully thin waist underneath. He began to write 'Love' on his knuckles in black ink, a weird habit that James described as 'just bollocks, Priory stuff'. He asked to be called Richard, not Richey, but as the band often called him 'Android' anyway this was largely ignored. The obsessive side of his nature began to break through again as well. Firstly he became embroiled in the life of the late Def Leppard guitarist Steve Clark, who suffered terrible stage fright and once smashed his knuckles on a wash basin so that he wouldn't have to go onstage. Richey told people he dreamed of chopping off his own fingers, and grave concerns were expressed when he returned to the entourage one day having bought a butcher's meat cleaver. When this phase passed, Richey became obsessed with the mad photo-journalist played by Dennis Hopper in *Apocalypse Now* – he even bought the same make of camera as he had and wore it round his neck in identical fashion.

His eating was also becoming a problem again. He would sit in a dressing room full of people and break up pieces of chocolate on to a plate, showing them that this was all he would eat all day. He also developed a large thyroid cyst in his neck, possibly a result of the pills he was taking to help him cope (one of which was the so-called 'wonder drug', the anti-depressant Prozac). When he read criticism in the newspapers from their recent support band, Dub War, claiming that the Manics were a sham, that they didn't drink as much as their reputation suggested, and that Nicky and Richey paraded around Blackwood like stars, his mood darkened even further. While Nicky was disappointed but could ignore these petty comments easily, as did James and Sean, Richey was crushed. The fragility of his self-esteem was further exemplified by the fact he was doing 1500 sit-ups a day.

Richey did seem to be controlling his drinking, but the discipline required only depressed him more because he missed what had been one of the few constants in his turbulent recent years. At one point he turned to Nicky and said, 'I can't do anything I want to any more.' At the show in Amsterdam, the set was so poor that everyone was gutted. Afterwards, Nicky noticed Richey was strangely cheerful, and became concerned. When he pulled up his friend's shirt he found a deep vertical gash down his upper torso. Nicky was devastated and Sean had to take the accompanying journalists out for a meal to distract them. Thereafter, Nicky would take Richey to one side before they retired to bed each night and say, 'Pull your top up, let's have a look.' On 4 December Nicky was called to the outside of their Hamburg hotel where Richey was repeatedly banging his head hard against the wall, with blood coursing down his face. Then, oddly, when some record company executives felt the tour was worth extending, Richey was the only one of the band who agreed. Sticking to the original schedule, they had three more gigs at London's Astoria left for the year and then they could finally relax, put 1994 behind them and start again.

London crowds are notoriously pretentious and hard to please, so although the Manics were glad to be home, they were understandably apprehensive of these Astoria dates, especially in the light of the fractured atmosphere in the tour camp. Their fears were exacerbated by sound problems with the house PA for all three nights, and strangely all four members suffered nosebleeds for all three days. Having said that, the mood in the camp was a little lighter; they enjoyed shopping along Oxford Street and were looking forward to a quiet Christmas rest. Supported by DJ Andy Weatherall, Strangelove, Whiteout, the Dust Brothers, and Marion, the Manics took to the stage in a massive air of expectancy for what were their first London dates since Richey's return. The first two nights were good, but it was the final show on 21 December that was to go down as a classic. The Manics were quite simply breathtaking. There was even time for some festive fun when James donned a red Santa hat and sang Wham's 'Last Christmas'. The rest of the gig was sheer, spine-tingling rock 'n' roll brilliance. At the end of the set the band smashed up their gear in a frenzy of destruction – this time it was their expensive instruments rather than the cheaper ones they often demolished. Richey was involved too, diving into Sean's kit and ending up smashing his guitar over his head and standing alone, centre stage, surrounded by the debris. 'That last five minutes of the last gig when we smashed eight grand's worth of gear and lights were five of the best minutes I've ever had in my life,' Nicky told *NME*. 'It was just brilliant. We were transported back to the days of "Motown Junk". Beautiful. It meant more than any of the songs. Until we saw the bill . . .' It was an amazing spectacle and the punters left that night knowing the Manics had reclaimed their reputation with panache.

That was the last gig Richey Edwards ever played.

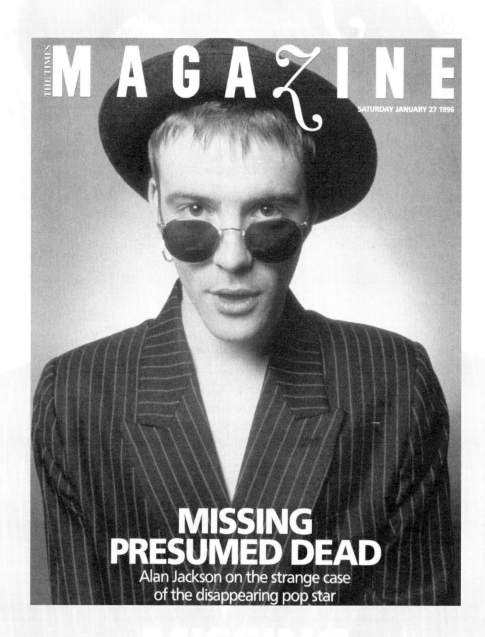

THE TIMES **MAGAZINE**

SATURDAY JANUARY 27 1996

MISSING
PRESUMED DEAD

Alan Jackson on the strange case
of the disappearing pop star

MISSING
PRESUMED DEAD
Alan Jackson on the strange case
of the disappearing pop star

CHAPTEЯ 10

'I still like to think of Richey as stronger than what he became . . . which is that he just . . . caved in.'
Nicky

'I suppose it was a gradual decline that led him to seeking treatment, but when he was at home he seemed reasonably happy and it was only later that we realised there was something seriously wrong.'
Graham Edwards, Richey's father

On 15 February 1995, the press received a Missing Person report concerning Richey Edwards, who had been absent since the first of the month. The report talked of his depression and of a previous suicide bid, and expressed concerns for his safety. If the Manics had received press attention almost continually throughout their career, this was to be nothing compared to the frenzy that surrounded them now.

The first shocking thing about Richey's disappearance was that there were no warning signs. He had driven home with Sean after the Astoria gigs and seemed quiet but reasonably content. He saw quite a lot of Nicky over the holidays and they exchanged festive presents as always. Friends of the family even saw him eat a Mars Bar and hailed this as a small step towards defeating his anorexia. It was apparent, however, that he was still not fully recovered.

Richey had disappeared before for short periods. For example, he had gone astray after the Glastonbury performance the previous year, and also he had vanished for a couple of days in January. Besides, he seemed to be enthusiastic about the forthcoming band work, and had been excited about starting rehearsals at the House in the Woods near Cobham, Surrey, in early January. They had worked on new, melodic material and started throwing ideas around for a soundtrack tune they had been asked to write for a film, *Judge Dredd*. Apart from his usual paranoid habit of phoning Nicky dozens of times to check the rehearsal time, Richey seemed at ease, vibrant and even happy. As they left the last rehearsal Richey gave each band member a present – Nicky received a Mars Bar and a copy of the *Daily Telegraph*, James got a CD and Sean something unspecified. This was nothing unusual – they did it all the time. He also handed over a folder full of lyrics which the band had seen before, as he had been working on them for a while. Nicky told him to give the lyrics to Sean and then Richey did some photocopies for each band member. Later rumours had it that Richey deemed the lyrics unworthy and threw 80 per cent of them into a river near his home, but this is not true. Nor was there any ritualistic burning of them.

'I can honestly say that the five days at the House in the Woods was the only time when I thought he was back to being Iggy/Keith Richards, as opposed to Ian Curtis. But that could have been because he was going,' Nicky later confided to a journalist from *NME*. With a 36-date, two-month tour of America coming up, Nicky felt all was in order and went for a short break in Barcelona. When he returned, in the middle of January, Richey was not around. His mother had believed he was in London with the band but they hadn't seen him. The next day he turned up, with his head poorly shaved, and claimed he had been in Swansea. He said he was very upset about the death of his beloved dog Snoopy earlier in the week. Shortly after, a friend saw him at a gig in Newport and Richey told him how bored he was, and the friend noticed how sad he seemed. The media made much of this (and of his university friend's suicide) in the light of later events, but James is unconvinced: 'I wouldn't make too much significance out of it – he was always adept at too much symbolism. It wasn't a breaking point, to be honest.' Nicky agreed: 'He was upset, but I felt good, actually. When he cried naturally, it was nothing to do with the Priory, it was just his pet had died.'

A week later, on 23 January, Richey conducted what is now known to have been his last ever interview, for the Japanese magazine *Music Life*, with fan and writer Midori Tsukagoshi. He attended the interview dressed in stripy pyjamas very similar to the ones worn by Nazi concentration camp prisoners. Four days later it was the fiftieth anniversary of the liberation of Auschwitz. He was wearing a pin-badge saying 'I miss my virginity' and had the word 'Love' written across his knuckles in black ink again. One further interesting point of detail is that he was wearing the same type of black canvas Converse trainers that Kurt Cobain was wearing when he killed himself. In the photographs Richey looked withdrawn, sad and wasted – in short, terrible. The interview itself has now been pored over meticulously and is quoted at length here.

'I was bored with my old hairstyle,' he said. 'It was irritating me. If I can't sleep I tend to have destructive ideas and I have to do something to root them out. I couldn't sleep and all I could think of was shaving my head, so I did.' (Later in the interview he said he shaved it because of his dog's death.) 'I can sleep now. I was almost in love with my hairstyle. But in the end I just felt like abandoning things like that.' He talked of being physically unable to get out of bed some mornings, and how much of a change it was not to be drinking anymore. He revealed that while he drank he couldn't bear the thought of getting a beer belly so he didn't eat to avoid it: 'I was always drinking and I felt sick all the time.'

His emotional instability was further highlighted when talk turned towards relationships: 'I'd love to love someone seriously, but considering what I'd expect and what would be expected of me it seems quite difficult. I feel nobody would want to live with me. To love somebody involves being trapped by jealousy. It's really hard. I've never wanted to love somebody insincerely – and I don't mean only sexually but intellectually and mentally too . . . seriously if I was in love with a woman, she'd have to be more attractive than Bette Davis, more than anyone else. I'd peel every picture off my walls.' Then he talked of the only girl he had ever really had such feelings for: 'I can speak to her more naturally than to anyone else. It means something. But I've never told her I love her. I've known her for years, but I've only kissed her once . . . once, twice. That's all.' This girl is believed to be called Jo, but otherwise remains anonymous.

He seemed reasonably optimistic about the future: 'The worst thing I did was to keep trying to be normal, which is how I ended up in hospital. Now I wake up in the morning and I know what I want to do – I want to write, it makes me feel better in myself . . . I value writing songs, I do regard myself as a good poet. I work hard. Songwriting is an art and I really try my best at it.' He finished by saying, 'The band is getting better and better, the lyrics are too. I've found better ways to express myself . . . I don't think I've changed what I say but maybe I'm saying it in a different way.'

Nine days later Richey vanished.

Only a few facts about the disappearance are certain. Richey checked in to the mid-range Embassy Hotel on the Bayswater Road on the evening of 31 January. The next day, he and James were due to fly out to America for a promotional tour which was to precede their biggest-ever attack on the US market. The band had spent the previous day demo-ing songs (several of which would later appear on the next album) and Richey seemed fine. That night he gave a book called *Novel With Cocaine*, by 'Ageyev', to a female friend and asked her to read it. The book was written under a pseudonym, and was a mystery in itself. It had been sent unsolicited to a Parisian literary journal for Russian emigrés, and was so brilliant in its depiction of teenage cocaine addiction that it won critical acclaim and widespread fame for the unknown author. 'Ageyev' had spent some time cooped up in mental asylums, so it was expected he would enjoy the acclaim, but he did not appear for the publicity stints and was never seen in public.

The two band members were given adjoining rooms, and James said he'd call Richey after they had freshened up. When he did so half an hour later, Richey was in the middle of taking a bath, so James said they would go to Queensway for the shops and the cinema a little later and Richey agreed. When the singer again knocked on Richey's door after another half-hour, Richey said he had changed his mind and would stay in after all. James went out with a friend and returned to the Embassy at just before midnight. He never saw Richey again.

Accounts of events after this are riddled with rumour and gossip, but certain facts can be deemed probable from police reports. Back in the Embassy, Richey wrapped up a box of presents for the girl he had spoken of so warmly in the Japanese interview the week before. Inside was a collection of reading material, and the videos of *Equus* and Mike Leigh's *Naked*. A note addressed to the girl said simply, 'I Love You.' He had frequently given her presents before but the relationship had never progressed past being platonic. Attached to the side of the box were a series of quotes and clippings. Beside the box on the bed was a packed suitcase, his bottle of Prozac and some toiletries. Richey then walked out of Room 516, leaving all these behind, and left the hotel without checking out, around 7am on 1 February, and drove down the M5 to his new flat in Cardiff, some 150 miles away. He left his passport, another bottle of Prozac and his credit cards on his unmade bed and then got back into his car. His exact movements after this are unknown.

Back at the Embassy Hotel all was confusion. Martin Hall, the band's manager, could not get any reply from Richey's room that day, and with his history of self-abuse, became concerned when no one knew where he was. The hotel room door was opened and the parcel found on the bed. Hall and the rest of the band spent the rest of the day frantically phoning round every friend or band associate they could think of, but all to no avail. The following morning Hall reported Richey missing at Harrow Road police station, and then drove to Blackwood to meet up with the guitarist's parents, Sherry and Graham (who last saw Richey on the 23rd, and last spoke to him by phone the day before he vanished). Next, they searched Richey's flat in Anson Court, Cardiff, and found newspapers which proved he had been home the day before, but otherwise no clues as to his whereabouts. Then there was a false alarm when a Richey Edwards was traced to a hotel in Swansea, but he turned out to be a middle-aged businessman. Hall cancelled the US promotional tour and the live dates, as well as two European gigs in Vienna and Prague and the track for *Judge Dredd*. For the immediate future, the disappearance was kept a secret, and the US promoters told that James was suffering from an ear infection.

The next morning Richey's family placed an advert in the local newspaper's personal column which ran for three consecutive days saying, 'Richard, please make contact, love Mum, Dad, Rachel.' The management company also hired a top private detective company to discover the musician's whereabouts, but both efforts proved fruitless. By 15 February, it was decided that by going public they might have more chance of finding him. Thus, on that day, the South Wales police statement was issued that told the world of the vanishing of Richey Manic. It mentioned his famous 'Useless Generation' tattoo, and said, coldly, 'Subject has made a previous suicide attempt and is taking anti-depressants.' On the reverse of the Missing Person report was a mention of the 'I Love You' note and a comment saying, 'Apparently subject would like to have a relationship with [her].'

While Richey's father appealed on BBC Radio One for his son to make contact, various friends, associates and industry figures expressed their shock and concern for Richey's welfare. His friend Byron Harris said in *Vox*, 'Richey would never do anything without a reason. He is a very intelligent man. He wouldn't just disappear like this under normal circumstances.' His father Graham said, 'Being in the rock 'n' roll business they are always under a lot of emotional stress, and I think that may have something to do with it. This is completely out of character and everyone's very worried about him. If he needs time to be on his own then that's okay. If he has any problems that we can help him with I hope he remembers he's always had strong support from his family and all the lads in the band.' From his record company Rob Stringer commented: 'What worries people so much is the fact that there were no indications. Richey seemed okay – there was no blow up, no row in the band, nothing. When he was ill last time his parents and his manager literally had to get him to hospital. Everyone saw it coming, but this time there were no signs.'

On 16 February the first positive news of Richey arrived – police reported they had found his abandoned silver L Reg Cavalier at the Severn View service station, near the Severn Bridge. The car had apparently been there for several days, and there were signs that it had been slept in, not least because the battery was flat. It had been reported by a security guard at the station on Valentine's Day and traced back to Richey on the national computer. The station manager, one Tom Cassidy, remembered nothing suspicious in the few days the car was left in his car park. Richey's father drove down to the bridge and took his son's car home. The service station had changed its name in 1991 from the Aust Service Station, so named for its proximity to the imposing cliffs overlooking the Bristol channel, where the 450-foot Severn Bridge was a notorious suicide spot (although not as 'popular' as the nearby Brunel Suspension bridge). Unsurprisingly, police admitted that they were now searching the Severn Estuary for a body, and they also contacted coastal authorities to see if any bodies had been washed up on the local shoreline. For the moment, the Manics made no public statement.

With the discovery of the car, the media and public gossip machines went into overdrive. Many people had at first thought he had simply gone to ground and would re-emerge given time, but with the discovery of his car, things seemed to become more serious. It emerged that Richey had withdrawn £200 a day from various cash machines for the two weeks prior to his disappearance. Some people concluded from this that he was planning to vanish, while others said that £2000 would not last long, especially as his bank accounts had not been used since he vanished. Moreover, he did not have his credit cards with him, but it is possible that he had saved some

Police report on Richey's disappearance

METROPOLITAN POLICE SERVICE

PNC W/M No:

Form 584 (C)　　　　Station Copy

Please use BLOCK CAPITALS / Do NOT fold
*Delete as appropriate

Stn. Ref. No: 584/21

Class class: *person missing / person, body found / absentee from care / mental absconder / hospital

Send photograph if available to B14 with Form 584. Original will be returned after copying

*LIMITED / ENQUIRY　Station: HARROW ROAD

| Surname: EDWARDS | Forenames: RICHARD | Male / Female / Unknown | DOB (if not known give age) 22 12 67 |

Ethnic appearance: White European / Dark European / Negroid / Asian / Oriental / Arab / Doubt　　Height: 5 ft. 8 ins

Alias:

Marks, scars, tattoos, physical peculiarities: SEVERAL TATTOOS

Birthplace: BLACKWOOD

ROSE 'USELESS GENERATION' ON LEFT ARM.

Nationality: WELSH

Warning signals: (drugs, suicidal, depressed, violent, etc.) ON ANTI DEPRESSANTS.

Habits / other characteristics: (smokes, drinks, etc.) SMOKES

Date of incident: 1 2 95 0700　Date of report: 2 2 95

Cross Ref., other person(s) involved:

Build: slim / medium / heavy / other

Hair: colour SHAVED length / SHAVED style

*Beard / moustache / wig / other:

Eyes: colour BROWN　*glasses / contact lenses

Complexion: PALE

Clothing — include full description and colour:

Jacket: Further tattoos - 2 ornate tattoos on shoulders (colourful but perhaps n/k).

Jumper: N/K

Shirt:

Trousers:

Footwear:

Skirt:

Other:

Topcoat:

Jewellery:

Address from which missing: LONDON EMBASSY HOTEL

Home address if different: 6 ANSON CT, SCHOONER WAY, ATLANTIC WHARF, CARDIFF

Circumstances: SUBJECT IS A MEMBER OF A BAND AND WAS STAYING IN LONDON EMBASSY HOTEL WITH ANOTHER BAND MEMBER BEFORE FLYING TO USA ON BUSINESS. SUBJECT WAS SEEN BY HOTEL STAFF LEAVING HOTEL ON 1 2 95 AT 0700 + HAS NOT BEEN SEEN SINCE. HIS PASSPORT IS MISSING BUT ALL HIS BELONGINGS ARE STILL IN HIS HOTEL ROOM. SUBJECT HAS MADE A PREVIOUS SUICIDE ATTEMPT + IS TAKING ANTI - DEPRESSANTS. Date / time last seen: 1 2 95 0700

School or Occupation: MEMBER OF POP BAND

Mental absconders: Order under S　MHA 19　NOT to be arrested after

Care Order: To　at　Social Services

INFORMANT Name:

Address 8 P...
UXBRIDGE

Publicity authorised:

Time 10 09

ACTION REFER...

Checks PNC

MSS Tp B14/B6(4) S

Time 1120

Transferred to:

Supervising O...

Time

CANCELLATION B14...

Supervising Of...

Time

M.P. 91

money before this elsewhere. Others speculated that with a band so close as the Manics, who even had their own personal nicknames for each other that no one else used, and who phoned each other every day, to disappear without saying a word was very strange.

People talked of other famous rock 'n' roll disappearances. Fleetwood Mac's Jeremy Spencer went missing from a hotel in Los Angeles hours before an important concert, purportedly for a pack of cigarettes, joined a religious cult called the Children of God and never played with the band again. Peter Green, genius guitarist with the same group, later gave away his millions and went to live with his mother. Joe Strummer of the Clash went AWOL in the early eighties and was eventually tracked down by a private detective in Paris, only to offer the explanation that he had simply wanted a break. With Richey's history of mental illness, other gory stories were rolled out as well, including Syd Barrett walking around with a penguin on his head before leaving Pink Floyd, and Julian Cope allegedly chasing members of the Teardrop Explodes around the Welsh mountains with a loaded shotgun.

Speculation heightened when it also emerged that for weeks Richey had been obsessed with the perfect disappearance. He had bought several books on the subject and watched many episodes of the *Reginald Perrin* TV comedy, about a rat-race middle-aged man who did exactly that. Leaving his car at a known suicide spot might have been a deliberate decoy, some said, and fans of Richey's held on to this theory, desperately hoping he was still alive. Other fans were not coping so well – only a fortnight after he went missing, there was a report of a copycat disappearance. Sixteen-year-old Sally Allen ran away from her parent's home in Skipton, west Yorkshire, having failed to return home from Swinton Comprehensive School. Her mother told police, 'She's a huge fan of Richey Edwards and she's not been right since he went missing. She's cut her hair off, she's virtually anorexic. Everything she's done seems to be down to this. We're very worried.' Three weeks later, Sally returned home, saying she had been on a pilgrimage to Bristol, Cardiff and London, but had decided to return after seeing Mother's Day cards in shop windows.

With no substantial new leads forthcoming, despite receiving over 100 calls a week at first, the police investigation continued fruitlessly. Many people had been found with far less information. Meanwhile, a spate of Richey sightings soon cropped up, and within a matter of months had blossomed into dozens of alleged sightings, as well as all manner of bizarre theories concerning his whereabouts. There are even hordes of questionnaires and theories flying around the Internet. While it is useless to mention every single detail (the one about being a workman in the north of England with a beer gut is as tasteless as it is laughable), there are several theories which are worth mentioning.

The first reported sighting came only four days after his car was discovered, on 20 February. A Guildford woman, Ms G. Williams, claimed to have seen a white man, about Richey's height, hitching eastbound from the Delamere Services on the M4, carrying a guitar case. Police in Avon interviewed her but it emerged she felt the man was at least 40 years old.

The very next day, another more probable sighting came to light. David Cross, himself a Manics fan from Mid Glamorgan, said that he saw Richey at Newport bus station on Sunday 5 February. He told *Vox*, 'I got off the bus alone and I usually buy the Sunday papers from a newsagent's shop which is a very short distance from the bus station. As I approached the newsagent's I saw Richey James Edwards. He was stood alone next to a silver-grey coloured car, I approached him as I was going to the shop. Although I do not know him I said to him, "Hello Richey I'm a friend of Lori's," and he said, "How is she, how's she doing?" I said, "She's fine." He looked at me and said, "I'll see you later." He was wearing a dark blue-coloured jacket. I am positive it was Richey.' Since Lori was a mutual close friend, and Cross's details seemed to fit, the police took this sighting seriously.

The most lengthy alleged contact with Richey was by taxi driver Anthony Hatherall. He claimed to have picked up a man resembling Richey at 7am on the morning of 7 February from the King's Hotel in the High Street in Newport. He described the passenger as 'a tall, slim man with a gaunt face' (though Richey was not tall) who got in the cab and asked him to go to Uplands. He also requested that they go via the scenic route, as he claimed he was always driving on motorways for his job. Hatherall said he was already suspicious because the man spoke in a Cockney accent, but one which was clearly fake, as it occasionally broke down into what was probably a soft Welsh dialect. He became even more concerned when the passenger asked if it was okay for him to lie down in the back seat while they drove. Unnerved, Hatherall asked for some money up front and was promptly given £40. He then proceeded to drive, as requested, to Uplands.

When they arrived, his passenger asked him to drive to Risca, and explained that he didn't know exactly where to go as he was looking for his boss who had broken down in a lorry. He asked where the nearest train station was and Hatherall said there wasn't one in Risca, so instead he drove to the bus station in Blackwood. On arrival there, the passenger snapped, 'This is not the place,' and asked to be taken to Pontypool train station, where he got out and said he would be five minutes while he made a phone call. Hatherhall was now very suspicious, as there was no public phone at Pontypool train station. On his return to the taxi, they then drove to Severn View Services via the scenic route where he dropped the man off. The total fare was £68, paid in full. Hatherall did not report this incident until 23 February because he said it wasn't until then he read about Richey's disappearance in the newspapers.

Another theory was that Richey was in America. The aforementioned Lori Fidler was embroiled in this theory, rather against her will, by an article in the *Sunday Times* which she later denied having been involved in. The paper alleged Richey was with her in New York and printed a photograph of the two together. Fidler, who had set up the Manics fanzine *Scream Tour Sigh*, denied this and said the photo was provided by a '"friend" who took advantage of my generosity and trust, and used her copy to submit to the paper'. Many people believed that Fidler was the girl Richey had left the note for in his hotel room – indeed, Fidler had been known to call him her 'babe' and there were rumours of jealousy among the band because she and Richey were so close. However, Fidler denied they were ever romantically involved, despite the police report naming her as the person most likely to be 'Jo'. Fidler claimed that Jo was, in fact, a fan of another band called Faith In Me, and she had refused to become Richey's lover. The badge saying 'I miss my virginity' and a book Richey carried in that final Japanese interview were alleged to have come from Fidler, although again she denied this. On 4 March, the police had received a phone call from a man in Irvine, Scotland who claimed to have seen Richey at Fidler's apartment in New York's East 21st Street. For her part, Fidler claimed she received a call which could have been from Richey. 'I was out at the time,' she told *Vox*, 'and my girlfriend took the call, the day after he went missing. There was that beep-beep on the line showing it was from overseas. The man on the other end just said "Hi Lori" and then hung up. I think it was him.' She also speculated: 'I think he's still alive in England and probably not far from home. Only back on 24 July, it was my birthday and I sat at home here in America all day waiting for him to call.'

Another detail to confuse matters still further was the claim by a German fan, Monika Pommer, that Richey had sent her a postcard, dated 3 March, from London. As evidence she sent another card Richey had posted her earlier, which was dated 13 December 1994, and which said, 'Thanks for all the presents, the coffee especially, take care of yourself, be happy, love Richey.' However, on being pressed, Pommer refused to send the actual March postcard saying it was too personal. She informed the police that on 20 August 1995 she would travel to Cardiff and throw flowers into the sea in his memory. Her partner Gregor Pommer wrote a letter to the police also listing twelve tangible reasons why Richey had probably committed suicide.

Other more protracted theories existed. One held that Richey was on a tour of Second World War concentration camps, on account of his interest in that part of history, the recent anniversaries of the camp's liberations, and the anonymity he could enjoy in Germany. One specific theory which was circulated to Manics fans tied in events in Richey's life with concentration camp dates of significance, and even gave an exact date, in May 1995, for his return. Then Cardiff police were told that Richey was staying at Henlow Grange Health Farm in Bedfordshire, and a withdrawn musician was found to be on the premises, but again, not Richey. Even Sinéad O'Connor had a theory, saying that she believed Richey was staying at the Hereford home of a schizophrenic fan – once again, the police checked it out and came back empty-handed.

People looked to the Manics' and Richey's literary tastes for hope and inspiration. In Allen Ginsberg's poem 'Howl', a tape of which the band used to play when going onstage in the early days of their career, a man jumped off Brooklyn Bridge and vanished into the hazy night of Chinatown. Others took solace in Richey's love of J. D. Salinger. After his novel, *The Catcher In The Rye,* Salinger locked himself in the basement of a New Hampshire redwood cottage for twenty years, refusing to see anyone or publish anything again, saying he was now writing only for pleasure.

The final possible sighting worthy of note was in Goa, India, over eighteen months after Richey first went missing. Vyvyan Morris, a 48-year-old media studies lecturer at Neath College in South Wales, claimed to have seen Richey in a hippie market there during November 1996. He told a Welsh newspaper, 'I was sitting having a Coke and I thought to myself, "I know that guy." He was a little worse for wear. His hair was a lot longer but he looked quite well and had quite a sun tan. I asked a bloke who was sitting nearby and he said, "That's Rick." He said he had come over to Goa about eighteen months earlier . . . he was wearing a kaftan top and jeans with matted and longish hair . . . I can't be 100 per cent certain, but I'm sure it was him.' Richey's sister Rachel revealed she had also been told of a reported sighting in Goa. Police talked to Morris but decided there were no new leads worth following, not least because Richey did not take his passport with him, although he could have obtained a false one.

There was even a false alarm when a body was found washed up on Beachy Head, which was the same size as Richey and had several tattoos. For a few agonising hours it seemed the desperate search had come to an end, but the body was identified as someone else's. Matters were complicated by an unusually high number of crank calls, prompted largely by Richey's celebrity. Det. Sgt Regan, one of the officers leading the investigation, told the *Daily Mirror*: 'One guy claimed that Richey was living at his house. He was obsessed with Richey and had made the whole story up.'

While all these rumours and possible sightings were investigated and subsequently dismissed, both the band and Richey's family kept a dignified and reserved distance. Richey's mother, for one, was not about to get her hopes up falsely: 'I don't believe in any of these sightings,' she told *Vox*. 'We are just carrying on with our lives and praying that one day the phone will ring and it will be him. I know he was not happy, but the circumstances surrounding his disappearance were nothing as bad as the tabloids have been trying to make out. We are just waiting to see if there is any sign of him, and so far it has been a long wait.' Likewise, his father said to the *Western Mail*, 'We haven't heard anything to tell us otherwise. We are like any other parents in this situation, trying to cope as best we can from day to day. The difficulty is that there is nothing there to help us deal with it. I have racked my brains trying to think of something that will bring Richard back to us and I can't.'

The band kept out of the public eye for months after Richey's disappearance. When journalists saw them around town no one dared bring the subject up. After a while though, they started to talk again, about their fears and hopes and theories. Nicky said it was his gut-feeling that Richey was still alive, and he even half-joked that he might be in a monastery somewhere. As a result of this, the rumours spread that Richey had been sighted at a monastery and there were reports of Manics fanatics touring such places to find him. In a revealing interview with the *Times*, the band opened up their thoughts. Nicky said, 'Though it's hard to speak on behalf of Richey, I mean, I've known him longer than anyone and I think of him as my best friend, but I still can't say that, deep down, I know him. I thought I did. The week before he disappeared he was in the best spirits I'd seen him in

During the months prior to his disappearance,
Richey constantly had the word 'Love' drawn on his knuckles

since the first breakdown, and I thought he was getting better. Sometimes now I think that he was happy because he knew he was going to do something.' Nicky also conjectured that Richey may have buckled under the pressure of being '4 Real', of living his songs, of being perceived (unfairly) as a fake.

Nicky also revealed how they had gone over Richey's possessions looking for possible clues: 'I went through a phase when I was just looking over and over 'cause there was collages in there and stuff. Me and James saw this picture of a house and it was like, "Is that where he is? It looks like a madhouse in Bavaria." We were going, "Perhaps he's there" . . . the front cover [of the box he left behind] is Bugs Bunny, so I thought perhaps he's in Disneyland. We went to a private investigator straight away, to try and track him down. You can go in his flat and you can look at every book, every thing. At the end of the day, you haven't got a clue.'

They took some solace that his car hadn't been found for twelve days, saying it was unlikely that he would drive around for so long and then suddenly decide to jump off the bridge. The location of the service station also meant he could have hitched a ride to anywhere in the country, or any number of ports within a few hours or days. He also looked to other similar cases: 'Having watched all these "missing" programmes recently and having spoken to Richey's sister about it all, it's not hard to go missing and completely change your life. There's so many people that do. One bloke moved from Middlesbrough to Newcastle, and he wasn't seen for eighteen years. They all thought he was dead – and there's only five miles between the two places.'

The band denied the rumours that they knew where he was, and scorned the dozens of fake sightings. James was also tired of the waiting: 'I just don't know, and I've tried to blank it out, to a certain degree. I won't give anybody the illusion that I'm sitting here waiting, 'cause we've all nearly fed ourselves up over it and I've developed some kind of immunity towards it. I'd rather be shocked than wait on something now. Because I can't wait round any more.'

Perhaps the last word should be kept for Nicky: 'Personally, I still think he's alive, although I've got no physical evidence or reason to think that he is. But I do. I've spoken to people about this who say you're just trying to block it out, that I've just got to accept that he's dead but how can you accept that he's dead, when there's no body, no evidence whatsoever? It's irrational.' He told Jon Savage: 'We slept in the same bed together for about six months. We shared a room in every hotel. I've know him since I was six but if someone wants to disappear, they can. It's not very hard at all. It really isn't . . . Wherever he is, he's made his own choice. Unless he's gone insane, he's made his own choice and he's doing what he wants.' Later in the year,

Nicky was found to be suffering from a stress-related illness, and doctors put much of it down to his inability to come to terms with Richey's disappearance.

In private, the police admitted that the likely cause was suicide, but they also acknowledged the possibility of the perfect disappearance: 'Obviously, if it was a vulnerable juvenile who had gone missing we would continue to search actively for him or her until they had been found. But you have to accept that every adult has the right to go missing.' At the same time, the hardened detectives on the case had seen many similar investigations over the years – at any one time there are on average over 300 missing person reports active. So their unofficial view was suicide, based on several facts: firstly, the discovery and location of his car; secondly, his mental history and the note and presents found at the hotel; thirdly, the difficulty for a man of his celebrity to remain anonymous for so long; fourthly, his apparent lack of money, a passport, his credit cards or his prescribed drugs; and fifthly, the absence of a body being no reason to suspect he had disappeared to start a new life – the Bristol Channel waters in that area are fast and swirling, and the current is known to be easily strong enough to drag bodies down and sweep them out to sea, never to be found.

The second factor was reinforced by his known interest in suicide – he would often quote statistics like the fact that 33 per cent of suicide jump victims have torn shoulder muscles where they jump off then grab for survival. In 1994 he said to *Melody Maker*, '[Suicide] is a subject that interests everyone. But most people . . . I wouldn't say they don't have the guts, but so many people rely on you, that's what stops you from doing it.' Shortly after the 4 Real incident, he had started collecting famous suicide notes, memorising the final words of many public figures. He particularly loved Tony Hancock's parting missive that 'things just went wrong too many times', which he described as 'one of the most beautiful things I have ever read'. Also, 27, his age at the time, was known as the average at which males kill themselves. Det. Sgt Morey, working on the case for the Metropolitan Police, said to *Vox* in 1996, 'Personally, and this is my own view, and not the view of the Metropolitan Police service, I believe that Richard Edwards may no longer be with us.'

MELODY·MAKER

April 8, 1995   75p

KURT COBAIN

RICHEY JAMES

FROM DESPAIR TO WHERE?

THE BOO RADLEYS, SLEEPER, PULP, S*M*A*S*H
and a panel of MM readers on a
year of suicide and breakdowns

ELASTICA ★ RADIOHEAD ★ PEARL JAM ★ SUPERGRASS ★ PAVEMENT ★ MN8

'Doctors keep saying, "You've gotta accept it, he's dead," but I don't think anyone can accept someone's dead without a body . . . I don't see it in terms of blocking anything out or putting a full stop on anything. I see it as an on-going situation that you've got to come to terms with.'

Nicky

In the immediate aftermath of Richey's disappearance, the letters pages of the music weeklies were flooded with mail, several containing horrific pictures of self-mutilation, including many bleeding limbs, mostly from girls, with some even written in blood. Such was the Manics' and Richey's impact that there was even more mail than when Cobain had committed suicide. In the context of the music of the time, these violent fan letters seemed all the more unsettling. Britpop was in full flow, with the cheeky, chirpy pop of Blur's 'Country House', Supergrass's 'Alright', and the general air of positiveness, that Damon Albarn himself had welcomed as light relief from the dour depths of grunge and 1994. The movement's overt disdain at celebrity miserabilists was most extravagantly displayed by Liam and Noel Gallagher of Oasis having a famous, and expensive, good time. In stark contrast to this was Richey's fan mail: 'I could burst and then I cut my skin and then everything's fine.'

When the grisly letters kept flooding in, the staff of the weeklies were so disturbed that they contacted the Samaritans to decide how best to help these people. *Melody Maker* held a debate about the so-called 'culture of despair', where it was discussed whether the Richey situation was an isolated incident, or whether it was indicative of a wider malaise. Even the mainstream media picked up on the issue, with BBC's *Six O' Clock News* featuring an ill-informed piece about the desperate state of the nation's youth and their music. The Samaritans were sufficiently concerned to highlight the problem in a national campaign, using the lyrics to R.E.M.'s 'Everybody

Hurts'. A compilation CD was later released to raise funds for this charity.

The fact that the majority of these letters were from girls highlighted a specific element of the Manics' career – their overt femininity. They had always been more feminine than any of their peers, right from their androgynous early days in make-up and blouses through to the harrowing *Holy Bible,* with its female focus in many songs. The fact that superficially their music had the testosterone look made this feminine side the more compelling. The band members acknowledged this aspect: 'I think they see us raging on their side,' Nicky told the *Times.* 'I hate men. Males don't seem to have any self control any more, something catches their eyes and they don't see why they shouldn't have it.' Richey's problems were largely, although not exclusively, ones endured by young women (particularly anorexia, and self-mutilation), and this added to the band's appeal, as seemingly scores of fans recognised someone they could relate to in the media who was going through the same as they were.

At the same time, the Manics had also always attracted a particularly obsessive type of fan. When they had released their first album, they received over 150 letters a week begging them not to keep to their threat of making it also their last one, with some efforts stretching to over 25 pages. It was not uncommon for female fans to wait for over 24 hours outside a venue where the band were playing. Richey in particular received constant sacks of mail. There were even two fans from Japan who were so keen on the Manics that they booked into the same hotels, flew over for each gig, and wrote to Nicky each day on a postcard telling him their thoughts. Once Richey had admitted his illness and *The Holy Bible* had been released, this 'cult of Richey' blossomed, with the devotion reaching extreme proportions. Richey fuelled the fire with his enigmatic quotes and theories and his looks – for example, in one *Melody Maker* photo shoot he was gaunt but still stunning, and wore a white boiler suit with the handwritten legend: 'A man who will mutilate himself is well damned, isn't he?' In return, he received sacks of letters, including one which said simply, 'Your beauty insults me because I can't touch it.'

Nicky felt that these fans were losing perspective: 'They want to believe that he was perpetually tortured, and any kind of ordinariness they just don't want to see,' he told *Kerrang!.* 'They'll never believe that Richey and me played cricket for hours on end. The last year of being in the band he definitely did go downhill. We got one letter which said "Why didn't you talk to him?" And I spent more time in my life taking to Richey and trying to understand him than I have done with any other person. He made my life a misery sometimes, because I was just worrying about him all the time.'

Nicky also revealed that Richey did not particularly enjoy this fan worship. For a start, he saw his self-abuse as a weakness, not something to be revered or copied. And he openly expressed weariness at the adulation he received: 'About four weeks before Richey went missing,' Nicky told *NME*, 'we were chatting. We had so much poetry off anorexics, and a lot of it was so shit even Richey was getting fed up – not another pile of this again. I said, "Look, I'm gonna have to write a song taking the piss out of their poetry." And he was laughing, he said, "Yeah." Even though he was one – or at least half anorexic, he could still see what I meant. He'd go, "Oh no, not another fucking poem about eating an apple in the morning!" Even though he was suffering, he still had it – the cynicism.'

In the whirlwind of media attention following Richey's disappearance, the band kept a deliberately low profile. Nicky became almost reclusive, entrenched on his settee with his television remote control and plates of chips and crisps. He later laughed at his new couch potato lifestyle with a track called 'Mr Carbohydrate', a nickname the band had given him because that was all he seemed to eat on tour. When he did wander out it wasn't to go to outrageous rock 'n' roll parties, but to play cricket or golf. Even his long-term addiction to fruit machines was over. He developed a preference for Marks & Spencer's food, largely because he was so paranoid about food poisoning, and he enjoyed sipping just one glass of red wine a day, 'for the blood'. He started wearing Pringle golf tops and casual trousers, and became even more of a sports fanatic. He was even addicted to housework in the marital home in Blackwood, only two miles from where his parents lived. He admitted that he dreamed about Richey.

Sean had also retreated, back to his girlfriend with whom he was living in Bristol, where he remained firmly out of the limelight, doing DIY and building a new room in his attic. James stayed in London, and found it difficult to cope at first: 'I was adrift,' he told *Mojo*. 'Suddenly the focus of my life for the last six years was gone. I'd get up, make some tea, walk around, go out, get pissed with my mates and then do it all again.' He also acknowledged he was drinking way too much: 'It was like I'd had an operation to fuse me to the bar. I knocked it on the head when the double chin started getting out of hand. It was slapping round my ankles.' Occasionally he visited the other two at their homes – as well as his mother, who had separated from his father – in Blackwood every three weeks or so.

Gradually, as the months passed by, thoughts of the band's future began to arise. Obviously this had never been considered when Richey first went missing, but as it became apparent that it was unlikely he was either still alive or coming back, the other three members started to debate their options. A meeting was arranged for May 1995 with the three remaining band members, Martin Hall and Richey's parents, where it was agreed that they should carry on. Admirably, there was no pressure from the record company either way. For one thing, Richey's father felt that new material might provoke a response from his son and flush him out. For another, the three band members felt they needed to carry on. Rehearsal space was duly booked at Sound Space Studios in Cardiff for the first week in May.

In fact, it had never been a certainty that the Manics would continue. Indeed, in the dark weeks immediately following Richey's disappearance, there seemed little option but to split up. The press gossiped that James was going to pursue a solo career, but this was never an option, and there was some talk of his joining Therapy? as a temporary guitarist. 'When Richey's car was found on the Severn Bridge we had to think . . . not so much about splitting up, but simply the prospect of everything being so dreadful,' Nicky confided in *Select*. 'We were just frozen in disbelief.' Until his car was found, most people felt that Richey would turn up, but with the discovery the future of the band took on a new perspective. The likelihood now was that Richey would either never return or would only do so after a long time away. James was perhaps the closest to calling it a day: 'I was stunned for six months. I waited for something to happen but nothing did and I definitely thought about giving up,' he told *Sky* magazine. 'I got pissed out of me head for a while . . . there was a spectre hanging over us and there were a lot of scary options to consider. Eventually we began writing some songs just to see if we could carry it off.'

The first song that was completed without Richey was a soaring anthem, and arguably their finest accomplishment so far. All three of them were inspired by it, and it gave them the strength to continue. That song was 'A Design For Life'.

'Eventually we began writing some songs just to see if we could carry it off.'

The band at C&A?

In typically realistic Manics fashion, the first rehearsals since Richey's disappearance were resolutely undramatic. They didn't cry through the set, or break down hopelessly after each song – they simply played some new ideas through and a few old songs, and then went shopping. 'After the initial upset, the studio became our refuge,' James told *Sky*'s reporter. 'Getting into that pattern of recording took our mind off a lot of things.' Before Richey left, they had already drafted the start for seven songs, and he had also completed some lyrics that they wanted to use, although none of these were from the batch he left just before he vanished.

The initial rehearsals strengthened their resolve to carry on, and so they reconvened in summer of 1995 to start tentative recording sessions for the next album. On 26 August, a statement appeared in the music press, with Nicky stating, 'We've sat down and discussed whether to record or not at great length, among ourselves and with Richey's family, and basically decided we would have a go. We have been rehearsing regularly for the last few months and have over twenty new songs which have been written over the last year. The last six months have been very difficult for us, but we feel ready to start recording. We're just going to go into the studio and see how things go. There's no rush.'

The studio they decided on was the Château de la Rouge Motte in Normandy, France. Initially they recorded a few ideas with Stephen Hague at the Real World Studio in London, but felt the results were too pop and too clean. Then they chose to work with Mike Hedges, after hearing his production work on the classic 'Yes' by McAlmont & Butler. He had also worked with Everything But The Girl, early Cure, the Beautiful South and Siouxsie. He owned the studio in France – it was small, with a wooden mixing desk which the Beatles had used in Abbey Road, and on which Pink Floyd had produced *Dark Side Of The Moon*. The first day recording here produced their contribution to the *Help!* album for the War Child charity, a version of Burt Bacharach's 'Raindrops Keep Falling On My Head', which had long been a favourite for James's live acoustic slot. The sessions were focused and highly productive, so that, in complete contrast to their earlier album sessions, they were largely finished within a month. In the second week of October they moved to a studio in Bath and then put the finishing touches to the record at the Abbey Road studios in London, where they added the string orchestration for the album. The only exception to that was the track 'No Surface All Feeling', which was left mostly as the version they had recorded with Richey at Cardiff's Big Noise Studios. Nicky for one loved the French sessions. He told Jon Savage, 'We recorded it in this little recluse in Normandy, which is like being in Wales. It's in this big chateau. It's such a relief when you can't speak the language because no one can speak to you. You just say a few words: Coke or Mars Bar, and that's it.'

Musically there was no problem without Richey. However, many people doubted that the Manics' lyrics would survive his loss. Nicky at first answered these doubters politely, but after a while resented their ignorance. 'The thing that's been glossed over,' he said to *NME*, 'is that people think I don't write lyrics anyway. They think Richey wrote everything.' James agreed: 'People come up to me and say, "What are you gonna do now – how are you gonna write songs?" I just say, "Well, before *The Holy Bible*, Nicky wrote half of the words anyway."' Nicky took up the theme with *Select*, 'If anything Richey going missing has freed us a bit. We don't feel the need to justify ourselves because we've done enough of that . . . it is our most complete record.' Moreover, the much talked-about lyrics Richey left behind were too dark – one line about cutting the feet off a ballerina seemed indicative of their depressing nature, and of the 50 or so songs-worth of lyrics, none were used – 'They were pretty heavy going,' Sean added. 'There wasn't a lot to pick out to be honest. Most of it was very fragmented and rambling.'

With the album completed by Christmas, the Manics' thoughts turned to playing live again. Just before the gigs, a press release was sent out explaining their decision to continue publicly, as well as their views on Richey's disappearance, and stating, 'It is hoped that this will avoid the need for future questioning on the subject.' The gig itself, albeit a support slot, could not have had a much higher profile – second on the bill to the Stone Roses at Wembley Arena in front of 11,000 Roses fans. There were, however, potential problems: the coachloads ploughing down the motorway from Manchester were never going to be charitable. Moreover, there were rumours that the Stone Roses were worried they might be blown offstage by the Manics and as a result only allowed their support act five minutes to soundcheck. But it would take a lot more than that to stop the Manics, and, in contrast, the Stone Roses were a band at death's door. When asked why they had not headlined their comeback gig, Nicky told *NME*, 'To be honest, we didn't want to face our own fans that early. The emotion of that.

We wanted to see if we could still do it.'

First up was ex-Stone Roses dancer Cressa in his dub reggae band Bad Man Wagon, but the crowd were largely uninterested. As the Manics walked on to an ovation, Nicky said modestly, 'What's up? It's only us.' The Manics played no songs from *The Holy Bible* and made no reference to Richey, which grated with some fans. There were also signs that the band had already changed enormously – gone were the combat clothes and make-up, instead replaced by James in a loose suit and Nicky in a Cardiff Devils ice hockey T-shirt. Gone too were the inflammatory between-song bursts they were so renowned for. In came keyboardist John Green to beef up the sound with lush new string arrangements. The idea was to make a healthy break from the difficult past and, with the five new songs they played, they achieved this ('Elvis Impersonator', 'A Design For Life', 'Enola Alone', 'Australia' and 'Everything Must Go'). It was a brave, dignified and inspirational performance. A footnote to the concert was that some fans thought Richey must still be alive, because the other three had said they could never continue playing if he were dead. A few even felt he might turn up at Wembley.

So the Manics' first Christmas without Richey was a strangely positive one. They had recorded the next album, with just a few last touches to be added, they had returned to the live arena with great success, and they carried an optimism that had been missing for months, even years. The feelings about Richey's disappearance were not about to suddenly go away, though – over Christmas, his sister Rachel did a number of televised 'Missing Person' appeals, including LWT's *Missing At Christmas* show on Richey's birthday, 22 December. Another upsetting reminder at the same time was the setting up of a trust fund for Richey, which would hold all his royalties for him in the event of his return. Nicky hated the clinical process involved: 'That was really depressing, doing all that legal shit,' he told *NME*. 'You've gotta wait seven years until he's declared dead. We were signing all these forms. We wanted everything to be proper. So if he ever turns up, it's all there for him. But doing that, it just makes him seem like a number. It was really sad.'

The first release by the Manic Street Preachers since Richey's disappearance was 'A Design For Life', in April 1996. Taken from the forthcoming album, the track was the pivotal point in the band's return, both because it inspired them to carry on and because it became their biggest hit to date. The track itself was about the pride of the working-class struggle and the patronising attitudes of the bourgeoisie. In light of the way Britpop often caricatured the British working-class, this was a refreshingly realistic record. Washed in lush, operatic strings and soaring vocals, it surpassed even 'Motorcycle Emptiness'. James remembered for *NME* the excitement when he first read the words: 'Lyrically, there doesn't appear to be much to that song, but the lines are so concise. As soon as I got those words I thought, "I've got to write the best tune ever." This was one of the first times in a while when I read a lyric it sent a tingle up my spine.' And he came up with a tune to match, very quickly according to what Nicky told Jon Savage: 'He phoned me up that night and played [the tune] down the phone to me, and he had the complete vision of how it was going to sound, an old Motown record, a bit of R.E.M., a bit of Ennio Morricone, which we don't always have. Fortunately, we're better players now and it's a bit easier to nail it.'

A track produced to back 'Design' pointed to a new interest for Nicky. As a lifelong fanatic of the movies, he increasingly felt drawn to writing his own film. He wrote a script about a serial killer with the hard-hitting *Cracker* television police drama in mind, but it got no farther than providing the idea for the B-side of 'Design'. The idea was based on a news story he had read about a man who walked on to a traffic island, died and was not found for six weeks. Nicky also said he might like to write a film about Owain Glyndwr, the Welshman who helped defeat the English in 1400 to 1402 and win his country a brief period of self-rule.

Despite the enthusiasm, James was still scared that no one would like 'Design'. After all, the band came with a lot of baggage. He need not have worried. The single entered the charts at Number 2 and was only kept off the top spot by Mark Morrison's huge-selling 'Return Of The Mack'. When James heard the news, he was delighted – previously, chart positions had not bothered him that much, but this was altogether different: 'When I woke up that Sunday and realised "Design For Life" was Number 2', he told *NME*, 'I felt the most relaxed I've been for a year and three months. Didn't jump up and down or anything, I just completely relaxed, watched sport on telly. It was gorgeous.' Nicky was predictably mowing his lawn when he found out, and celebrated by having tea round his parents' house. Before that however, he rang Richey's parents to tell them the news, and they were typically and admirably delighted.

With Richey gone, James realised he had much more to do than just write songs

The record sold 93,000 copies in its first week and went on to sell more copies than all their preceding singles put together. Although the subsequent *Top Of The Pops* performance was strange without Richey, the band's new-found success reaped many rewards. Locally, they were recognised much more – one of Nicky's neighbours even offered the services of his brother, as he'd heard they were looking for a new keyboard player: 'He plays on the ferries you know.' Nationally, it meant the seemingly impossible burden of the past had not made the band fall at the first hurdle. With such a brilliant taster, the anticipation for the next album was immense.

Before it came out, however, the band played another gig – their first headline show since Richey's disappearance – at Leeds Sound City Festival. It gave more signs that they were moving forward, and BBC Radio One's live broadcast was of sufficient quality for bootlegs to start turning up soon. The gig was notable also for the return of Nicky's mouthy attitude, apparent when he heavily slammed Terrorvision during the show. With interest in the album growing, and the band apparently back on track again, some critics admonished them for continuing, and asked if Richey was to return would they let him re-join. The band's united answer was an unequivocal 'no'. Their remarks seemed cold-hearted at the time and upset many fans, but they had to take this attitude in order to progress: 'We were best mates,' James said to *Mojo*, 'and while I couldn't bring myself to be friends with him anymore there's still a part of me that will always think of him as a best mate.' Sean revealed they never now considered what Richey might want: 'That was never an issue for me, because it's to do with the three of us, rather than the four of us now. Richey isn't in the band any more.' Nicky said to *NME*, 'The barriers that he's put there are so great now. They say that's the worst thing about trying to get back in touch with people. The longer it goes on, you're just building up.'

This break with the past upset many fans, and they began to receive hate mail. 'I was out having a drink in London,' James recalled to *NME*, 'and someone says to me, "How can you be out having a drink?" I say, "What the fuck are you on about?" He says, "If I was you I'd be in my room chopping myself up by proxy for Richey."' James disdainfully calls such people 'full-on Richey-philes'. The band were sick of people telling them how they should have reacted, that they should have taken action sooner, that they let Richey down. It was all misinformed nonsense, of course. James went on to reveal that one of the worst thoughts was 'that perhaps he just didn't like us any more . . . Perhaps one morning he just woke up and said we're a bunch of dickheads, fuck off. That would be really upsetting wouldn't it?' Despite this, he was still adamant about his withdrawal from their friendship: 'I couldn't be friends with him again. Just for the sake of us three. If it went off again, just imagine how much it could fuck you up. It's my biggest nightmare – what would I do if Richey turned up and wanted to know me again? It's really scary.'

With the Manics now definitely reborn, comparisons were inevitably made with the Joy Division/New Order story. Joy Division's enigmatic lead singer Ian Curtis had hung himself on 18 May 1980, on the eve of a lengthy American tour that was promising to be the band's biggest success ever. The band were one of the few acts who had the same degree of musical gravitas as the Manics. After the death there were a handful of copycat suicides, and people talked about the 'cult of the young boy outsider' which Curtis was seen as representing. Then the remaining band members slowly re-shaped their music with a less introspective slant. And so, when the artwork for the next album was being designed, the Manics had this comparison very much in mind. Nicky acknowledged the influence of the abstract and simplistic cover design of 'Ceremony', the first single the older band had put out after Curtis's death, by then also having changed their name to New Order. 'We decided to use Mark Farrow, who'd done work for M People and the Pet Shop Boys. We tried to make it . . . not New Orderish as such, but we definitely wanted to go for that non-image . . . yeah – that was a conscious decision [to replicate "Ceremony"].' James also said to *Select* magazine, 'With this album we just craved anonymity and the one-dimensional presentation gave us that. We just want to diffuse the chance of anybody reading anything symbolic into the artwork or the way we looked, put the wannabe rock mythologists off the trail.'

One way the band did not follow Joy Division, obviously, was to change their name: 'We did consider changing the name and starting over again,' Nicky told Jon Savage, 'and we probably would have done if we knew he was dead. It would be more like a Joy Division/New Order thing then. It was an imponderable position really to consider changing our name.'

'In the band at the moment it's a matter of giving ourselves some human grace, the chance to show emotion other than disdain or hate and not be ashamed of it. Breathe a bit more. I think we've survived under a heavy load of self-censorship.'

James

'Between the three of us we can still be very sarcastic and piss-taking about the whole thing and ourselves, and that helps. It's the New Order school of thought – "Ian Curtis was a twat 'cause he ruined our American tour . . ."'

Nicky

When the Manic Street Preachers' fourth album, *Everything Must Go*, was released in June 1996, another difference between their story and that of Joy Division/New Order became starkly apparent – this record was nowhere near as bleak and desperate as 'Ceremony'. Many people had expected the new record to be in memory of Richey, but the album was in fact dedicated to the Tower Colliery. The miners had bought this pit from the National Coal Board in the face of closure and in the first year alone turned the business's losses into a profit of £3 million, prompting rumours that a Hollywood film was to be made of their story.

Change ran throughout this record. For a start, emotionally it was a massive move away from the nadir of *The Holy Bible*. Musically, too, it was far removed from much of their previous material. Although the album was washed with lush strings similar to those on *Gold Against The Soul*, its more sophisticated and powerful polish meant it was never as bloated. Lyrically, the album was much less obscure than the previous ones, and, most strikingly, Nicky's contributions in particular were far more uplifting and positive than much of their previous work. When Richey had been writing the devastating personal insights of *The Holy Bible*, Nicky was getting married, buying a house and setting up a marital home, so he felt little affinity with the themes of death and morbidity that Richey had focused on. As a consequence, Nicky had built up quite a backlog of material that now found an outlet on *Everything Must Go.*

The album opened unfortunately with what was probably its worst track, the pathos-ridden 'Elvis Impersonator: Blackpool Pier'. A subtle acoustic intro slams into a barrage of rock and raucous feedback, portraying the discrepancy between a rosy romantic ideal of America and the tatty reality, shown here as a pathetic Elvis impersonator in a run-down English seaside town. A rough version of this track had been completed when Richey was still around, one of four such tracks on the record. Then came the classic 'A Design For Life', which raised the standards as high as possible. Taking its title from a Volkswagen advert, the second track on the album was the first that had no input from Richey.

Next was another Richey track – the lyrically fascinating 'Kevin Carter'. Its subject was a Pulitzer-Prize-winning photo-journalist whose critically acclaimed pictures vividly captured the horrors of the modern world, in particular the Rwandan Civil War atrocities. His most famous work was a stunning shot of a dying young girl, curled up, while a huge vulture waits hungrily nearby. Carter returned from Rwanda with his nerves shattered, and could not reconcile the fame and fortune that his work brought him with the problems it documented. After being accused of exploiting tragedy, he took to wildlife photography but could not satisfy his conscience. Eventually he blew his head off with a shotgun. Richey was fascinated with this story, even more so on the last tour when he was wearing the Dennis Hopper-style camera round is neck. The track itself has a sparkling melody, lifted by Sean's trumpet lines and a strangely funky musical setting.

'Enola/Alone' was prompted by another sad tale. Nicky was looking at his wedding photos one day, when he saw a picture of himself with Richey and Philip Hall, neither of whom were with him any more. The track he wrote as a result drips with melancholic beauty, and is one of the album's highlights. For Nicky the words represented an unusually personal exposé; they also speak of the importance of carrying on in the face of such loss, seen by some diehard Manics fans as a betrayal of Richey. Next up was the title track, which was perhaps the most optimistic song the Manics had ever recorded. Once again written by Nicky, the lyrics are explicitly about the band, highlighting the terrible disaster of losing Richey and the band's dilemmas and choices which resulted from that loss. Then came Richey's best track on the album, 'Small Black Flowers That Grow In The Sky'. He wrote it after seeing a BBC documentary about zoo animals, which had moved him to phone Nicky to talk about it immediately afterwards. The captive animals' insanity struck a chord with Richey and the song is indirectly revealing about his own frame of mind. Although Nicky does not believe that Richey was drawing any direct analogies between himself and the animals, it is possible that he saw himself as being like a caged animal with no privacy from a gawping public. It is perhaps one of the few tracks here that could have fitted on to *The Holy Bible*.

'The Girl Who Wanted To Be God' was the album's most infectious song, a soaring anthem lifting the tone again after the gloom of the previous track. Although he wrote it with Richey, Nicky claims to have no idea of what the song is about, and indeed the track offers few clues – one suggestion in the media was that it concerned American poet Sylvia Plath, the wife of fellow poet Ted Hughes, who killed herself in 1963 and one of whose biographies had the same title. The next track, 'Removables', was the oldest one on the album, having been written three years before recording. The band had tried to complete the song several times previously, all unsuccessfully. Then while they were recording in Britannia Studios (where Ian Curtis had made his bleakest records), they heard the news that Kurt Cobain had committed suicide. The news provided the idea for an 'unplugged'-style backing and Nirvana feel to the track, as its themes of personal distaste and misery are similar to much of Cobain's work. The track was completed in one take.

'Australia' was about the need sometimes to get away from everything, maybe in this case from Richey's celebrity, maybe from the uncertainty over his whereabouts. Ironically, after Nicky wrote the track he decided a break would indeed be good for him but he only made it as far as Cornwall, as his chronic fear of flying made Down Under highly unlikely. The track is the record's brightest pop song, despite its lyrical theme. Then 'Interiors' darkens the mood again, talking about Alzheimer's Disease and the effect it had on the brilliant Dutch-born Abstract Expressionist painter Willem de Kooning. Again inspired by a documentary, Nicky was fascinated by de Kooning's determination to carry on painting despite the disease, and the medical astonishment when his condition started to improve as a result. A delicate song, the bass line again drew up comparisons with New Order.

The next song was the first-ever Manics love song, 'Further Away', and another sign that the rigid self-imposed restrictions were relaxing all the time. James revelled in this feeling, as he told *Select* magazine: 'This time we realised that we couldn't always be so intense about the artwork and make every album like an encyclopaedia. Once upon a time we couldn't have done a song like "Further Away", which is almost a love song. It is healthy to be able to do whatever we like without always having to think, "Wait a minute, we're the Manic Street Preachers."'

The album closed with 'No Surface All Feeling', another Nicky Wire lyric, about the changing relationships within the band, and how they must look to the future to progress. Richey had heard this track and indeed played on a full demo version at the House in the Woods in Surrey. As a tribute to their missing friend, the band used that version here, almost in its entirety, save for a slightly changed ending. It is an eerie and unsettling way to end what is otherwise an uplifting and very positive album. 'It's about for the first time in my life I don't want to be with you two,' Nicky explained to *Q* magazine. 'Not "I hate you", but it's not like it used to be. I'd say everything's changed because of Richey going. Apart from onstage and in the studio, although we're still the best of friends, we've got different lives.'

Everything Must Go is a subtle, luxurious and accomplished record, perhaps three qualities that many Manics fans thought they would never get from them. Sean revealed their pride in the album to *Mojo*: 'Our first three albums were a build up to this one. They're all flawed, mind, occasionally naive records but they were important . . . it has changed definitely. Without Richey we've become more optimistic on record, more positive.' For a record with such an impossible burden of expectation, and with so many pitfalls to avoid, the end result was incredible. Not only had the Manics recorded easily their best work to date, they had also released probably the finest album of the year. It was a remarkable achievement.

Before their headline tour for the album, the Manics first did a series of gigs with Oasis, who were by now the undisputed kings of British rock, following the success of *What's The Story (Morning Glory)?*, and were playing a number of large-scale concerts through the summer. Between then and Christmas, the Manics seemed to become Oasis's support band by appointment, warming up the crowd at colossal shows at Knebworth, Maine Road and Loch Lomond, as well as relatively smaller ones at Cardiff International Arena and the Point in Dublin.

Nicky at the Brit Awards, early 1996

Before the Maine Road gig a secret warm-up show was arranged for the Manics, at Manchester's Hacienda club. It was only announced on the same morning and as a result only real fanatics managed to get to it, but the fans loved it and the press raved about the performance. The band, however, hated it. The realisation that Richey would never join them onstage again hit home with a new force. At one point Nicky stumbled into James and laughed, then looked over to where Richey would have been standing and his face dropped like a stone. Afterwards, he was in tears, inconsolable.

James said simply of the show, 'It was an awful thing,' and later in the tour he said, 'Occasionally when you're playing live, you catch yourself thinking, "We shouldn't be doing this," but you quickly stop yourself.'

The Oasis gigs were a strange experience for the Welsh band. On the one hand they were a great opportunity to play before a huge section of the population, but on the other the towering dominance of Oasis overshadowed everything and made them feel very much second best. Rumours spread that the Manics hated these dates, and indeed many of their performances seemed lacklustre and non-communicative, while the Oasis fans appeared oblivious to the angst, irony and emotion in their songs and only perked up when the Manics played 'Raindrops Keep Falling On My Head'. Things were not helped by the Oasis fans constantly shouting, 'How's Richey?' and there was even a football-style chant of 'Where the fuck is Richey?'

James did, indeed, hate the Knebworth show, saying, 'It made us think the whole of southern England was just a fucking shithole. There was no magic to it,' but contrary to the gossip the band generally enjoyed the dates. They reflected honestly and modestly on these shows to *Q* magazine. 'Oasis have made me a fan again,' said Nicky. 'They've completely revitalised British music. But yeah, we do like to think it could have been us. Perhaps we didn't have the guile.' He also said to *Select*, 'Musically I do genuinely love Oasis. They're so natural, I think its above criticism. But I now know that we're too difficult for that. They have something that hits you like an elemental force. In many ways Oasis are the band that we wanted to be, but never could be.' James was also very complimentary about the Mancunians: 'It made me realise that we were becoming a big band, but we were nowhere near becoming a phenomenon and we never would.' He continued: 'Maine Road showed us our allotted position. I knew what we would never be after that gig. People have just taken Oasis to their heart, independent of anything like a marketing push. Anything at all. It just seemed uncontrollable, totally inspiring.'

With the Oasis dates over, the headline tour for *Everything Must Go* was a comprehensive sell-out of all 40,000 tickets available. One of those tickets was sold to Arthur Scargill, who came to the show in Liverpool and gratefully received a donation from the band for his new Socialist Labour Party. The band's initial unease with playing live again gradually dissipated, as it became apparent that the new set was stronger than anything that had gone before it. Each gig started with an instrumental of 'A Design For Life' before a huge projection screen flashing images, including ones of Richey, as well as pictures connected with the album. They played some of the bleak *Holy Bible* tracks as well, another sign that they were coming to terms with their new situation. Noticeably, Nicky and James never wandered over to stage left where Richey used to stand. As for a new rhythm guitarist, Nicky said with a wry smile, 'They wouldn't exactly be queuing up for that one, would they? "Guitar player required. Must mutilate himself onstage and carry impossible demands on shoulders forever . . ."'

After the shows the band flew to America for what should have been their big push over there. Again they were supporting Oasis for a series of arena dates before embarking on their own small club tour. This time, however, the controversy came from the headliners, not the Manics. Shortly after the tour began, Noel Gallagher announced he was to quit playing live with the band, and after rows with his brother gleefully reported by the tabloid media, he returned home on Concorde, leaving both Oasis's future in doubt and the Manics' tour in tatters. With typical resolve, though, the Manics soldiered on, playing over twenty more gigs throughout the autumn, albeit to moderate response.

Ever since they had played in the States in 1991 with T-shirts declaring 'All rock 'n' roll is homosexual' the feeling was that America just didn't understand the Manics. Undoubtedly comments about John Lennon's death and complaints about the lack of a release for their third album or any lengthy tours did nothing to endear them to the music-buying public. Despite their success in Europe, the Manics struggled to sell out 500-seater clubs on this tour. They were so little known that they could always walk straight through the front door just before a gig without being recognised. A likely reason for their failure to impress the States is that they were caught between the pop and rock markets, neither alternative enough nor mainstream enough – a theory reinforced by the fact that *Generation Terrorists* sold four times more than *Everything Must Go* in the US, and even that only represented a miserly 12,000 copies.

Their gruelling schedule continued on their return home in October between when and Christmas they played another 30 dates, including some on the Continent. The high point was a 6000-capacity headline gig, their biggest ever, at Cardiff's International Arena. The only hitch on the tour was at the Trossingen Strange Noise Festival when they refused to play in the pouring rain for fear of electrocution. For these UK dates the Manics chose to assist younger Welsh bands by being supported by some of the finest of them: Super Furry Animals, Catatonia and Stereophonics. 'It's just nice,' Nicky told *Melody Maker*, ''cause when we started there was a lot of ridicule just for being Welsh. Every headline either mentioned a daffodil or a Dai or

a boyo. Everything was derogatory. There's always been a lot of creativity in Wales, but people thought that Welsh music was Bonnie Tyler or Tom Jones or Mani. It's good that that's changed.'

The first of two London Christmas shows saw Kylie Minogue finally co-operating with the Manics when she climbed onstage at the Shepherds Bush Empire to sing 'Little Baby Nothing' (was it a coincidence that the Manics' records now outsold hers by ten to one?). The last gig of what had been easily their most successful year to date came at the Kentish Town Forum, where Liam Gallagher joined them onstage for a few songs. Swigging from a beer bottle, he engaged in a mock fight and snogging session with Nicky and then smashed the bottle on the floor. As with many of the dates on this tour, James introduced the band in a comic, over-the-top cabaret style. When the time came for the band to play 'Yes', he dedicated it to 'our Richey'.

Although the gigs were warmly received, the band still felt they had some progress to make. Nicky told *Q* magazine, 'Live we know we haven't reached the heights of excitement we had with Richey. The sound and the playing are good but in terms of us looking at one another and knowing we could take on the world, change people's lives . . . we haven't regained that and without Richey, without the aura, perhaps we never will.'

Consistent with their policy of releasing quick-fire singles, this lengthy spread of dates supported not just the album but three single releases. First up was 'Everything Must Go', which reinforced the band's newfound mainstream appeal by reaching Number 5. The video for the single, which delayed the record's release a few weeks, contained a screen backdrop displaying yet more images, again including ones of Richey. Of this James said to *Mojo*, 'People said the album title *Everything Must Go* was about catharsis and letting go of the past. For us that video is a way of showing that we're not proposing to forget. There are people who will knock us for using it, but that history is ours.' Then in September, while they were struggling through the America/Oasis crisis, they put out 'Kevin Carter', which was another success at Number 9. The year was rounded off by the release in December of the rather more forced 'Australia', which despite its rather corny appeal was yet another Top Ten hit. Only Celine Dion and Boyzone also enjoyed four Top Ten hits that year. There were yet more new songs on the various formats. Most notable was 'Sepia', a track clearly about missing Richey. Nicky said of it: 'We kind of feel that gap. This is not like a dreadfully unhappy song – it just says "Miss you" in a friendly sort of way. There's nothing complicated about it. It's not melodramatic, not trading on any situation. It's a natural type of reaction, a delayed reaction. It's a bit of yearn.'

In October, James co-hosted BBC Radio One's *Evening Session* with their old adversary Steve Lamacq, and on air he talked of Super Furry

Animals as 'the greatest rock 'n' roll Welsh band since Badfinger'. This programme happened a week after the airing of a Channel Four documentary, *The Vanishing Of Richey Manic*, a half-hour piece shown as part of a *Fame Factor* season. Other shows in the series looked at star stalkers, paparazzi, tribute bands and Brian Connolly of the Sweet, who had fourteen cardiac arrests in one night (and who was to die of ill health in 1997). No Manic Street Preachers music was used for the show and the band did not participate.

Despite the fact the Manics had enjoyed a monumental year, and had performed something of a miraculous recovery from a position few bands could have survived, they still had their detractors. Where once they were criticised for being too glam, too mouthy and too politicised, now they were belittled for being too quiet, too mundane and too apolitical. The snide nicknames of 'The Band At C&A' and 'Littlewoods Street Preachers' were thrown at them regularly. Many of the cult-of-Richey fans now disowned them. Onlookers laughed at the fact that Nicky phoned his mum everyday on tour, and the fact that their gigs were now full of 30-somethings when they had originally denounced anyone over 25 as irrelevant. Instead of writing about revolution, they were talking about people like the Welsh cricketer Matthew Maynard, and even considered a tune about the golfer Ian Woosnam. James was discussing being trained at athletics, and Sean, who owned two houses, talked enthusiastically about his designer clothes from Paul Smith and Katherine Hamnett, which he could buy with his Harvey Nichols chargecard. Others claimed that the culture of despair had given way to the culture of sympathy and that *Everything Must Go* was only so warmly received because of this charitable feeling towards the three remaining members. Where once they wanted to work with Pubic Enemy, now they actually worked with Kylie and the Lightning Seeds. In short, they said the Manics had sold out and softened up. Such accusations, of course, were utter rubbish, and the Manics treated them as such.

1997 continued as successfully as 1996 had left off. The band won two Brit Awards for Best Album and Best Single ('A Design For Life'), and were nominated for two more. Although they had once announced that if they ever won such an award they would 'Get our dicks out and piss on it,' they were delighted. At the awards ceremony, Nicky draped himself in a Welsh flag (the same one he covers his amp with nowadays), and dedicated their win not to Richey but 'to every comprehensive school in Britain which the government is trying to eradicate. They've produced everything – the best bands, the best art, the best everything, and the best boxers too!' These prestigious awards followed a spate of other accolades given to *Everything Must Go*, including a Mercury Award nomination, and scores of 'Best Album' awards by magazines like *Q*, *Vox* and *Select*. When Shaun Ryder of Black Grape presented them with their *Q* Award he said, 'It's always good when you get one of these and give it to somebody that really deserves it.' Basking in the glory, Nicky told *Melody Maker*, 'It's ironic how it's finally okay to like us! We always evenly divided the critics in the past . . . maybe we're just acceptable because we've been hanging around for five or six years now. I dunno, perhaps it's because we've actually made the best record.' Perhaps most impressive of all was the fact that James walked into his mother's betting shop one day and overheard some labourers whistling 'A Design For Life'.

After these awards, the band played yet more UK dates, including a benefit concert at Anfield to support the families of the Hillsborough football tragedy, and a massive Nynex gig at the end of May, supported by Mansun, Audioweb and Embrace. James and Nicky worked on a new 808 State single called 'Lopez' and had also started work with Kylie Minogue in the studio, recording material for a proposed 'Greatest Hits' package due out in late 1997. James also appeared at a concert in aid of the National Missing Persons Helpline at Brixton Academy in May, alongside the Charlatans and Monaco, Peter Hook's new band. James expressed the wish to carry on producing after his first attempts with Northern Uproar on their debut single 'Rollercoaster', and Nicky collaborated with Ian Broudie's Lightning Seeds on the track 'Waiting For Today To Happen'. The band's esteemed songwriting was further acknowledged when they won an Ivor Novello Award in the early summer for Best Contemporary Song for 'A Design For Life'. A batch of summer festivals, including a headline slot at Reading, was then to be followed by a break until the New Year. Although the band signed a £1 million deal with ATV music for their publishing rights, one of the biggest deals of the year, no newly recorded material was planned for 1997, and with Nicky telling all who would listen that he was fed up with touring, extensive live shows also came to look unlikely for the immediate future.

CHAPTER 13

'We didn't achieve much of our original manifesto,
but one thing we always said we wanted to be was the
most important rock band of the decade – and I think
that's the one thing we probably have achieved.'

Nicky

In the wake of *Everything Must Go*'s multi-platinum success, a renewed interest in the band's back catalogue led to post-'A Design For Life' sales of 110,000 for *Generation Terrorists*, 75,000 for *Gold Against The Soul* and 62,000 for *The Holy Bible*. Nicky, for one, took great satisfaction in this fresh appreciation of their history. 'People have been genuinely enthused by it all,' he said. 'Especially *The Holy Bible*. 'Cause it never sold any, really, except for a thousand weirdos buying it every year, like a Joy Division record.'

Everything Must Go eventually shifted 1,125,000 units – 800,000 of those in the UK alone – and bestowed lifelong financial security upon Nicky, James and Sean.

One of the Manic Street Preachers' last shows that year was a Saturday main-stage headlining slot at Reading Festival, where Nicky performed in a dress for the first time since 1993 (a see-through number that would feature on the covers of both *NME* and *Melody Maker* the following week). While *Generation Terrorists*-era footage of a lipstick-smeared, coal-eyed Richey flickered across the huge stage screens, the eighteen-song set climaxed with the soaring double-whammy of 'A Design For Life' and 'You Love Us' – the latter song now evolved into a triumphant and entirely un-ironic call-to-arms.

As the promotional duties and live dates in support of *Everything Must Go* finally wound down, so did the band. Nicky retreated into a reinforced domestic bubble of family, sport, and a self-confessed obsessive-compulsive approach to cleaning. 'I love Dysons,' he opined, in reference to the three vacuum cleaners he owned (one for upstairs, one for downstairs, and one spare). 'They are a work of art.' (He had infamously collected the group's

1997 Brit Awards wearing a T-shirt made by a Swedish fan that bore the spray-painted slogan 'I [Heart] Hoovering' rather than the once-traditional 'Spectators Of Suicide' or 'Culture Slut'.)

James bought a flat in London and pursued the kind of boozy bachelor lifestyle afforded a man of his inclinations and recent success. He later described the low-key indulgences the sales of *Everything Must Go* allowed him: 'I don't drink Bells. I drink Jameson. When I buy a record, I'll buy the CD and the vinyl if I can. When I buy a book I'll buy the hardback instead of the paperback.'

Sean, living with his long-term girlfriend on the outskirts of Bristol, indulged his love of redecoration, gadgets and new technology. 'I want everything to look like it's just come out of the wrapper. I love the smell of, say, a Walkman when you first unwrap it. If it gets a scratch on it, that's it. That's the way I am. And I've always got to get hold of the next best thing. I don't care about money.'

It had been over a year and a half since 'A Design For Life' marked the beginning of a victorious and unprecedented new Manics chapter. The band's largest audience yet awaited their next move.

Production on the Manic Street Preachers' fifth album commenced in August 1997, when the band convened at London's Whitfield Street Studios to begin demoing tracks, none of which were destined to make the final cut. (One of these, a duet with Sophie Ellis-Bextor entitled 'Black Holes For The Young', would appear as a B-side on 'The Everlasting' single.) Production duties were shared by Mike Hedges (*Everything Must Go*) and Dave Eringa (*Gold Against The Soul*). In early September the band flew from Big Noise Studios in Cardiff (where Sean laid down several drum tracks) to Château de la Rouge Motte. Nicky spent his downtime in France following the Glamorgan cricket team's county championship success on satellite TV, and congratulated the victorious players by sending them a hamper of champagne. Between December and January album tracks and B-sides were recorded before a return to Rockfield Studios in Wales, then London for final mixing. The LP was deemed complete in June, ten months and seven studios after work had begun on the initial demos.

The resulting thirteen-song collection would be the first LP to feature no lyrical input from Richey. The task of writing the words that formed the backbone of James and Sean's compositions was shouldered by Nicky alone. Success – both its privileges and trappings – had initially left him unsure of how to approach his solo lyric-writing. In 1996 he told Manics biographer Simon Price: 'I'm finding it really, really hard to write lyrics . . . I've got writer's block. In terms of content, I worry about us because I've never been in a position where things have gone relatively well, I've been successful financially, so I'm kind of . . . it's hard to know what to write about.'

Though he undoubtedly felt the burden of living up to Richey's lyrical legacy, he ultimately approached the writing process with characteristic pragmatism. 'There's just me now,' he told *NME*. 'To write twenty lyrics now, on my own, it's like writing a novel . . . The language is simpler, but the content is probably more complex. Each song has two or three themes.'

These themes included the conflicts inherent within Welsh identity ('Ready For Drowning'), Nicky's own often fierce dislike of touring ('You Stole The Sun From My Heart'), the Hillsborough disaster ('South Yorkshire Mass Murderer'), the normality of depression within modern culture ('Black Dog On My Shoulder'), and a male longing for the perceived freedom of womanhood ('Born A Girl'). The elegiac slow-burner and first single 'If You Tolerate This Your Children Will Be Next' was inspired in part by George Orwell's *Homage To Catalonia*, an account of the writer's experiences during the Spanish Civil War, and the Clash song 'Spanish Bombs', which also alluded to that conflict. Nicky described 'Tolerate' as 'a grower, the most subtle thing we've ever done'.

Although the achievements of *Everything Must Go* had been revelatory, a rebirth on a scale that scarcely could've been imagined, the band remained intensely aware of the demands that went hand-in-hand with their new situation; not only in terms of their accelerated sales and increased profile, but also the fact that – more than three years after Richey's disappearance, with a new album and huge tour behind them – they were still adjusting to the realities of life as a three-piece. 'The biggest pressure was knowing it was now totally just the three of us,' Nicky confessed, 'that any goodwill we might have had because of the situation we were in – which we didn't expect but I'm sure there was – would be gone.'

James professed to have found a new degree of personal contentment in singing Nicky's lyrics, one he was swift to admit would have been unthinkable had Richey remained in the band. During a November 1998 interview with *Esquire*, he elaborated: 'Singing Nick's lyrics is a purifying experience for me and they lend me a certain humility and humanity. Richey's lyrics were a challenge and they were always confrontational to my nature . . . maybe [had he stayed] I'd have plunged into Richey's lyrics again, allowed him to go further and further, and I think that might've ripped the band apart. I don't think it was a staple diet we could exist on.'

This Is My Truth Tell Me Yours took its title from a speech made by Welsh British Labour Party politician Aneurin Bevan, which Nicky had heard a recording of whilst attending a rain-soaked celebration of the National Health Service's fiftieth anniversary on Treclegar Mountain during early 1998. The album, he believed, achieved previously beyond-reach levels of 'beauty and purity', while James felt that every element of the LP was 'completely realised'.

'We wanted to make it less uplifting and epic,' Nicky revealed prior to its release. 'We're very happy with it. If it sells 10,000 copies we'll probably think it's shit; if no one likes it or buys it, then you've got to reassess your position. But we're egomaniac enough to think that everything we do is perfect.'

This Is My Truth . . . was a restrained, multi-instrumental affair that largely lacked the melodic bombast of the album that had launched them into the mainstream. The Manics knew as well as anyone that their increasingly pronounced soft-rock tendencies would further alienate some fans, but also knew that their past could not be reproduced.

'We're 29 now,' Nicky offered. 'It sucks that real urgency out of you.' When pressed regarding the visual and aural chasm that existed between the Manics as they now were and the Manics as they had once been, he simply said: 'It's alright for a fan to want to freeze us there, still going about in combats playing "Die In The Summertime", but if we were frozen there we'd probably all be dead.'

Certainly the new album, awash as it was with omnichords, tampuras, wurlitzers, sitars, mellotrons and accordions, shared little common ground with the *The Holy Bible*'s bilious punk-metal savagery. Nicky claimed that age had tamed their more nihilistic urges, arguing that Richey was a good example of why anger provided inadequate sustenance in the long-term.

Opening track 'The Everlasting' was a sombrely paced reflection upon the band's career whose title Nicky had appropriated from his brother after trying and failing to think of one similar to Joy Division's 'The Eternal' and Blur's 'The Universal'. The New Order-esque beat and playful melody of 'You Stole The Sun From My Heart' belied that song's melancholic lyric, which explored the notion of being forced to do something that repels you. Sitar-driven mini-epic 'Tsunami' was inspired by the case of June and Jennifer Gibbons, the so-called 'Silent Twins' who, having ceased to communicate with anyone but each other at a young age, unsuccessfully pursued literary careers and became involved in petty crime before being committed to a psychiatric unit at Broadmoor Hospital. Opening with a baroque organ swirl, 'Ready For Drowning' ('the most complete song I've ever written', Nicky stated at the time) lyrically sought to do for the Welsh what 'A Design For Life' had done for the working classes. Penultimate track 'Nobody Loved You' obliquely mourned the loss of Richey within a harmonic squall of guitars, and acted as an obvious companion piece to *Everything Must Go*'s 'No Surface All Feeling'.

'Basically we're an experiment gone wrong,' Sean dryly informed *The Face* in a knowing response to the now-common accusation that the band had become everything they once despised. 'We were going to do one album and split up, and as time's gone on we've become this five-album thirty-something everything-that-we-didn't-want-to-be.'

Released on 24 August 1998, the melodious, string-laden sigh of 'If You Tolerate This Your Children Will Be Next' was an instant success, providing the band with first-week sales of 176,000 and their first Number 1 single, and finally delivering something akin to the prestige and commercial impact they'd hungered for since their early declarations that *Generation Terrorists* would sell twenty million copies. Nicky, who upon learning of their chart position had knocked back four glasses of champagne, wanted to phone people with the news, 'but then I realised I didn't have any friends'.

Though Wire revelled in the fact that his band had topped the charts with a song about the Spanish Civil War, the achievement did not come without particular regrets. 'It would've been better if "Faster" had been Number 1,' he said, 'at our mental peak, *Top Of The Pops*, fire and balaclavas . . . pretty implausible, really.' Warming to this nostalgia for missed opportunities, he told *Select*: 'I feel like we're still on the first stage, but that the success was a bit delayed. If "Motorcycle Emptiness" had been around at the height of Britpop, we would have had a Number 1 record, but unfortunately it came out during the grunge era – a terrible time for music.'

James, who had confessed to touching wood 30 times a day before the release of 'A Design For Life', said, 'The first time I've actually felt any astonishment was with this single. But I didn't know how to react, so I just didn't react . . . I was just relieved – not to be a bridesmaid anymore, a perennial bridesmaid. It's nice to be taken off the shelf. But even now, I'm not quite sure. It's only one single: it could all go fucking wrong.' In economic terms, at least, his fears proved unfounded. The album followed the single's example, shifting 140,000 units in its first week and entering the charts at Number 1, a position it would maintain for the next three weeks in the face of less than ecstatic reviews.

On 29 August they performed their third live show since recording had been completed; a high-profile gig at Dublin's Slane Castle in front of around 80,000 people, supporting headliners the Verve and playing on the same bill as James, the Seahorses and Robbie Williams. The sprawling audience was decorated with a smattering of Welsh flags, and one fan took it upon themselves to hurl a copy of Jean-Paul Sartre's *Nausea* onto the stage. For the majority of the Manics' set, however, the crowd's reaction left a lot to be desired. It was not until the penultimate 'A Design For Life' that they showed signs of life, prompting James to chide, 'Oh, so at last it's one you know?' Backstage before the show, Nicky met Mo Mowlam, then Secretary of State for Northern Ireland, who was apparently surprised by the bassist's ability and willingness to discuss politics with her.

A subsequent European and UK arena tour fuelled the band's prominent media profile and, somewhat inevitably, ensured a further spate of Richey 'sightings'. During November 1998, on Fuerteventura in the Canary Islands, Tracey Jones, a British woman working in a Corralejo pub called the Underground Bar, reported that a patron had drawn attention to a thin man who was drinking in the tavern by shouting 'You're Richey from the Manic Street Preachers!'

'The man,' Jones said, 'just started to run towards the door and within seconds he was gone.'

The same month, 'The Everlasting' was released as a single (it reached Number 11 in the UK charts, breaking the Manics' unbroken run of Top Ten entries), and *Esquire* published a substantial article on the band in which an uncharacteristically drunken and emotional Nicky elaborated upon his continued grief over Richey's disappearance – his candidness apparently sparked by a recent visit to the house the pair had shared whilst attending Swansea University more than ten years previously. 'We wrote "Motorcycle Emptiness" in that house . . . There was a review by some knob who said the band had benefited from Richey's disappearance, but they don't realise how my personal life has been completely and utterly fucked. They don't realise that every time someone rings and hangs up without speaking, I press 1471 hoping it's Richey.'

It became apparent that the unremittingly bleak core of the situation could not be escaped. 'He fucking drove off in a Cavalier to the Aust motorway services,' a tearful Wire told the interviewer. 'You're not fucking pissing around when you do that. You're fucked out of your fucking mind.'

He also admitted that he found the band's all-conquering mainstream success anticlimactic; he'd spent his entire adult life craving it, but even now, with so many of those lofty goals achieved, reality remained a poor substitute for fantasy. 'Today is the first time I've ever been bored. I must admit that I never thought success would avalanche into some kind of mediocrity . . . I've wished for this kind of success since the age of sixteen, since I gave up football. It's the one thing that kept me going. Trying to be better than everyone else. And now it's happened, it's a bit of a let-down. People think our lives should be perfect. I wish mine was.'

At the 1998 *Q* Awards the Manics won 'Best Act In The World Today' and, despite their slight embarrassment at coming face-to-face with the former focus of one of Nicky's most notorious public displays of vitriol, posed for photographs with R.E.M.'s Michael Stipe. Their year's touring concluded with two headlining shows at Wembley Arena, followed by a three-night homecoming residency at Cardiff's International Arena. During the final show on 22 December, an acoustic 'Black Dog On My Shoulder' segued into a cover of Wham!'s 'Last Christmas'. The band also launched into 'Revol', getting as far as the first two lines before abandoning the song, because 'it's Richey's birthday'.

CHAPTER 14

'*So now it's the old fucking cliché, it's only indifference that's hard to take.*'

James

'*I think we've probably changed people's lives. For better or worse . . . I don't know if we've actually changed anything, but I think we've changed the perception of what a band can do . . . But unfortunately twenty to 50 per cent of that historical importance is probably because of Richey going missing.*'

Nicky

January 1999 witnessed a sequence of shows in Australia (including a performance at Melbourne's Big Day Out) and Japan. From March to June the Manics steadily toured Europe. Their headlining set on the Saturday night of that year's Glastonbury Festival was criticised for favouring tour-hardened efficiency over emotion – all surface, no feeling, an accusation with which James would later agree after watching a recording of the show. 'I thought, "Oh my God, this is horrible,"' he admitted. 'It looked like we knew everything backwards and there wasn't even the possibility of the art of falling apart.' The Glastonbury weekend also prompted a sniggering press backlash when it emerged that the band had requested their own toilet backstage, one which apparently bore the handwritten notice: 'These facilities are reserved exclusively for the Manic Street Preachers: Please respect that.' Having chanced upon the portaloo in question, politicised punk-rock veteran Billy Bragg was quick to draw attention to what he saw as a snobbish betrayal of the festival's longstanding we're-all-in-this-together idealism. During a subsequent July performance at Scotland's T in the Park Festival, Nicky introduced 'Tsunami' by spitting: 'This is for Billy Bragg. I wouldn't let him piss in my toilet for all the money in the world. Go back to the army, you dickhead, and stop stealing Woody Guthrie's songs, you big-nosed twat.' The toilet incident was dubbed 'Crappergate' and became prime fodder for reaction-hungry interviewers. Years later, James claimed that the offending sign had been placed there out of spite – the band had keys so didn't need one. Nicky remained unrepentant, telling *Q*: 'I don't want any snorting of coke or, even worse, smoking of spliffs in my toilet. If we'd done that in 1991 everybody would have thought it was brilliant.'

Upon reaching the end of the European summer festival circuit, the Manics flew out for a twelve-date American tour, starting in New York and ending in Los Angeles. 'We're wise enough to think that after five records if it hasn't happened, it may not happen,' Nicky admitted in reference to the eternal question mark that hung over the band's 'breaking' America.

A three-month reprieve from touring gave the Manics ample time to recover their energies before the biggest non-festival show of their career. On 31 December 1999 they ushered in a 'Manic Millennium' at the recently opened Cardiff Millennium Stadium before a 60,000-strong audience. (The stadium was, at the time, the largest in the UK, making that night the largest ever British indoor gig.)

After support performances from Shack, Patrick Jones, Feeder and Super Furry Animals, the Manics' appearance onstage was prefaced by a video reel of Welsh figureheads including Tom Jones, John Cale, Arthur Scargill, Max Boyce, Charlotte Church and Shirley Bassey. The band emerged to the strains of Joy Division's 'Incubation' and launched into 'You Stole The Sun From My Heart', during which Nicky – resplendent in leopard-print scarf, pink miniskirt, electric-blue eyeshadow and sleeveless 'Culture Slut' T-shirt – bounced up and down ecstatically. The set was comprised of fourteen songs before midnight and a further eight after the New Year had been welcomed. It included 'Faster', 'La Tristesse Durera', 'Of Walking Abortion', 'Motown Junk', 'You Love Us' and imminent single 'The Masses Against The Classes' amongst expected cuts from *Everything Must Go* and *This Is My Truth Tell Me Yours*. James dedicated his solo acoustic rendition of 'Small Black Flowers That Grow In The Sky' to Richey, 'The best and coolest companion of the decade.'

The night, epic in every sense of the word, united old fans, new fans, parents, and children; housed an abundance of tiaras, glitter, eyeliner and feather boas; was supplemented with emotional footage of the band's decade in the spotlight, and descended into a spectacularly lit morass of sing-alongs, screams, beers, applause and tears. The gig concluded during the first hour of the new millennium with the inevitable, climactic onslaught of 'A Design For Life', which James introduced by declaring Cardiff to be 'the most beautiful place in the world – tonight at least'. His guitar strap broke during the first chorus, forcing him to sing several lines without the backing of his trusted white Gibson. As the song reached its crescendo, Nicky pushed over his speaker stack and shooed away a cameraman before smashing his bass and handing the splintered pieces to the crowd.

'That was kind of our Knebworth,' Wire would say of the show eight years later, 'as close as we're ever gonna get to being that powerful. So from then on in it has been a struggle to follow. We'd kind of reached the apex of all our dreams. If there ever was a time to split up, it would have been then. That's retiring with your 100 per cent record intact.'

'The Masses Against The Classes', a Dave Eringa-produced stand-alone single that portentously featured the Cuban flag on its artwork, provided Manic Street Preachers with their second UK Number 1 – and the first Number 1 of the new century – on 16 January. An impressive feat given that it received no direct promotion from the band, was deleted from wholesalers on the first day of release, and the fact that the song itself was a sleazily melodic return to, if not quite their glam-punk roots, then at least a worthy, FM-accessible facsimile of the 'Motown Junk'-era. Replete with quotations from political dissident Noam Chomsky and perennial Manics favourite Albert Camus, the single – its title derived from a quotation attributed to nineteenth-century British Prime Minister William Ewart Gladstone ('All the world over, I will back the masses against the classes') – featured a multi-tracked vocal harmony that echoed the breakdown of oft-covered classic 'Twist And Shout', a barrage of fuzz-box power chords, and lyrics that vied between the despondent and triumphant. Whether viewed, as it inevitably was, as either a long-overdue return to form or a misguided attempt to recapture former glories, the song and its chart success marked the end of one era and the far-off approach of another, and would be the last the listening public heard from the Manics for over a year.

'I think at the end of *This Is My Truth* we went off ourselves a bit,' Nicky reflected. 'You know when your favourite band gets liked by someone you really hate? Well the Manic Street Preachers were always my favourite band.'

In February of 2000 Sherry Edwards, Richey's mother, published an emotional open letter to her son in the *Sunday Mirror*. 'To see you walk through our door or even hear your voice again would make me the happiest person in the world,' she wrote. 'When you went away you took a huge part of me with you and I will never be able to reclaim that without you.'

It was exactly five years since Richey had abandoned his room at the Embassy Hotel, and the Edwards family had spent every day of each of those years in an agonising limbo, one which it increasingly seemed they would have to learn to live with permanently. 'I can never give up hope that you will return one day,' Sherry concluded, 'and, wherever you are, I hope the pain you carried inside has gone away. You are my precious son and I will never give up looking for you.'

Preliminary work on album number six had begun as early as November 1999 in the Manics' usual studio in Wales' Monnow Valley, but what the trio would later describe as the 'epicentre' of the LP's recording did not take place until they flew out to Spain for six weeks of recording at El Cortijo studios during the summer of 2000. When they weren't working, there was ample recourse for relaxation – they swam, watched television, and slowly worked their way through the 200 packets of Golden Wonder and Brannigan's crisps they'd had shipped over especially.

Going straight into the studio without rehearsing the new compositions beforehand, the band worked under a self-imposed limit of five takes per song, though the majority were recorded in as few as two. James described their approach to recording this time around as both 'bloody-minded' and 'relaxed', citing the boredom that had plagued them towards the end of the previous album as the impetus necessary to rebel against creative inertia. While writing lyrics for the new material, Nicky confessed that he had listened to *The Holy Bible* with the intention of capturing Richey's lyrical 'spirit of adventure', and appeared to have acquired a firmer belief in the strength of his own written output. 'I know Richey would've loved this record. Lyrically I've caught up with him. I can stand on my own two feet. That makes me very, very proud.'

His lyrical agenda for the album in broader terms concerned the 'malaise' of a world degraded and disillusioned by capitalism, and contained the by now expected wealth of cultural references, including allusions to post-communist Eastern Europe, Afro-American singer and left-wing activist Paul Robeson, Buddhist icon the Dalai Lama, the Bay of Pigs, the *Daily Mail*, the Cubist art movement, and T. S. Eliot. He was aware that the socialist stance of many of the songs – coming as it did from someone in so privileged a position as his – would draw out bile from the band's detractors, but remained unfazed. 'I decided I'd rather be called a hypocrite than just be called crap,' he retorted. 'The idea that you stop being a socialist when you become financially secure is not true for me.'

The intensely personal 'Ocean Spray' was the first lyric James had ever contributed to the band; a melancholic ode to his mother Sue, who had succumbed to cancer one and a half years previously. 'When you're very ill and you've had lots of operations, they always make you drink cranberry juice,' he explained. 'It's one of the best things to keep infections away. Of course, my mother – who had a seven-year bout with cancer – was in the hospital and every day she would say, "Can you get me some Ocean Spray?" Five times a day, I'd be going up and down these lifts in the hospital with bottles of Ocean Spray. The fact that she was so obsessed with drinking it just showed how much spirit she still had left, that she put so much faith in something so small, that drinking cranberry juice would keep her alive. It inspired me in a way, in the face of something which is so devastating.'

Finishing touches were applied to the LP mix at London's Abbey Road Studios during January 2001. 'Baby Elian' (whose lyrics were inspired by the case of Elian Gonzales, a Cuban child who had been the subject of a custody battle that evolved into an international dispute between Cuba and the United States) was the final song to be completed. The record, which ran to a bloated sixteen tracks and had in many ways shaped up as an antidote to *This Is My Truth*'s soft-rock passivity, wasn't, Nicky admitted, 'going to go down very well on the Asda racks'.

Know Your Enemy was the first Manics album to be completed after every member of the band had turned 30. Just as *The Holy Bible* had been an exquisitely vitriolic and uninhibited reaction against *Gold Against The Soul*'s compromised, in-search-of-a-hit studio polish, so *Know Your Enemy* was touted as a return to ambition and artistry after the languorous arena-rock that had characterised *This Is My Truth Tell Me Yours*. The 'enemy' of the title was, Nicky stated matter-of-factly, 'What we had let ourselves become.'

The LP's marketing campaign sprang into suitably attention-grabbing action with the announcement that the Manics would return to the live arena by performing at the Karl Marx Theatre in Havana, Cuba, on 17 February, making them the first major Western rock band to play in one of the world's last remaining communist republics, a place where, in the past, rock music had been repeatedly outlawed for inciting civil unrest.

Accompanying the band, their management and a handful of label executives were a camera crew and a small army of writers and photographers from London's music media. The entourage arrived in Havana three days prior to the scheduled performance, leaving ample time for filming, press conferences, interviews and meetings with delegates from the Cuban Ministry of Culture.

This heavily publicised show of solidarity with an infamously anti-American nation carried the subtle-as-a-sledgehammer political overtones of the Manics' youth; a calculated move, and one that Nicky, who had re-embraced his role as group mouthpiece with aplomb, saw as symbolic of their reinvigorated sensibilities, at once lyrical, musical and political. 'It doesn't seem that people so principled exist anymore,' he told *NME* from his suite within the faded glamour of Havana's Hotel Nacional. 'It's unfashionable to have political principles and few people have the guts to declare any. Whatever anyone says about us, it takes guts to come to Cuba and openly ally yourself with the last successful communist regime. It's not winning a war, but I love the idea of making a huge impact just by saying something you believe in.'

Whether the concert and the surrounding media furore was itself a valid and worthy opportunity to highlight the global threat of Americanisation or merely a shrewd publicity stunt was a question few were afraid to pose. During a press conference the day before the gig, Nicky did his best to quell accusations that this wasn't a matter of politics so much as highly imaginative self-promotion. 'Cuba has been a major influence on me . . . This is not like a student Che Guevara thing – it's just that Cuba for me is the last great symbol that really fights against the Americanisation of the world.'

When quizzed about his band's apparent endorsement of a dictatorship in which free speech was prohibited and anti-government sentiment punishable by imprisonment (and one that an estimated 83,000 people had died trying to leave), Wire was on appropriately acid-tongued form. 'Every sad *Lonely Planet* cunt who travels a thousand miles before they think they've seen the "real" Cuba believes that every [Cuban] they see is gazing across the Gulf of Mexico wishing deep down that they were on a boat . . . if that was true, there wouldn't be anyone here.' Nicky was adamant in his conviction that, for all its flaws (over the years the country had amassed an alarming array of human rights violations), Cuba was an admirable example of the achievements and benefits of socialism – 'the nearest thing we have on this planet to a true socialist state'.

When a journalist pointed out that had Wire – with his known penchant for make-up and cross-dressing – been in Cuba during relatively recent periods of government paranoia and militancy, he would have probably faced imprisonment, he witheringly replied, 'Do you really think I don't know that? I'm not stupid.' (He had, in fact, been strictly forbidden from wearing a skirt onstage.)

A local radio interview culminated in an enthusiastic DJ playing 'The Everlasting', which he informed the group he considered to be the best representation of their work; an awkward moment, as by unfortunate coincidence, it was also the song that the Manics had recently disowned and vowed never to play live again (a fate that had previously befallen 'Love's Sweet Exile' and 'Revol').

Between rum cocktails in the hotel bar, sun-bleached meet-and-greets, and camera crew-documented bouts of sightseeing, James expressed his nervousness about the impending performance to writer Ted Kessler. 'I have no idea who's coming to the gig. It could be a load of international journalists and some government officials. It could be two Cuban kids and a dog. It could be 200 British Manics fans in feather boas. We just don't know and we're very much on edge about that.'

In Cuba the Manics were promoted as 'El famoso grupo de rock británico', and the largely adolescent crowd who poured into the 5,000-capacity Karl Marx Theatre paid the equivalent of 17p a piece for their tickets. Other members of the audience were 'asked' to attend by the authorities to ensure that the venue was full. (Apparently local awareness of the Manic Street Preachers was not quite what they or Cuba's government might have hoped for, expert propagandists though the two doubtless were.)

Fifteen minutes before the band were due to take the stage, they were intercepted by the Cuban Minister of Culture, who asked, 'Would you like to meet someone very, very important?'

James, Nicky, and Sean were led into a brightly-lit room and sat on a sofa beside Fidel Castro, the 74-year-old Cuban President, revolutionary, dictator, and one of the most iconic and enigmatic political figures of the twentieth century. Through an interpreter (he was able to speak perfect English but had vowed never to do so) Castro – wearing his trademark green military uniform, septuagenarian face half-hidden behind his infamous thick grey beard – informed the band that he had come early to meet them and, despite a later prior engagement, hoped to be able to witness their performance.

'It might be a bit noisy,' Nicky informed him.

'Nothing could be louder than war,' Castro replied, a statement he would retract in the ear-ringing aftermath of the concert, and the much-repeated quote that provided the DVD being filmed with its title: *Louder Than War.*

Castro then appeared in the second tier of the auditorium before the band took to the stage, and provoked the kind of crowd response more often afforded rock stars than political figureheads. Five thousand Cubans whooped and screamed, saluting their leader with little red 'Manics in Cuba' flags that had been handed out in the theatre's foyer. 'Tony Blair doesn't get a reception like that anywhere,' said an impressed Nicky.

The Manics walked onstage in front of an enormous Cuban flag and launched into 'Found That Soul'. The crowd, most of whom had no idea of how to behave at a rock show, greeted the Stooges-esque grind of the opener with polite applause. Second song 'Motorcycle Emptiness' provoked scattered dancing, and by the show's mid-point people were headbanging, rising out of their seats and batting inflated condoms around. Nicky's scissor-kick during 'Kevin Carter' induced thrilled screams; a solo acoustic rendition of 'Baby Elian' – added to the set-list at the last minute after Castro had expressed admiration for the lyrics backstage – provided the most poignant moment, and caused the President to rise from his balcony seat in ovation. A feather boa wrapped snake-like around his microphone stand was Nicky's only concession to the band's glamour-puss roots. He, like Sean and James, was dressed casually, and understandably *sans* eyeliner.

'It was absolute insanity,' said James post-gig. 'Never in my life have I been so distracted while singing. It did seem like – ha! – our destiny.'

Backstage, an elated and adrenalin-pumped Nicky provided eyebrow-raising quotes for journalists ('He [Castro] has an enormous cock. They call him the Horse') and later reflected on his meeting with the living legend. 'He was just like the greatest pop star I've ever met! There's only two people I've ever come across who really have that special aura. One was Muhammad Ali and the other was Fidel Castro. I never want to meet anybody I admire because they let you down. I'm sure I've let people down, but meeting him, he didn't let me down at all.'

The following day, the publicity campaign continued unabated, with Castro inviting the hungover band to attend the opening of a state university. 'It's a mutual contract,' Nicky said, speaking frankly of the reciprocal benefits of the Cuba trip. 'He's getting some propaganda out of it, we're getting a DVD.' Castro, it was claimed, intended to use the Manics' visit to show the world that Cuba was changing, and his direct involvement with them was predicated on the fact of their being vocally anti-American and anti-imperialist. The time Nicky had spent with Castro had also provided him with a valuable appraisal of his new lyrics. 'I think the best thing was that he talked about "Baby Elian", the track on the album, and he actually just said to me, "You must know a lot about Cuba to write those words." That made me feel really relieved, because you're always worried about using situations as a lyricist, and I did really try to research the situation. I'm fucking glad I did, because I wouldn't have liked to be in a bullshit situation there! With Fidel, as I call him now.'

Years later, James would ultimately deem the Cuba trip a 'failure' and 'the biggest anomaly a band can have', citing it as making him realise that an interest in politics doesn't necessarily qualify one to be a politician. Critics frequently paid lip-service to what they perceived to be the smirk-worthy irony of the Manics attempting to revive their fortunes by meeting with a faded revolutionary. 'We thought it worked at the time,' Nicky reflected in 2008, 'but Christ, it's always there lurking in the back. It's fine for Bono to shake hands with George Bush, but shaking hands with Castro seems like you're a living endorsement of all his bad policies over the years.' Wire's last – and perhaps most telling – word on the matter was: 'I just think we looked so shit. That's what ruins it for me.'

CHAPTER 15

'Put it this way – if the world ended tomorrow, if the human race ended tomorrow, I wouldn't have any regrets about it whatsoever; because I don't think we've contributed anything whatsoever, in the entire history of this planet, that's worthwhile. At the end of the day, everything's dust, and that is it.'

Sean

'Virtually every band in Britain has become really self-indulgent. We've got to that terrible point where every new band is more interested in playing their instruments well rather than making some grandiose, interesting statements. Lyric-writing at the moment is in dire straits.'

Nicky

Less than a fortnight after the Cuban gig, two singles were released ahead of *Know Your Enemy*, both on 26 February. 'Found That Soul' was a stripped-down garage-rock number taut with staccato piano lines and distorted solos; 'So Why So Sad' a shimmering, mournful pop song awash with Beach Boys-indebted harmonies. The songs charted at Number 7 and 8 respectively, and both had dropped out of the Top Twenty by the following week. 'If we'd released one single it probably would have been Number 3,' said Nicky, 'which would have been even more frustrating. There's just a natural drop-off. When you've had two huge albums, it's pretty impossible to sustain that level. It just feels good to have a bit of failure. *The Holy Bible* was an utter commercial disaster, and it almost gave us strength.'

Know Your Enemy was released on 19 March 2001 and – like *Everything Must Go* – entered the UK album chart at Number 2. The LP's musical eclecticism divided fans and critics alike, with some praising as diversity what others derided as scattergun inconsistency. The dichotomy implied by the twinned release of 'Found That Soul' and 'So Why So Sad' was more audibly extreme on the full-length record, with the band road-testing such a variety of styles and approaches it at times resembled a high-sheen karaoke compilation, or was at least the sound of a group pointedly unafraid of wearing their influences on their sleeves.

The Picasso-influenced 'My Guernica', with its Sonic Youth-invoking shards of guitar and hailstorm of cymbals, was, in Nicky's words, about 'making a political statement through art', while borderline pastiche dancefloor-filler 'Miss Europa Disco Dancer' was the album's obvious weak moment; frequently singled out by reviewers as an at best ill-advised and at worst cringe-inducing detour into white-boy funk territory. (The track achieved a somewhat juvenile redemption with Nicky's expletive-ridden spoken-word outro.) 'Wattsville Blues' was a misanthropic ode to the village in which Nicky was raised, and featured his first ever lead vocal for the band, sung in a deadpan voice that, as the *Guardian* observed, 'manages to make Mark E. Smith sound like Mariah Carey'. 'Let Robeson Sing' – all twanging acoustics and sugary melodies (and eventually the fourth and final single to be taken from the album) – addressed the eight-year period during which singer and civil rights campaigner Paul Robeson had his passport confiscated by the US State Department. The splintered alt-rock guitars and pokerfaced vocals of 'Intravenous Agnostic' had been built around lyrics that Nicky claimed summed up *Know Your Enemy* as a whole: 'It's about maximum intake of reality. My life is based in reality, unlike most rock stars. I take a lot of interest in everything. Maybe too much.'

Sean's take on the mindset behind the album's sprawling sonic aesthetic and reclaimed political sensibility was that the Manics didn't want to keep doing things in the same way. Experimentation, and the inevitable failure that often goes with it, was a necessary process for any band, or at least any band hoping to evolve in the long-term. 'It's fashionable to say that we've lost it . . .' the drummer shrugged. 'There's other places for us to explore. There's still that undercurrent of bile bubbling away. But the older you get, the more you want to unleash it in a controlled, focused way.'

In Havana Nicky had compared the boredom and lack of self-expression that can come with reaching contentment in life to the failings of a political party who, once they've achieved power, forget what they wanted to do with it. The Manics, he felt, had always been about too much of everything, and on the last album they'd been about too little. 'We've now made an album that achieves what we want,' he said, going on to claim, with motor-mouth running at full-throttle: 'I've been telling people that this isn't just our best album ever. It's one of the best albums ever.' This statement would ultimately prove untrue and, if nothing else, confirmed the band's unquenchable, forever-evolving appetite for rhetoric and self-contradiction. Nicky, always the first to admit this, reflected years later that *Know Your Enemy* was 'a deeply flawed, highly enjoyable folly'.

Following their return from Cuba, Manic Street Preachers embarked upon a British and European tour that was to last for the majority of the year's remainder. Given that on previous tours the band had performed in front of arena audiences running into tens of thousands, these down-sized theatre shows provided fans with a rare chance to witness the Manics live spectacle in comparatively intimate settings.

During a March date at the Manchester Apollo, Nicky lambasted journalists 'who think I'm trying too hard with my lyrics'. Clad in a tennis dress, he spat, 'It's just because I'm more intelligent than you, that's all,' and proclaimed, with the lipstick-and-Babycham bile of his 21-year-old self, 'You just want to fuck me, but you can't!' At the same gig James preceded 'Motown Junk' by playing a few bars of the riff from 'Sweet Child O' Mine' – a sly nod to the ubiquitous Guns N' Roses song that had inspired 'Motorcycle Emptiness' during the Manics' infancy.

Fourteen dates, reaching from Helsinki to Vienna, originally booked to start in early October were cancelled in the wake of the 9/11 World Trade Centre attacks. No specific reasons were given by the band's management, through it was rumoured that Nicky's well-documented fear of flying had been heightened by the global terror situation and temporarily eliminated the possibility of foreign travel. This sudden live hiatus lasted for almost year.

1 February 2002 marked the seventh anniversary of Richey's disappearance. Missing persons who have not been seen, heard from, or the subject of any confirmed sightings in seven years can at that point be declared legally dead by their next of kin. In this instance, Richey's parents and sister refused the option, saying that they still had hope of seeing him again, no interest in the songwriting royalties a death certificate would have granted them access to,

and insisting that the investigation remain open. 'We want our son back, not the money,' Graham Edwards told the *Mirror*. 'As far as we are concerned he is still alive and we have always felt the same.'

The date had been well anticipated by the UK media, resulting in a deluge of articles re-treading the now exhausted ground of his depressive history and subsequent vanishing. At this time the *Big Issue* printed the last known picture of Edwards in a fresh plea for information. Chris Coleman – the PC who had been in charge of Richey's case up until this point – told *NME*: 'It's totally up to his family, and usually, that's only if people want to get access to his bank accounts and personal things like that. But even though there have been no new supposed sightings for years, I think the family will just want the file to be kept open on Richey as a missing person. If any leads come in, then they will be followed up.'

Sony issued a statement to the effect that for Richey's family and the band, nothing had changed, and he remained 'missing'. 'The family chose not to,' James informed a *Guardian* journalist, 'and I don't blame them. But that's not a decision taken by us or anything. And it's not a decision I'd like to take.'

A month later, in March, a fisherman discovered a size-eight Diadora trainer containing remains of human foot bones near the River Severn. The *Daily Star* published this information – making the connection with Richey's case – without forewarning his family. (James branded the paper as 'Cunts. Fucking cunts.') When contacted, Richey's sister Rachel told police that, despite the trainer being Richey's size, she did not think it could be his. Diadora then established that the trainers in question had not been manufactured until 2001, which ruled out the possibility that the remains were Richey's. ('I think it hurts us a million times more than we would ever let on and even realise ourselves,' said Nicky.) DNA testing eventually revealed that the foot bones belonged to 24-year-old Damien Allen, a missing hospital patient.

During this prolonged period of band non-activity, Nicky became a father for the first time when his wife Rachel gave birth to a daughter, Clara. In August 2002, Manic Street Preachers made their live return by headlining the MTV Stage at the V Festival, and in October released *Forever Delayed*. This 22-track greatest hits package took its title from a line in 'Roses In The

Hospital' (Nicky: 'It's just so beautiful. So much depth in it') and featured two brand-new songs: 'There By The Grace Of God', a restrained electronica number that dipped its toes in distinctly Depeche Mode-esque waters and owed a lyrical debt to Marilyn Manson's 'Coma White', and 'Door To The River', a mournful ode to lost innocence that had originally been recorded during the *Know Your Enemy* sessions.

Released as a single, 'There By The Grace Of God' reached Number 6 in the UK charts. Two weeks later, *Forever Delayed* charted at Number 4, and drew considerable ire from critics and fans who felt that the band had composed a shameless, corporate-minded selection of songs that all but overlooked critical aspects of their history ('Faster' was the only track from *The Holy Bible* to be featured) and wallowed in the mid-tempo, radio-friendly rock that had consolidated their place in the mainstream (singles from *Everything Must Go* and *This Is My Truth Tell Me Yours* were predictably predominant). The songs were not arranged chronologically, and several tracks – including 'Little Baby Nothing', 'Motorcycle Emptiness' and 'The Everlasting' – had their length digitally trimmed so they could all be included on one CD. The *NME* declared that releasing *Forever Delayed* was 'like remaking *A Clockwork Orange* without the ultra-violence' and awarded it a scathing zero out of ten. Nicky maintained that the collection did no more or less than what it had been intended to do. 'We just wanted to do it within the parameters of a greatest hits record. We didn't want to dilute it in terms of picking our favourite album tracks and various things. The greatest hits was meant to be the big corporate greatest hits, we're quite honest about that.' The *Forever Delayed* tour took in both arena and academy shows, and culminated – familiarly – with two consecutive nights at Cardiff Arena on the 15 and 16 of December.

In July 2003 a human skeleton was discovered in a Severn Estuary, part-buried by mud. The band and Richey's family were alerted once more, but an examination of the teeth confirmed that the remains were not the missing guitarist. By this point there had been supposed sightings in Goa, Fuerteventura, Liverpool, Shropshire, Swansea, London, and numerous other locations, but no substantial evidence; no proof. The same month, *Lipstick Traces (A Secret History Of Manic Street Preachers)* was released. A double-CD of rarities, B-sides and covers that derived its title from American rock critic Greil Marcus's 1989 book *Lipstick Traces: A Secret History Of The Twentieth Century*, the album acted as a fan-appeasing antidote to the 'hits'-based *Forever Delayed*; complete with leopard skin-print artwork designed by Nicky. One of the most anticipated tracks included was 'Judge Yr'self', a brittle, anthemic rocker that had originally been intended to appear on the soundtrack of 1995 Sylvester Stallone vehicle *Judge Dredd*, and was the last song ever recorded by the band as a four-piece; complete with post-*Holy Bible* Richey lyrics that referenced Dionysus, the Greek god of wine and ritual madness. The video released to accompany this track, which prominently featured Richey, was cut-together from early performance footage and behind-the-scenes outtakes, including the band's notorious April 1994 trip to Thailand. The release of *Lipstick Traces* was supported by performances at a handful of European festivals (including a second-from-top Sunday night billing on Glastonbury's Pyramid Stage) before the band began production on their seventh studio album, working title: *Litany*.

CHAPTER 16

'I've let go of people expecting things from us. Some people want you to be a cartoon version of yourself forever, and if you can't be that then you've got to split up.'

James

'We are haunted by ghosts. We're haunted by the way we looked – the symmetry, the four of us – everything was perfect.'

Nicky

Studio sessions for the LP took place in New York with renowned David Bowie producer Tony Visconti, though only three of the tracks he worked on ('Solitude Sometimes Is', 'Emily' and 'Cardiff Afterlife') made the final cut. Further recording was undertaken in Wales with producers Greg Haver and Tom Elmhirst. The band admitted that the recording process became somewhat clinical, with each member laying down their parts separately and spending nowhere near as much time together as previous album sessions had necessitated. 'On *Lifeblood* we barely played in the same room,' James told *NME*. 'It was created in some kind of virtual studio space. We wanted something that sounded detached, we just didn't quite know what *from*. That was the problem.'

This sense of detachment – from each other, from their musical history, even from the songs they were creating – was to become a defining component of the *Lifeblood* period. 'The Love Of Richard Nixon' was exemplary of the 'elegiac pop' that Nicky believed characterised the album. Underscored with programmed beats and a barely existent chorus, it featured no guitar tracks – a first for a Manics single. Having taken initial inspiration from the fact of President Nixon being more remembered for his role in the Watergate scandal than, say, any of his positive achievements in international relations, Nicky told *Repeat* fanzine: 'The main thrust of the song is the idea of being tarnished with a certain part of your life forever. With us, people might think of Richey's disappearance, or 4 Real.' Album opener '1985' held its title close to its chest; a luminous, pulsating synth-pop opus that name-checked Morrissey and Marr whilst rifling through a well-stocked New Order collection, it showcased an introspective lyrical approach that had been largely absent amidst *Know Your Enemy*'s frenzy of rhetoric. ('It wasn't necessarily the year we started making music,' Nicky told XFM of the era in question, 'but it was the year we started making our own world.') 'Emily', inspired by the plight of suffragette leader Emily Pankhurst, was about losing hope in politics; Wire admitted having come to terms with the fact that 'communism doesn't work'.

Though, since Richey's disappearance, many of Nicky's lyrics had referenced or alluded to the missing guitarist (as early as 1998 he claimed to have an album's worth of unheard lyrics written about him), 'Cardiff Afterlife', *Lifeblood*'s final track, was the first completed song publicly intended to address Richey, and was seen by the band as an opportunity to reclaim him as a friend, rather than some mythologised rock 'n' roll martyr. 'There's no way you could write "Cardiff Afterlife" straight after Richey's disappearance because the song and the sentiments would be coloured with so many bad emotions,' James told *Billboard.com*. 'The other reason we felt like it was the right time was that we wanted to reclaim him for us a tiny bit. The idea or myth Richey represents to some people isn't right.' Nicky explained that the song – its baroque, melancholy acoustics ornamented with lilting harmonica lines – was intended to deal 'with the feeling of being kept dangling. There's not a body, there's not a grave, but there's hope.' Patrick Jones, Nicky's brother, made a sombre video for 'Cardiff Afterlife' which featured some of the band's personal photos of Richey, including one taken at Nicky's wedding. Nicky admitted that, whatever his original intentions, *Lifeblood* did little to lay those particular ghosts to rest. 'There are no answers.'

It seemed that the personal contentment the band had once identified as being antithetical to their creativity had reared its head once again. (Nicky was now a father, and James had married his partner Mylene in a secret ceremony in Florence, Italy during July of 2004.) And it was perhaps unsurprising that an album whose gestation had been moulded by detachment and resignation would meet with a largely passionless public reception. 'We've given ourselves the freedom to fail with a smile this time,' Nicky somewhat prophetically stated. 'Our albums were always full of hate.

For the first time, I think there's a bit of love on this album.' The central quotation adorning *Lifeblood*'s sleeve came from René Descartes, the so-called 'Father of Modern Philosophy': 'Conquer yourself, not the world.' 'That's where we are now,' Nicky told the *Guardian*. 'Twelve years ago we'd have said, conquer the world and fuck yourself.'

Released two weeks before George Bush's second victory at the US Presidential elections, on 18 October 2004, 'The Love Of Richard Nixon' reached Number 2 in the UK charts. Any presumption that this boded well for its parent album was quashed when *Lifeblood* – 'a concept album about death', according to Nicky – charted at Number 13, delivering one of the most mediocre sales performances of the Manics' career (even the notoriously poor-selling *The Holy Bible* had peaked at Number 6) and dropping out of the Top 75 two weeks after its release. While not as damning as these swiftly plummeting chart positions might suggest, critical reception rarely rose above the lukewarm. The Manics were on the receiving end of the very thing they'd spent their career raging against: indifference.

In early promotional interviews, James had expressed satisfaction that the LP was receiving a relatively gentle push from Sony ('I don't want to make this album join the army if it doesn't want to'), but it's unlikely that he or the rest of the band anticipated the label all but abandoning promotion of the album after the release of second and final single 'Empty Souls' (like its predecessor, this song outperformed *Lifeblood* itself, charting at Number 2), which is what ultimately happened.

'We nearly pushed ourselves over a cliff with *Lifeblood*,' Nicky reflected in 2008, 'because we became a band that no one really recognised . . . I think the barometer of being fucked as a relevant band is: are you headlining Guilfest? And I think we were offered it the year of *Lifeblood* but we went, "No way are we doing that." Nothing against Guilfest . . . but I just felt mortally wounded. The attention on the band at that point was dead.'

In December 2004, a month after Nicky had provided *Lifeblood* with one of its core journalistic sound-bites by describing it as '*The Holy Bible* for 35-year-olds', the album that, for better or worse, had remained the band's defining work was given a ten-year anniversary re-release. The triple-disc set included a digitally re-mastered mix of the LP, a previously unheard US mix that warped the razor-wire tightness of tracks like 'Yes' and '4st 7lb' with a beefed-up, alt-rock aesthetic – one that the band admitted they felt improved upon 75 per cent of the original mix – and a DVD comprised of retrospective interviews and *Bible*-era live performances.

'It was probably the most definitive period for us,' said James. 'We've never been scared to admit that. And we've never been scared to admit that since Richey hasn't been with us, that element of us, that visual symmetry that we used to share as a band, was never going to be there after he left.'

In the enclosed interview Nicky reflected on the forces that drove the album's recording ('We needed to have the freedom of failure again – commercial failure, not artistic failure. And it was a purely artistic experience'), Sean claimed that the opportunity to re-examine and repackage the album had been a welcome one ('It gives us a chance to reflect on past glories. At the time, we didn't think there was much glory to reflect on'), and James conceded that revisiting the period induced pangs of something more poignant than nostalgia ('It's painful to look back at yourself when you're thinner, and younger. It makes you realise that the indestructibility of relative youth gives you such an armour and such an identity . . . It's something you can't reclaim. You've got to go with the onward march of age').

As well as live recordings and early demos of songs including 'Die In The Summertime' (Nicky: 'the most frightening song on there, musically and lyrically'), the anniversary pack contained an excellent piece by journalist Keith Cameron which examined the album's near-perfect musical and lyrical synthesis, and concluded by describing *The Holy Bible* as 'a triumph of art over logic; a vindication of intelligence'.

History had recognised *The Holy Bible* as a triumph, and in confronting the intensity of their past, the band, it seemed, had been forced to admit something of the mediocrity of their present. *Lifeblood*'s chrome-hearted AOR sheen had stimulated few critics and – if its sales figures were anything to go by – fewer fans. The Past-Present-Future tour of UK arenas that they undertook in support of the album struggled to shift all of the available tickets; the first time the band had failed to sell-out venues of that size since 1996. These dates also saw the Manics doing what they had avoided for the best part of a decade: employing a second guitarist. (Abbey Road studio engineer Guy Massey had previously worked on *Everything Must Go* and *Know Your Enemy*.) This decision carried obvious weight and was viewed as a betrayal by those fans who felt that, even onstage, Richey's absence was still a presence more powerful than any hired hand could provide. 'It was a difficult decision but we just needed another guitarist desperately,' said Nicky. 'We always have done. It's not like he's replacing Richey, good God, no. Nothing's ever gonna replace Richey. It's just a musical thing.'

The band were a week and a half away from flying out for a four-date tour of Japan on the tenth anniversary of Richey's disappearance in February 2005. When asked if the three of them would be doing anything particular to mark the occasion, Nicky told the *NME*: 'No, I don't think we're that kind of people. We'll talk to each other on the day and we'll remember something funny or stupid or sad. That's the impossibility of the situation anyway, there's no centred thing to fix yourself on. It's a personal thing between the three of us, and his mum, dad and sister.' There was still no definite end to Richey's story, rather a fragmentation, a fade out, and the apparent permanence of this not knowing was something that the Manics had, in some ways, come to depend on. 'We're cursed between the idea of hope and closure,' Nicky told *Mojo*. 'Can't honestly say I want closure, I prefer the hope. If you want closure you've got to kill the hope, and I dunno, maybe I should? Richey's not blamed, I don't blame him for anything. He did what he did.'

A further sequence of UK shows commenced in April, and the Past-Present-Future tour culminated at London's Hammersmith Apollo on the nineteenth of that month. Songs from *Lifeblood* were notable by their almost total absence. (Only '1985' and 'Cardiff Afterlife' received an airing.) As a 'thank you' to the fans who attended, 300 copies of an EP entitled *God Save The Manics* were handed out before the performance. Rapturously received rarities 'Stay Beautiful' and 'Ifwhiteamericatoldthetruthforonedayit'sworldwouldfallapart' propelled the concert towards its climax before the stutter-punk finale of 'Motown Junk' was preceded by an abbreviated cover of Guns N' Roses' 'Paradise City'. During the show, the band announced that this was to be the last time they'd play live for at least two years. 'After *Lifeblood* we decided that people deserved a rest from us,' James later explained.

Less than six months after its release, the album had, for all intents and purposes, been abandoned. The band, disappointed by the LP's performance and once again disillusioned by what they had let themselves become, needed a change, and it eventually became apparent that only by looking back would they be able to move forward.

CHAPTER 17

'When success comes, the Welsh find it very hard to cope with. When our Oasis-at-Knebworth moment came – around the time of This Is My Truth Tell Me Yours *in 1998, when we were selling out the Millennium Stadium – we didn't enjoy it like we should have. We asked, "If we're this popular, does that mean we're shit?" Something in the Welsh psyche rejects success: there's a self-destructive streak. The place is littered with people like us.'*

Nicky

True to their word, the Manic Street Preachers' musical output over the ensuing period was limited. In September 2005, new song 'Leviathan' was recorded for inclusion on the War Child charity album *Help!: A Day In The Life* – which broke the then-held record for fastest-selling download album ever. Lyrically, the song saw Nicky return to political literature for inspiration, in particular a work by fifteenth-century English philosopher Thomas Hobbes entitled *Leviathan* – the book credited with establishing the foundation of Western political philosophy. In March 2006 they provided a cover of 'The Instrumental' for a tribute album to cult eighties pop act the June Brides entitled *Still Unravished*. During this time James, troubled rather than relieved by the prospect of a prolonged sabbatical from music, had devoted himself to writing and recording a solo album. Released in July 2006, *The Great Western* was a well-received LP of soaring pop-rock that drew persistent – and complimentary – comparisons with *Everything Must Go*; comparisons that the synth-laden sugar-rush of mini-anthems like 'That's No Way To Tell A Lie' and 'Bad Boys And Painkillers' did much to perpetuate. *NME* declared that it sounded 'like a man freed from the shackles of history'. The album, which debuted at Number 22 in the UK charts, took its title from the train line that ran between London and Cardiff. 'I was spending so much time travelling back to Wales,' said James, 'and I realised that the songs on the album were all about people I'd met who had changed me either in west London or in Wales.' He claimed that he had previously considered his lyric for 'Ocean Spray' a one-off, specifically inspired as it was by his mother's death, and when asked about how he re-approached the songwriting process on his own terms after spending two decades shaping music around other people's words, he said, 'I just had to find my own style, and I think the main difference between my lyrics and Nick and Richey's is that they write a lyric from a very high degree of understanding of what they're talking about, whereas when I write a lyric, I'm writing it *to* try and understand the subject.' 'An English Gentleman' was written in tribute to Philip Hall, while 'Which Way To Kyffin' was inspired by the work of famed landscape painter Kyffin Williams. James toured minor venues up and down the country in support of the album, and frequently silenced the constant shout-outs for Manics songs by playing tracks including 'Ocean Spray', 'This Is Yesterday' and 'No Surface All Feeling'.

In September 2006, nine months after he first made one of his songs available to download via the Manics' official website for a single day, Nicky Wire oversaw the low-key release of his self-produced solo album *I Killed The Zeitgeist*. 'This is my crusade,' he deadpanned, adding: 'No one's listening anyway.' The LP was a thirteen-track collection of fractured indie-pop oddities that Nicky described as 'cheap, amateurish, [and] drenched in feedback with a Lou Reed-style vocal'. His inspiration had apparently come from such disparate stimulus as Teenage Fanclub, *Watership Down*, J.D. Salinger and Plastic Ono Band, and he played all of the instruments himself (save drums – provided by Manics producer Greg Haver). Titles such as 'Goodbye Suicide', 'Everything Fades' and 'Stab YR Heart' were considered particularly reminiscent of *Generation Terrorists*, a vibe Nicky embraced when he played an acoustic version of that album's 'Condemned To Rock 'n' Roll' during his debut solo performance at the Hay Festival. Clad in a pink suit and clutching a half-drunk bottle of wine, Wire asked the crowd, 'Have any of you been to James Dean Bradfield's solo shows? Well, this is going to be a lot rougher.' During his run of solo performances, he also promised that the forthcoming Manics album would be no less than 'our *Appetite for Destruction*'.

    I Killed The Zeitgeist track 'Kimono Rock' was purported to be part-inspired by ex-Libertines frontman and tabloid mainstay Pete Doherty, the classically 'troubled' rock figure whom some journalists had taken to comparing with Richey (though he was known for favouring crack and heroin over starvation and self-harm), a tenuous link reinforced when it emerged that a teenage Doherty had written to *NME* expressing his admiration for Edwards. 'Withdraw Retreat' saw Nicky singing the praises of disillusion-fuelled solitude, while 'Bobby Untitled' alluded to iconic IRA hunger striker Bobby Sands.

Although the LP did little to trouble the charts, pleasantly surprised reviewers were almost unanimous in their praise for *I Killed The Zeitgeist*. *Q* labelled it 'a future cult gem', the *Guardian* was taken with its fusion of 'romantic poetry and ragged art-punk', while the *NME* concluded, 'Best Manics album since *Everything Must Go*? Possibly.'

Almost nine months before its release, Nicky told the *NME* that the band's eighth studio album was shaping up to 'sound like *The White Album* played by Guns N' Roses – pure melodies mixed with rock 'n' roll. A mix of *Generation Terrorists* and *Everything Must Go*, that's what we're after.' He added that, on reflection, the Manics now considered their last few years of activity to be their 'wasteland period'. Writing for the album dated back as far as late 2005, while studio sessions had actually commenced during March 2006, months before Nicky and James began promotional duties for their respective solo efforts. ('Both our albums helped us focus on what we love most,' said Nicky. 'They were an exercise in de-cluttering and musical vanity.') Once again the band worked with old friends Dave Eringa and Greg Haver. Recording took place at Grouse Lodge in Ireland, a luxurious residential studio replete with in-house massage therapists that had recently hosted sessions by Muse, R.E.M. and Bloc Party, and the by comparison far more basic Stir Studios in Cardiff. The initial 30-song collection amassed for the album was trimmed down to a final ten tracks after intensive bouts of editing; a means of slicing away the excess fat they now felt had weighed down previous albums. 'We've been trying to reduce ourselves to a pile of rubble,' Nicky wrote in an essay posted on the band's website. 'When we started this album it was the three of us, in a room, making a right old racket. Sometimes you have to learn from your own past. James playing huge guitar solos without me and Sean going, "Stop wanking!" We just felt liberated.'

On 8 December 2006 the band performed their first gig in nearly eighteen months – a set at the Manchester Apollo as part of XFM's Winter Wonderland shows, in support of homeless charity Shelter. Anticipation was rife enough to ensure that a collective of feather-boa-clad diehards were camped outside the venue in freezing temperatures the night before the gig in order to secure their place on the barrier. James arrived onstage with a pre-emptive apology for their potentially rough-around-the-edges performance before the band kicked off with 'You Love Us'. Pandemonium ensued. Their tight 45-minute headline set necessitated a race through the familiar ('From Despair To Where', 'Motorcycle Emptiness', 'Yes') and the unveiling of the brand-new ('I'm Just A Patsy' and 'Autumnsong'). 'It's fucking amazing to be back,' James told the crowd, going on to declare that their prolonged hiatus appeared to have done Sean the world of good. 'Sean suddenly looks about twelve years old. We're calling him Sean "Dorian Gray" Moore.' The new album's title was revealed as *Send Away The Tigers*, and before the finale of 'A Design for Life' the Manics promised to be back in 2007, 'tighter, more vicious, more fucking angry'.

Musically, the new material sought to recapture the exuberance and idealism of the band's early years, to reclaim the original meaning of what they'd set out to create with Manic Street Preachers; the possibilities of self-belief and glorious failure, or, as Nicky described it, 'fabulous disaster'. The medium: power chords, squealing solos, incisive lyrics and anthemic choruses. The message: don't be afraid of doing what you do best. *Celebrity Skin*, Hole's 1998 album of hyper-polished pop-rock, was cited as a massive sonic influence. Sean channelled the drumming technique of his twenty-something self. Nicky looked to the lyrics of the Who's *Quadrophenia*. James dug out his old Jeff Beck LPs. Inspiration was drawn from the memory of the 'I Am A Cliché' guitar-strap Richey had once worn. 'We've learned to accept our true nature,' said Bradfield, 'not to try and delineate and deconstruct everything we do. Just admit what we are: a punk rock 'n' roll band.'

Send Away The Tigers was mixed in America by Green Day and My Chemical Romance collaborator Chris Lord-Alge, whose brother Tom Lord-Alge had been responsible for the much-admired US mix of *The Holy Bible*. Its title was a direct lift of a phrase British comedian Tony Hancock often used in reference to his longstanding battle with alcoholism. Hancock killed himself with an overdose in 1968, and in his suicide note wrote that 'things have gone wrong too many times', a line Richey had once expressed admiration for that appeared in the first verse of the album's title track.

Retrospectively, the Manics identified 'melancholia that made you feel good' as one of the key ingredients to the success of their earlier material, and now sought to revisit this precision balance of sadness and uplift. Lead single 'Your Love Alone Is Not Enough', a glacial burst of call-and-response power-pop in which James duetted with Cardigans singer Nina Persson, was lyrically intended by Nicky as a 'two-way conversation in my head about love, religion, democracy and Richey', and arrived as a genuine shiver-down-the-spine moment – the sound of a band finally coming up for air. In a *Guardian* interview Nicky freely admitted to using Richey's memory in 'an almost cynical way' as a songwriting trigger, and wrote of him in relation to the single: 'He was in a successful band, he could have had a nice girlfriend if he wanted, and we all loved him. But it wasn't enough.'

'Send Away The Tigers' referenced not only Tony Hancock's 'alcoholic demons', but also an incident that occurred in Baghdad Zoo in 2003, when 300 animals were released during fighting between coalition forces and the Iraqi republican guard. After the zoo had closed, American soldiers held a party in its grounds, and a drunken soldier attempted to touch a rare Bengal tiger, who retaliated by mauling his arm and biting off his finger, only for the animal to be shot dead by a second soldier. Nicky drew parallels between this scenario and the Tony Hancock idiom in that both represented misguided and ultimately corrupt notions of liberation.

'Underdogs' was a bristling, glam-punk thank-you to the 'freaks' who'd supported the band over the years. 'Rendition' addressed the process of 'extraordinary rendition', by which the CIA extradited terror suspects to countries in which more extreme methods of interrogation could be employed. The militant six-string strut of 'Imperial Bodybags' saw Nicky empathising with the plight of American soldiers and their families, while with 'Indian Summer', the band confessed to finding themselves firmly back in 'A Design For Life' territory via a waltz beat, cathedral-wide string arrangements, and lyrics that celebrated their enduring friendship and the human need for idealism even in the face of cynicism, subject matter Wire admitted was 'really un-Manics'. He described fiery, amped-up ballad 'Autumnsong' as being 'based on the same sort of ideals as "Sweet Child O' Mine" – it's falling in love with your girlfriend at the age of sixteen. I needed a lot of regressive therapy for that.' 'I'm Just A Patsy' was an exploration of political stooges that drew inspiration from the case of Lee Harvey Oswald – who was accused of the 1963 assassination of President John F. Kennedy before himself being murdered in a similarly public shooting.

The band, apparently no longer laughing at his premature demise, included a cover of John Lennon's 'Working Class Hero' as the album's hidden track. The LP's artwork – a photograph which depicted two young girls in devil and angel costumes walking side-by-side in front of a bridge Nicky later revealed to be located in New York – was perceived by some to be an indirect allusion to Richey's hypothesised fate on the Severn Bridge, an interpretation the band dismissed, claiming that they wouldn't engage in such 'heartless' use of a 'bad memory'. They did, however, concede that they now felt ready to address Richey's legacy in a more positive and redemptive way. 'I was obsessed by the band not using him,' confirmed Nicky. 'Now, I just feel people are missing out if they don't know about him.'

Having always argued against the media defining Edwards with the terrible question mark that hung over his departure, the band felt able, for perhaps the first time, to champion his talent and achievements, untainted by the paranoia – of seeming insensitive, opportunistic or manipulative – that had once made them wary of publicly discussing him. 'As time passes, obviously Richey is still our friend,' said James, 'but he seems more an icon now than a former friend.'

'If this one doesn't make our audience happy, then perhaps we should call it a day,' said Nicky before *Send Away The Tigers* was released. 'Luckily, I think we might have pulled it off.'

Having already charted at Number 26 on early downloads alone, 'Your Love Alone Is Not Enough' received its physical release on 30 April 2007, and – in a scenario long familiar to the Manics – subsequently took up residence at Number 2 in the UK charts (this time they were kept from the top by 'Beautiful Liar', a duet between ubiquitous R&B powerhouse Beyoncé and Colombian pop songstress Shakira). The reviews for *Send Away The Tigers* were the best the band had received in years, with the general consensus being that it was their most focused and accomplished work since *Everything Must Go. NME* claimed it was 'in many ways the quintessential Manics album – the cathartic regeneration the band really needed to become

relevant again'. *Uncut* thought the album saw 'the brain of the Manics reunited with their strongest qualities: their heart, humanity and soul'. The *Guardian* felt that the 'gung-ho vitality of the music – full of nods to the Stooges, Guns N' Roses and the Ramones – helps grant the band a little absolution'. The album's 7 May release was supported by a 23-date British tour that promised 'Springsteenesque long sets, working-class rage, make-up and dumb punk fun'. Tickets had sold out more quickly than any of their previous tours, prompting all-round sighs of relief from a band who'd been away too long to be able to rest on their laurels. 'We were scared putting the tickets on sale,' James admitted to the *Guardian*, 'and we're still fragile in confidence.' He claimed that their old songs, unplayed live for such a long time, now seemed new, and Nicky delighted in the prospect of delivering a nightly trawl through their back catalogue. 'The Manics still stand for something,' he said, 'the concept of what we were at the start – which was giving people something that didn't exist. I think we still do that; occupy our same space. We've never been part of any fashions or trends. That's why we have longevity. We stand for something that stands alone.'

The first night of the tour, at the Cambridge Corn Exchange the day after the album's release, saw the band making good on Nicky's promise of a return to their roots. 'Born To End', 'Motorcycle Emptiness', 'Faster', 'From Despair To Where', 'La Tristesse Durera', 'Everything Must Go', 'Kevin Carter', and James introducing what was to become a fixture on the subsequent dates; a squalidly beautiful acoustic version of 'Yes' ('the greatest lyric I've ever sung'). Nicky, his hair dyed a shade of fiery red reminiscent of the bottle-auburn fringe Richey had worn during the latter half of 1994, returned to the stage for the encore wearing a miniskirt, and revealed that he'd had an offer from the BBC to take part in a reality show in which participants learn how to be a conductor at the proms. 'I told them I'd do it if I could say, "Fuck queen and country!"' he grinned.

Send Away The Tigers charted at Number 2 in the UK, only 690 copies shy of the top spot. 'It's a bit more frustrating knowing we were so close,' Nicky said. As the tour progressed, the rigours of life on the road left him with a torn calf muscle and a gashed leg (courtesy of some pint glass-hurling audience members in Preston who took exception to his miniskirt), while James's overeager stage-hopping led to an injured knee. 'It's great to be playing songs like "Slash 'N' Burn" and "Roses In The Hospital" again,' said

Bradfield. 'You fall out of love with songs over a period of time, but it's great to be playing them again.'

'Bradfield's solos are truly heroic,' claimed Wire of his bandmate's gig-toughened musical focus, 'the spirit of Slash has re-entered his body and soul, he sounds like Jeff Beck on steroids.' Downtime on the tour bus was filled by listening to bands including Gallows, Babyshambles and the Hold Steady; watching *A History Of Violence*, *The Football Factory*, and *The Good, The Bad And The Ugly*; and – in Nicky's case – reading Kurt Vonnegut's essay collection *A Man Without A Country*.

The Manics live spectacle moved through Scotland and Wales before taking in three nights at three different London venues, the second of which, on 30 May, was performed at the Astoria, the first time they'd played the theatre since their final trio of gigs with Richey in December 1994. The air heavy with expectation – old scars ready to reopen – they began with the vitriolic euphoria of 'Stay Beautiful' and progressed through a considered and lengthy set-list that left fans salivating. 'Faster' was dedicated to 'the genius of Mr Richard Edwards', while at the conclusion of 'A Design For Life', James moved his microphone stand to Richey's place at the side of the stage.

At the end of the following month, via the completion of the first leg of the UK tour and a handful of festivals in Sweden, Switzerland and Germany, the Manics arrived in Glastonbury. At the Worthy Farm site, which was – as per its reputation – rain-lashed and half-sunk in oozing mud after three days of Biblical weather and Babylonian revelry, the band played a Sunday evening main-stage set (before Kaiser Chiefs and the Who) under a sky swollen with cataract-grey clouds. 'You get to Glastonbury and the mud takes a quantum leap into the unknown,' James commented backstage before their performance. Addressing the band's past love-hate relationship with the festival, he added: 'We've bitten the hand that lets us play a couple of times – there was the bypass [comment], there was Crappergate, there was me wearing a balaclava. We've had a chequered history with this festival, and that's kind of why it's exciting. I'm feeling scared, and when you're feeling scared you know the stakes are high.'

A swarm of soggy Welsh flags thrashed above the audience for the duration of opener 'You Love Us', and Nina Persson joined the band onstage for an anthemic 'Your Love Alone Is Not Enough'. 'If it's any consolation,'

James told the damp but not dispirited crowd, 'we just did two gigs in Germany and it was pissing down there as well.' He introduced 'La Tristesse Durera' by telling the audience he hoped they would excuse his 'cod French' and dedicated penultimate song 'Motown Junk' to Richey. 'We first played Glastonbury in 1994. One of us was hammered before the gig, during the gig and after the gig. That man was Mr Richey James. This one is for him.'

At the Rock'n Coke Festival in Istanbul the band were thrown by the sight of 10,000 Turkish fans singing along to 'If You Tolerate This', and James indulged in what Nicky referred to as 'the most stadium rock thing I've ever seen' when he allowed the crowd to sing the second verse of 'A Design For Life' alone. In September the Manics performed at the Vodafone Live Music Awards at Earl's Court and the *Q* Awards at London's O2 Arena, winning 'Best Track' for 'Your Love Alone Is Not Enough' at the latter. During his acceptance speech Nicky (who had recently become a father for the second time after the birth of his son Stanley) thanked Clash bass player Paul Simonon, the Argentinean rugby team ('for putting honour back into sport') and TV presenter Jeremy Paxman ('for *Newsnight*').

After two nights at Brixton Academy, which Wire played hammered on champagne ('I do firmly believe that champagne afflicted playing is better – for me anyway'), their year's touring concluded in Brighton on 14 December. That same month Manic Street Preachers were named as impending recipients of *NME*'s 2008 Godlike Genius Award. Previously bestowed upon the likes of the Clash, New Order and Primal Scream, the prize sought to honour an 'outstanding, innovative and unique career in music', and was a source of considerable pride for the three boys from the valleys who had grown up reliant upon the magazine in question for their early link to the wider musical world. 'When our manager told us about it, I just genuinely felt humbled and excited,' Nicky gushed. 'We've won four Brit Awards, Ivor Novellos, but it's vindication. It feels like the best one because *NME* is what I grew up with, and for all its faults it still means a lot to me. It's so fucking brilliant, honestly. It's really made me feel fantastic.'

In the years since *This Is My Truth Tell Me Yours*, the Manics had been locked in a somewhat tempestuous relationship with the *NME*. The band were no longer androgynous rent-a-quote press darlings, or even unlikely Britpop conquerors gleaning commercial success from tragedy, and the publication that had once been unable to go a week without printing a

hyperbolic or fawning MSP piece had spent many years sniping at their perceived irrelevance and repeated musical *faux-pas*. 'I know we could have been cynical about it and said, "Oh, they ignored us for ages,"' said Nicky, 'but it just doesn't matter.'

Send Away The Tigers had done much to repair the damage of those years spent – as some would have it – in the middle of the road. And the Manics' last-gasp resurrection couldn't have proved timelier. The *NME*, lifelong advocates of the build-'em-up-to-knock-'em-down school of journalism, were apparently ready to recant and put the band back on a pedestal with as much overstatement as the 'Godlike Genius' accolade implied.

James was swift to admit that, had the award been offered during the *Lifeblood* era, for example, it would have felt less like a vindication and more like a 'nail in the coffin'. 'It was the perfect scenario really,' he said. 'It's been given to bands that have split up, it's been given to other bands who maybe don't know where they're going at that point, and I think it's been given to us at exactly the right time.'

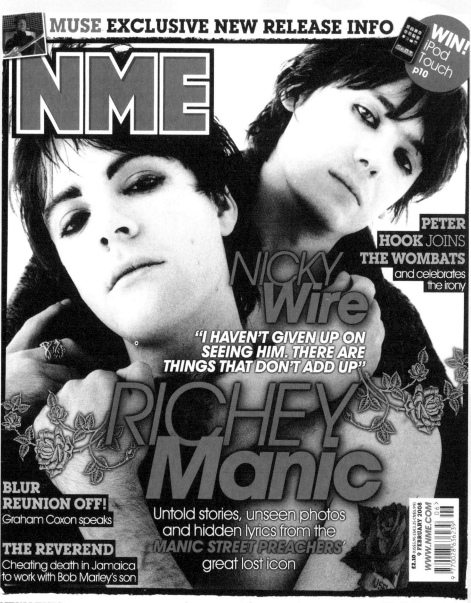

NME

NICKY
Wire

PETER
HOOK JOINS
THE WOMBATS
and celebrates
the irony

*"I HAVEN'T GIVEN UP ON
SEEING HIM. THERE ARE
THINGS THAT DON'T ADD UP"*

RICHEY
Manic

**BLUR
REUNION OFF!**
Graham Coxon speaks

Untold stories, unseen photos
and hidden lyrics from the
'*MANIC STREET PREACHERS*'
great lost icon

THE REVEREND
Cheating death in Jamaica
to work with Bob Marley's son

£2.10 (US$5.95 (SK£2.95 CN$5.99)
WWW.NME.COM
9 FEBRUARY 2008

NEW MUSIC GET CAPE. WEAR CAPE. FLY | GLASVEGAS | HOT CHIP | THE TING TINGS
HERCULES AND LOVE AFFAIR | LET'S WRESTLE | JEFFREY LEWIS | THE COOL KIDS

521 UK GIGS
LISTED

CHAPTER 18

'Nothing will ever correlate with the mad idea that myself and Nick had when we were fifteen years old and wrote our first song. We had a preposterous fucking big ready-made myth in our heads. I don't think anything we ever do will live up to that.'

James

'The biggest misconception about Richey was that the last six months of his life was how he was all the time. It just wasn't, y'know.'

Nicky

Richey's fortieth birthday would have fallen on 22 December 2007. For nearly thirteen years he had existed for others only within the confines of memory, photographs and video footage – the one that got away, a rock 'n' roll ghost, the eternal lost boy.

Before the *NME* Awards ceremony, which was due to take place in February, Nicky gave an extensive cover interview to *NME* writer James McMahon. Entitled 'The Lost Godlike Genius', it dealt solely with Wire's feelings about and memories of Richey – perhaps the first interview published since February 1995 to do so. 'Richey was unlike any other rock star of our era,' Nicky said. 'He towers over so many people in popular culture. I was reading this piece by Mark Lawson the other day – he used to do *Newsnight Review* – and he said that, when you mix high art with low art, both are just as important and deserving of scrutiny. When you combine them both, that makes the most interesting art. That's what Manic Street Preachers had the ability to do. And no member more so than him.'

During the interview Nicky reflected upon Richey from the perspective of both friend and fan, mourner and celebrant, revealing that one of his biggest regrets was that Richey wasn't around to enjoy success when it came. Wire's curiosity about how Edwards would have behaved in the glare of the country's media spotlight still needed him. 'I would have loved to see him at the Brit Awards when we won for *Everything Must Go*. Can you imagine him onstage at Cardiff Millennium Stadium in 2000? For all his emptiness at the end, he did really enjoy certain elements of stardom. It's not all about the negative question mark that is his end.'

Nicky insisted that against the odds, against the pessimism of logic, against the dead weight of all the time that had elapsed, he still hadn't surrendered hope of seeing his friend again. 'I know that everything leads to suicide, and I think that nine out of ten people would think that he's not alive anymore. But knowing his brain as I think I did, I can never actually convince myself that there is any outcome yet. There's still things that don't add up.'

Beyond his loss, the band's loss, the Edwards family's depths of despair and sense of 'utter abandonment', Nicky predicted that, were he still around, Richey's knowledge and artistry would have undoubtedly reached exceptional and profound heights. 'I genuinely think he would have been uncontrollably creative. I think we would have seen acceleration in him mastering his art . . . I think he would have been a writing machine. I think he could have written the most amazing novel. I would have loved to have seen that blossom. There's so many great things he could have done.'

On 28 February 2008 the *NME* Shockwaves Awards took place. The ceremony during which the band were presented with their Godlike Genius gong was located in the Indigo theatre in London's O2 complex, while the subsequent 'Big Gig' occurred next door, in the cavernous O2 Arena. Nicky found the experience of the day most comparable to Cuba seven years previously: 'One of those things that just flashed by in an instant, that you just wish you could suck it all in.'

Talking to interviewers outside the theatre, an ever-humble James said, 'Some cynics might say that if you hang around long enough, you'll get that award . . . We're music press nerds. Even when the *NME* was criticising us, and hated us, I still kept reading. It was always our bible.' Nicky, who spent far longer on the red carpet than his bandmates, admitted: 'We're not used to being loved. Sometimes we deal better with hatred.'

During the ceremony, Nicky mingled with the assembled throng. Bloc Party guitarist Russell Lissack was keen to express his admiration for *The*

Holy Bible, while Franz Ferdinand frontman Alex Kapranos whispered, 'Nicky Wire is the biggest prick I've ever met' to an *NME* journalist (Nicky: 'He should have shouted it'), and Wire even found time to converse with Billy Bragg – burying the Crappergate hatchet.

The Godlike Genius Award, presented by Welsh boxing champion Joe Calzaghe, was accompanied by a video montage during which personalities including New Order bassist Peter Hook, Welsh rugby captain Ryan Jones, and journalist Steve Lamacq paid tribute. (Kylie Minogue and Super Furry Animals had recorded messages that couldn't be broadcast due to technical problems.) During an emotional speech, Nicky produced a copy of the Manics' first-ever *NME* cover, and indulged in what he referred to as a 'Gwyneth Paltrow' moment by thanking a reeled-off list of individuals that reached all the way from Tennessee Williams to Philip Hall, and, of course, Richey, 'who's not here today, and we love him to bits. He's one of the greatest boys I ever knew. He wrote my essays in university! And James and Sean for putting up with me being an insane fucker all my life.'

Afterwards James admitted, 'I nearly had an Oscar moment,' while he and Nicky were left somewhat dazed by the prospect of having to re-psych themselves and perform another gig, having done a four-song set during the ceremony itself. 'We've shot our load now. We're done,' Bradfield joked. 'I just want to go to sleep . . .'

In the O2 Arena before the main attraction, the crowd witnessed performances by the Cribs, Klaxons, Bloc Party and Kaiser Chiefs. The Manics arrived onstage after an entourage of leopard skin-clad bagpipers and drummers had performed a rabble-rousing instrumental piece, and launched into 'The Masses Against The Classes'. It was perhaps no coincidence that they chose to open the gig with this – the single that featured the Cuban flag on its cover – during the same week that their old friend Fidel Castro announced his resignation. The Enemy's Tom Clarke joined the band on guitar for 'You Love Us' (briefly occupying Richey's stage space), while Nicky, in white skirt and gold glitter eyeliner, strutted the length of the stage during their cover of Rihanna's ubiquitous chart-smash 'Umbrella' ('this song is fucking genius'). A run through the Cult's 'She Sells Sanctuary' segued into 'Motown Junk', and ex-Catatonia singer and sometime Manics associate Cerys Matthews filled in for Nina Persson during 'Your Love Alone Is Not Enough'.

'We're fucking happy taffs tonight!' a visibly emotional James announced. After 'A Design For Life', an explosion of glitter cannons sequinned the arena air. The last slogan to flicker across the vast stage screen was George Orwell's 'Hope lies in the proles'. When asked how he intended to celebrate post-gig, James's succinct three-word reply was: 'Jameson and Coke.'

There would be no further live appearances until June, when the lucrative summer festival season began once again. The band started work on new material in the immediate aftermath of the *NME* Awards. James phoned Nicky the following day to try and sketch out a rough idea of what their next move would be. A subsequent studio jam session yielded raw, jagged soundscapes that Nicky described as 'miserable and dirty', and saw as a reaction against the acclaim and elation invoked by the Godlike Genius Award. 'When we feel we're being loved a bit too much we have a natural tendency to think that something must be wrong,' he told *NME*. The new songs apparently vied between the bone-scraping abrasiveness of *The Holy Bible* and mellower, stripped-down acoustic works.

On 2 June 2008 they played their first show since February, supporting Foo Fighters at the City of Manchester Stadium. Festival appearances ensued in Switzerland, Germany, Croatia, Poland, Romania, Ireland, Latvia, Russia, Finland, Austria, and Belgium. In August the band headlined the *NME*/Radio One Stage at the Reading and Leeds Festivals. Before playing a serrated cover of Nirvana's 'Pennyroyal Tea', Nicky told the crowd: 'I think we last played this here in 1994. Richey was in hospital then, we had to play it as a three-piece, just to pay the bills.' James dedicated 'La Tristesse Durera' to Edwards: 'So, Reading Festival number five for us. Richey only played one of those with us. But it feels like he's been there for a lot longer than that.' He went on to tell the crowd that Reading was the only festival that 'truly feels like home'.

In a subsequent blog Nicky informed fans that the band had booked studio time at the end of September with the intention of beginning recording of their 'dark' ninth album, which was also the last the band owed to Columbia Records under their current contract. On the twelfth of that month, they played a unique set at the Forever Heavenly Festival at London's Royal Albert Hall – an event held to mark the eighteenth anniversary of

Heavenly Records. The Manics performed the six songs they had originally recorded for the label almost two decades previously ('Motown Junk', 'Sorrow 16', 'We Her Majesty's Prisoners', 'Starlover', 'Spectators Of Suicide' and 'You Love Us'). After 'Starlover', which had been played live only once before, Nicky grinned: 'You can tell me and Richey were nineteen when we wrote those lyrics. You have to make a fool of yourself when you're young.'

On 4 November it was revealed, via the official Manic Street Preachers website, that the lyrics for the forthcoming album would be drawn entirely from writings left behind by Richey. Not only that, but the band were recording with visionary producer Steve Albini, an industry veteran renowned for his back-to-basics studio techniques who had most famously worked on Nirvana's ragged swansong *In Utero* – a longstanding Manics favourite. As Nicky wrote: 'We have been in the studio with Mr Steve Albini recording live – to tape – analogue – no digital hiss – no Pro Tools – no safety nets. Quite scary, daunting but invigorating. All the songs we are recording are lyrics left to us by Richey. Finally, it feels like the right time to use them.'

The work-in-progress was initially given two working titles: *Journal For Plague Lovers* and *I Know I Believe In Nothing But It Is My Nothing* (the former bearing a resemblance to the name of Daniel Defoe's 1722 novel *A Journal Of The Plague Year*, a fictionalised account of a man's experiences in plague-ravaged London during 1665; the latter being derived from a key line in 'Faster').

The lyrics that Richey had written in the weeks before his disappearance (some of which had, allegedly, been left behind in his room at the Embassy Hotel) had occasionally been alluded to or discussed by the band over the years, but never in any real detail. In 1998 Nicky told *Esquire*: 'He left 50 or 60 songs. Three to five weeks before he went missing. Richey gave us these songs. It's pretty hard to look at them . . . Some of them are pretty fucking astounding. If we use them, they're going to a million times overshadow mine, which I can deal with.' In the same interview, he described a piece called 'Doors Closing Slowly' as 'absolutely amazing. Total Ian Curtis.'

Though the November 2008 announcement was not the first time Nicky had drawn comparisons between new material and *The Holy Bible* (overzealous comments made before the release of both *Know Your Enemy* and *Lifeblood* being a case in point), it now seemed that the oft-hinted at and fan-hungered-for 'Holy Bible II' was on its way to becoming a reality, complete with brutal sonics and a holy grail of unread but already iconic writing. 'We've had these lyrics for fourteen years and we all felt compelled that this was the right time to do it,' he told *NME*. 'It's a follow-up to *The Holy Bible* in a lot of ways, and I did write 25 per cent of the words on *The Holy Bible*, but on this one it felt proper that they're entirely Richey's. There's a small amount of editing involved, because some of them are prose and they needed to be made into lyrics, but no, they're all Richey's.'

Some of the tracks being readied for inclusion on the LP were named as 'Jackie Collins Existential Question Time', 'William's Last Words', 'Peeled Apples', 'Me And Stephen Hawking', 'Pretension/Repulsion' and 'She Bathed Herself In A Bath Of Bleach'. Musically, Nicky said the material had the most in common with the 'very intense post-punk rock of *The Holy Bible*', while at the other end of the spectrum, the acoustic works were reminiscent of the bleak beauty of 'Small Black Flowers That Grow In The Sky'. 'Steve Albini was perfect,' said Nicky. We've been listening to *In Utero* a lot . . . Everything's played live . . . We wanted to push ourselves again.'

In the past Richey's 'lost' writings had been viewed to an extent as incoherent and obscure – even unsuitable for use in songs. Nicky had claimed that 'The lyrics in the last file he gave us were more poetry of a sort. There was a lot of ranting,' and at one point had ruled out the possibility of using any of the writing purely because it was 'way too personal'.

Wire, who still confessed to being mystified by some of *The Holy Bible*'s Richey-penned content, now said of the new songs: 'Lyrically, some of it is pretty impenetrable even to us, and we knew him pretty well. We don't know what he's talking about all the time because he's not around to tell us.' He told MTV Asia that 'they [the lyrics] were ingrained in me anyway, and he left them to us, and I always knew they were good . . . It was inspirational to read those words again.' Working with Richey's lyrics signified a personal and creative homecoming of sorts, and Nicky maintained that the themes contained therein remained 'really relevant' even after fourteen years. 'It's not all doom and gloom, you know? They've got a lot of surreal humour too, and a lot of references that you might not get unless you research them . . . I think there's something more humane about it,' he concluded, 'a more human role.'

When the final, thirteen-song *Journal For Plague Lovers* tracklisting was revealed, so too was the fact that the band would be releasing no singles from the LP. The album's artwork, a painted portrait depicting the dazed and blood-smeared face of a young girl with a pudding-bowl haircut, had been provided by Jenny Saville, whose work famously adorned the cover of *The Holy Bible.* 'I think it just conveys that sense of innocence as well as some kind of violence,' Nicky said of the chosen painting. 'That's what the record is. At times, even though it's dark and heavy, there's a sense of innocence and it's quite uplifting, but there's always a sense of menace and threat in the background.'

On 23 November 2008, less than three weeks after the existence of *Journal For Plague Lovers* had been announced, the *Mail On Sunday* published a one-page article bearing the heading: 'AFTER 13 YEARS, PARENTS OF RICHEY THE MISSING MANIC ADMIT HE'S DEAD'.

The piece revealed that Graham and Sherry Edwards had been granted a court order for their son to be legally declared 'presumed dead'. The family's lawyer, David Ellis, said the decision reflected 'an acceptance that his affairs have got to be sorted'. But he was careful to clarify: 'That's not the same as an acceptance that he is dead.' The Probate Registry of Wales issued a document stating that Richey James Edwards had died 'on or since' 1 February 1995. His parents would inherit his estate, which the article claimed stood at £455,990 (reduced to £377,548 after death duties). It was unclear if this amount included or was in addition to his share of the songwriting royalties amassed by the Manic Street Preachers' record sales since 1995.

At the time, neither the Edwards family nor any band members were prepared to publicly discuss the situation, though Terri Hall spoke briefly to the *Mail On Sunday*. 'The band has been aware this was coming,' she said. 'It is hugely emotional for all of us. This is the parents' choice and the band is happy to go with what the parents decide is best. We all dream Richey will come back one day. You hope he is still around somewhere. But it is no longer a realistic hope and if this offers some kind of closure then the band will be content with that.'

The following week a series of obituaries and articles flooded Britain's national press, the same facts and falsities that had been the preserve of every piece written about Richey in the intervening years appeared once again: 4

Real, the perpetually unplugged guitar, Rimbaud, Kafka, Camus, Plath, the parallels with Curtis and Cobain, depression, self-mutilation, anorexia, alcoholism, hospitalisation, the empty hotel room, the abandoned Vauxhall Cavalier, the Severn Bridge, the sightings, the myth, the band's subsequent success; the confirmed, the unknown, and the imagined. The obituaries inevitably ended with some variation of: *Richard James Edwards, guitarist and lyricist: born Blackwood, Gwent 22 December 1967; declared dead 23 November 2008.*

The small flickers of hope that Nicky had still felt were bound up with his friend's loss only ten months beforehand had – even if only publicly and legally – been extinguished. The case of Richey Edwards as a missing person was closed, and the legal documents, death duties, and obituaries that followed in the wake of his family's decision had granted the story an official if inconclusive finality, even if the answer to the question of his ultimate fate remained as frustratingly out of reach as it had always been. Whether by suicide or some grander design, he had successfully walked away from the world. The few clues he had left; the years of search, hope and speculation, had amounted to nothing. It seemed that no one but Richey himself would ever know what happened, and whatever his state of mind in February 1995, whatever choices he had made, whatever he believed he was doing, and whatever impossibly slim chance now remained for his safe return, it's hard to imagine that he would have wished such incalculable pain upon his loved ones.

EPILOGUE

'All you can do is leave clues throughout history towards something better. Towards progress.'

Nicky

In many ways, the Manic Street Preachers' career has been that of the epitome of a modern rock band. Four close friends from the provinces, fired up on revolution and music, make an assault on the capital, announcing they are there to change the world. With some success but their initial goals in tatters, they produce a bloated second album. They soon denounce it and follow it with a harsher return to their roots. Drink and mental problems take hold. One member in particular falls apart, crushed by the very intellect that makes him a genius, and eventually going missing just after writing his masterpiece. The remaining band members return triumphantly and reach new levels of success.

The Manics have always been so intense, so sincere, and so thoughtful that they have stood apart from their peers, uncompromised by the likes of Britpop, New Wave, grunge or baggy. From day one they have shunned fashion, but that has been their strength. Although their music has often flagged behind their brilliant lyrics and biting live shows, the Manics' story is full of intelligence, venom, drive and gravitas. Even when they have overstepped the mark, or flagrantly changed their minds, they have done so with confidence, honesty and an ability to use the media. With obvious exceptions, their records have been admirably inconsistent, but the Manics have mastered one quality which so many other bands never capture: the ability to make people think. To have then survived such a catastrophe as Richey's disappearance and returned even more successfully is a triumph indeed – to do so with their integrity and passion intact is better still. Their story, even as it continues to unfold, has been comprised of highs and lows that few artists could – or would want to – aspire to. When the Manic Street Preachers first exploded on to the British music scene with 'Suicide Alley', there was no other band like them. Today, despite a career dogged with controversy and tragedy, triumph and acclaim, they still remain unique.